GREAT HORSEMEN
OF THE WORLD

DAVID & CHARLES' EQUESTRIAN TITLES

GREAT
HORSEMEN
OF THE WORLD

Guy Wathen

DAVID & CHARLES
Newton Abbot   London

TO THE HORSE
Without whom there would be no
great horsemen

This book could not have been written without the co-operation of its living subjects, and I am extremely grateful to the following who have been kind enough to find the time for interviews or to answer questions by telephone or letter: Lester Piggott, Pat Eddery, Steve Cauthen, John Francome, Jonjo O'Neill, Peter Scudamore, Willi Schultheis, Reiner Klimke, Christine Stückelberger, Pierre Jonquères d'Oriola, Hans Günter Winkler, Bill Steinkraus, Piero d'Inzeo, Raimondo d'Inzeo, David Broome, Alwin Schockemöhle, Paul Schockemöhle, Nelson Pessoa, Joe Fargis, Pierre Durand, Nick Skelton, Michael Whitaker, Richard Meade, Bruce Davidson, Mark Phillips, Lucinda Green, Mark Todd, Ginny Leng, and Ian Stark.

It could not have been illustrated without the assistance of those who have not only supplied photographs but also advised on their selection, and I am especially grateful to Bob Langrish, Bernard Parkin, Leslie Lane, Findlay Davidson, Brian Hill (*Eventing Magazine*) and Guy de Burgh Wilmot (W.W. Rouch & Co.)

To Theresa Fitzgerald and Betsy Burroughs, librarian and photo librarian respectively of *The Blood Horse* of Lexington, Kentucky, USA, I am indebted for information and pictures of North American jockeys.

Finally I am very grateful to the following who have cast their expert eyes over the manuscripts of the introductory chapters to the five parts of the book, and who have suggested improvements to the text: John Oaksey (flat and National Hunt racing), Jane Kidd (dressage), Judith Draper (show jumping) and Jane Pontifex (the three-day event).

GUY WATHEN, Burley, February 1990

British Library Cataloguing in Publication Data
Wathen, Guy
Great horsemen of the world.
1. Horsemanship. Biographies. Collections
I. Title
798.2092

ISBN 0-7153-9370-7

© Text: G. L. Wathen, 1990

Typeset in Plantin Light by ABM Typographics Ltd, Hull
and printed in Great Britain
by the Bath Press Ltd,
for David & Charles Publishers plc
Brunel House Newton Abbot Devon

CONTENTS

WHO ARE THE GREAT HORSEMEN? 7

Part I
FLAT RACING 9

Origins · Matches · Fordam · Wragg · Elliott · Smith · Mercer · Starkey · Carson · Cochrane · Swinburn · Sloan · Maher · Longden · Arcaro · McCarron · Antley · Pincay · Baeza · Velasquez · Cordero · Asmussen · Poincelet · Wooton · Breasley · Williamson . Moore · Cumani · Dettori · Roberts

The Great Names

Fred Archer (GB) 20 · Steve Donoghue (GB) 27 · Sir Gordon Richards (GB) 37 · Lester Piggott (GB) 42 · William Shoemaker (USA) 51 · Yves Saint-Martin (France) 55 · Patrick Eddery (Ireland) 57 · Steve Cauthen (USA) 60

Part II
NATIONAL HUNT RACING 69

Distinguishing the good from the great · Stevens · Mason · Rees · Stott · Wilson · Rimell · Marshall · Dowdeswell · Molony (T.) · Francis · Dick · Mellor · Gifford · Biddlecombe · Davies · Barry · Brabazon · Molony (M.) · Taaffe · Carbury · Uttley · Kelleway · Broderick · Smith-Eccles · Powell · Dunwoody · Anthony · Walwyn · Smith · Fenwick · Saunders · Sherwood

The Great Names

Fred Winter CBE (GB) 82 · John Francome MBE (GB) 90 · Jonjo O'Neill (Ireland) 96 · Peter Scudamore (GB) 104

Part III
DRESSAGE 109

The meaning of Dressage · From a means to an end to an end in itself · Xenophon · Grisone · de Pluvinel · The Duke of Newcastle · de la Guerinière · Caprilli · Fillis · Boltenstern · St Cyr · Hartel · von Langen · Lesage · Marion · Jousseàume · Bürkner · Linsenhoff (L.) · Neckermann-Boldt · Lörke · Günther · Springer · Grillo · Uphoff · Theodorescu-Linsenhoff (A-K.) · Moser · Fischer · Chammartin · Filatov · Kizimov · Petushka · Tuttle · Galvin · Gold · Williams · Hall · Johnstone . Loriston-Clarke · Bartle · Bartle-Wilson · d'Esmé · Otto-Crépin · Podhajsky · Jensen-Törnblad

The Great Names

Willi Schultheis (Germany) 119 · Reiner Klimke (Germany) 122 · Christine Stückelberger (Switzerland) 128

Part IV
SHOW JUMPING   132

Caprilli · Corry · O'Dwyer · Ahearn · Rodzianko · Talbot-Ponsonby · Hasse · Momm · von Barnekow · Brinckmann · Cortéz · Ansell · Llewellyn · Nicoll · Carr · White · Stewart · Robeson · Smith · Pyrah · Thiedemann · Schridde · Wiltfang · Simon · Sloothaak · Mancinelli · d'Orgeix · Lefrant · Rozier · Robert · Cottier · de Balanda · Goyoaga · Hayes · Wade · Ringrose · Macken · Heins · Weier · Chamberlin · Nishi · Wiley · Chapot · Morris · de Nemethy · Matz · Brown · Homfeld · Elder · Vaillancourt · Millar · Smythe · Coakes · Moore · Shapiro · Robbiani · Johnsey · Lefèbvre · Townsend · Drummond-Hay · Bradley · Edgar · Greenhough · Monahan · Burr-Lenahan · Jacquin · Mairs · McVean · Bacon

The Great Names
Pierre Jonquères d'Oriola (France) 150 · Hans Günter Winkler (Germany) 154 · William Steinkraus (USA) 160 · Piero d'Inzeo (Italy) 166 · Raimondo d'Inzeo (Italy) 170 · David Broome OBE (GB) 175 · Alwin Schockemöhle (Germany) 181 · Paul Schockemöhle (Germany) 186 · Nelson Pessoa (Brazil) 188 · Joe Fargis (USA) 191 · Pierre Durand (France) 195 · Nick Skelton (GB) 199 · John Whitaker (GB) 201 · Michael Whitaker (GB) 204

Part V
THE THREE DAY EVENT   209

Background · Pahud de Mortanges · Fanshawe · Rook · Hindley · Weldon · Hill · Hough · Willcox · Somerset · Roycroft · Morgan · Crago · Davidson · Plumb · Le Goff · Blixen-Finecke · Kastenmann · Busing · Lutke-Westhues · Ligges · Schultz · Karsten · Rethemeier · Erhorn · Baumann · Kaspareit · Ehrenbrink · Allhusen · Holderness-Roddam · Gordon-Watson · HRH The Princess Royal

The Great Names
Richard Meade OBE (GB) 219 · Bruce Davidson (USA) 225 · Mark Phillips CVO (GB) 231 · Mark Todd MBE (New Zealand) 238 · Lucinda Green MBE (GB) 246 · Virginia Leng MBE (GB) 253 · Ian Stark MBE (GB) 258

WHAT MAKES THE GREAT HORSEMAN?   264

BIBLIOGRAPHY   267

INDEX   268

WHO ARE
THE GREAT HORSEMEN?

The author who undertakes to produce a work with this title faces two problems: the first, to define a great horseman, is the easier of the two to solve; the second, to select those who fulfil the criteria, rather more difficult.

The scope of this book is limited to five competitive equestrian sports: racing, both on the flat and over fences, and the three main competitive disciplines controlled by the International Equestrian Federation (FEI) – dressage, show jumping and the three day event. It is also confined to riders. This does not imply that there are not great horsemen engaged in other forms of competition such as carriage driving, harness racing, showing, polo, even the rodeo, or indeed in non-competitive sports such as hunting.

Certainly there are those entitled to be called great horsemen who are not riders – at least not primarily. As trainers of horses or instructors of riders, or as both, they may well have made as significant a contribution to their respective sports as the riders themselves. And when we speak of horsemen we include those elegant and proficient members of the fair sex, among them Olympic, World and Continental Champions.

The horseman is unique among sportsmen. The athlete must train himself, coached and assisted by experts, to a peak of fitness and technical competence so as to produce the ultimate level of performance at the required time. He knows what his goal is and he knows when he must reach his peak, so he can programme himself accordingly. The horseman has to develop a partnership with a four-legged animal, who, though he may have a mind of his own, has no idea what his goal is or what the future holds for him.

The horseman must himself (or herself) be physically fit, but it is the horse who is the real athlete. The rider must train the horse and develop his natural ability, bringing him to a high level of technical competence. Then in competition he must ride him in such a way as to give him the best possible opportunity of returning the best performance of which he is capable.

The horseman also differs from many other sportsmen in that there is neither physical contact with his opponents, such as there is in boxing, nor is he playing directly against his opponent, as he is in tennis or on the running track. Only in racing is he measured directly against his rivals, and in a close finish there may of course be inadvertent physical contact, while in going for gaps the jockey may be in direct confrontation with others. In dressage, as in figure skating, he is striving for an individual performance that impresses the judges more than those of other competitors. In jumping and in the three day event, as in downhill skiing, he is matching himself against the course, rather than directly against the other competitors, though the speed at which he overcomes the problems set by the course designer may in the end be decisive.

So what are the criteria by which we can judge a horseman? What separates the great from the very good? First we can tabulate his results, his victories in major competitions – the Classic races, on the flat and over the jumps, the Olympic Games, World and Continental Championships, major Grands Prix or the equivalent, and major team events. But except in racing, where each year's riders' Championship is decided solely by the number of victories, quantity counts for less than quality. Even in racing, a Derby, an Arc de Triomphe or a Grand National is worth dozens of lesser races, and elsewhere an Olympic Gold Medal may be worth its weight in that precious metal (from which it is no longer made!)

A single important victory, however, is not enough, and it is questionable whether even a series of victories on the same horse stamps a rider as a really great horseman. And to justify inclusion amongst the world's élite, a rider should really have dominated ·or at least been very prominent in his sport over a considerable time-span.

So, we suggest that a great horseman is one who has achieved outstanding success over a considerable period of time on several different horses.

In considering each sport we review its history, mentioning the many riders who have played a significant part in its development. Then we examine the careers of those selected as 'Great Horsemen of the World.' Here the aim is not so much to chronicle their victories as to pinpoint the reasons for their success. And in the case of those still with us, it is interesting to record their views on the state of their own sport today, the improvements that they would like to see introduced, and their advice to young riders who would like to follow in their footsteps.

We do not claim that our list of great horsemen is complete, merely that all those whom we include do deserve that label; that this is a selection of great horsemen from five equestrian sports. Any many of today's riders will emerge as great horsemen in the future. In our final chapter we endeavour to identify what really makes the 'Great Horseman'.

Part I

FLAT RACING

ASCOT, THE CURRAGH, CHANTILLY, Aqueduct, Sha Tin or Flemington, wherever the racegoer finds himself, in England, Ireland, France, North America, Hong Kong or Australia, or anywhere else in the world, he is unlikely to be far from a racecourse. Flat racing, the 'Sport of Kings', is enjoyed around the world at some two thousand tracks where millions of racegoers come to watch or to wager on some three hundred thousand horses in training. From simple beginnings the sport of racing has developed into a major industry which generates a huge turnover in betting.

There is little resemblance between Royal Ascot, symbolising the traditions of English racing, and Sha Tin, opened in 1978 on land reclaimed from the sea in Hong Kong's New Territories and surrounded by high-rise office blocks. And conditions for racegoers at some of the modern American courses with enclosed air-conditioned stands bear little relation to those at some of the country courses in Australia. But however grand or simple the facilities, and whether the racegoers come primarily to bet or to watch the racing, the one common factor is the horse. And he cannot perform without a very special breed of horseman – the jockey.

The breeders and owners spend their millions, the trainers produce their charges fit to run for their lives, but it is the jockey in whose hands lies success or failure once the stalls are opened. As in most equestrian sports, it is the horse who is the athlete, and it is his rider's job to bring out the best performance of which he is capable. Some jockeys do this better than others; many will win on almost any good horse; the best will win on moderate horses too. The good jockey doesn't lose races that he ought to have won; the great jockey wins races that it would have been no disgrace to lose.

Man first tamed the wild horse for his own use in warfare and then as a means of transport, and it was from the horse's use in war that the origins of racing are to be found. Chariot races were originally popular because they were so spectacular, and when ridden horse racing was introduced it consisted mainly of matches between two good horses. But one of the earliest formal race meetings was one that continues in much the same form to this very day; the Palio di Siena in Italy is still run round the cobbled main square with bareback riders who represent the various wards of the city.

The first recorded race in England took place in 1540 in Chester, Queen Elizabeth I attended racing on Salisbury Plain, and James I went racing at Newmarket, but it was Charles II who soundly established the 'Sport of Kings' and who actually moved his court to Newmarket for the major meetings. It was during the eighteenth century that racing became formalised in England, and the first meetings were recorded in Ireland

Royal Ascot, England (Bernard Parkin)

and France. In the nineteenth it developed also in Australia, North America, Germany, Hungary, Italy, New Zealand, and Japan.

Since it was in England that formal racing first developed, it was here that the first great jockeys emerged. Perhaps the first to establish himself as a great jockey of his time was **George Fordham** (1837–87), who won the Cambridgeshire Handicap aged fifteen and went on to win seven 1000 Guineas, five Oaks, three 2000 Guineas and eventually, at the age of forty-two, the Derby on a 20-1 outsider. His great rival was **Fred Archer** (1857–86) (see p20), who though twenty years younger died a year earlier, and was the first of four jockeys who completely dominated the racing scene in their times.

The second was **Steve Donoghue** (1884–1945) (see p27), who rode his first winner (in France) in 1905, three years after the birth of **Harry Wragg** (1902–85), who was known as 'The Head Waiter' for winning races from behind with a late run, and who won thirteen classics including three Epsom Derbys before retiring in 1946, riding three winners on his last day in the saddle. (He then trained six more classic winners before finally retiring at the age of eighty.) **Charlie Elliott** (1904–79) had the misfortune to be born in the same year as **Gordon Richards** (1904–86) (see p37), but it was he who broke Steve Donoghue's ten-year run of Championships, and he won three Derbys, eleven other classics and the French Derby.

Doug Smith (1917) rode the first of his 3,112 winners in 1931, and was Champion five times, and his classic victories included two in royal colours. The career of **Jo Mercer** (1934) was overshadowed by that of **Lester Piggott** (1935) (see p42), but he won thirteen European classics and had the good fortune to partner the great Brigadier Gerard for Dick Hern to seventeen wins from eighteen races.

Greville Starkey (1939) is one of those unfortunate riders whose one well publicised second place (on Dancing Brave in the 1986 Epsom Derby) has outshone his undoubted achievements. He will also be remembered for the extraordinary incident at Ascot in 1988 when his mount Ile de Chypre was put out of action when in the lead by what was alleged to be a stun gun concealed in a pair of binoculars wielded by someone in the stands! He should, however, be remembered for the 1975 Arc de Triomphe on Star Appeal, the 1978 Epsom and Irish Derbys on Shirley Heights, and eight other classics.

Willie Carson, OBE (1942), the ebullient Scot who is one of the great characters of English racing, only came into racing because he was too small to do anything else. He started his career slowly, with a mere twenty-one winners in his first three seasons, and only 107 in his next three, but in 1971 his score shot up to 145 and he finished second in the jockey's table behind Lester Piggott. Then in 1972 he became one of the few jockeys to dethrone Piggott when he took the title with 132 winners. He retained his title the next year, and in 1974 he nearly pulled off a treble of Oaks victories; having won the Irish and Yorkshire Oaks on Dibidale, the filly's saddle slipped at Epsom; first the number cloth disappeared, then the weight cloth, but somehow Willie contrived to remain on board and finish third, only to be disqualified for loss of weight.

Greville Starkey (GB) before winning the King George VI & Queen Elizabeth Diamond Stakes at Ascot 1982 on Kalaglow (Bernard Parkin)

Willie Carson, OBE (GB) on 'the best horse I ever rode', Nashwan, before winning the 2000 Guineas, 1989 (Bernard Parkin)

That was probably his greatest feat of horsemanship, but he regards as the greatest moment of his career the day he won the Oaks for HM The Queen in 1977, her Silver Jubilee year. The day started moderately when he was involved in a car crash on the way to the course, and he arrived only just in time to weigh out. Then Dunfermline got away to a poor start and it was only his strength and skill that drove her through to win; and they then went on to beat all the colts in the St Leger. The year 1978 brought another championship, and in 1979 he won the 200th Derby with Troy, together with the Irish Derby, the King George VI & Queen Elizabeth Stakes and the Benson & Hedges Gold Cup.

A second Derby followed with Henbit in 1980, when he also won the 2000 Guineas and the Oaks. Champion again that year and in 1983, he had to surrender the title to Steve Cauthen in 1984. But a continuing stream of important winners over the next four seasons culminated in a unique feat in 1988 when he won his third St Leger with Minster Son, a colt that he had bred himself. Small in stature he may be, but the Thoroughbred Breeders Association must have had their collective tongue in cheek when they awarded him the accolade of 'Small Breeder of the Year'!

A year for Carson to remember was, undoubtedly, 1989, for it was the year of Hamden Al Maktoum's Nashwan, and together they won the 2000 Guineas, the Derby, Sandown's Eclipse Stakes, and the King George VI and Queen Elizabeth Diamond Stakes at Ascot. Trainer Dick Hern and his owner decided to forgo the chance of the Triple Crown, probably fortuitously, since the St Leger was transferred from Doncaster to Ayr because of subsidence on the Yorkshire course, and aimed for the Arc de Triomphe instead. But in a preparatory race on the Longchamp course Nashwan disappointed and was withdrawn from the big race. Nevertheless, it was a great year for Willie Carson.

One of the most determined riders, he pinpointed one of the differences between the average jockey and the great one. 'Most jockeys don't really know why they've lost a race; when I come back in I know exactly what I've done and why I've won or lost.' Now nearing his half century (in years) he is still able to make the likes of **Steve Cauthen** (see p60) and **Pat Eddery** (see p57) fight for the jockey's title.

The 1988 English and Irish Derby double on Kahyasi was a triumph for Northern Ireland's **Ray Cochrane** (1957), and some compensation for two unlucky but severe injuries early in his career. He has now won four classics, and since being retained by Luca Cumani, has been snapping at the heels of the Championship leaders. **Walter Swinburn** (1961) was another who achieved the Anglo-Irish Derby double, on Shahrastani in 1986, and but for a suspension he might well have recorded the same double on his 1981 Derby winner, the ill-fated Shergar, as well. In 1983 he rode Daniel Wildenstein's filly All Along to victory in the Arc de Triomphe, and then travelled to the States with her to win the Washington International, and two other big races.

The first American jockey to hit the headlines in England was **Tod Sloan** (1874–1933), whose short crouching style was shown to be more effective than the old English straight-legged upright method depicted in the sporting prints of the time. He enjoyed brilliant success, and was a great influence on jockeys everywhere, and had he not fallen foul of the authorities because of his dubious gambling coups might well have become one of the greatest.

Ray Cochrane (Ireland) scored an English–Irish Derby double with Kayashi in 1988 (Bernard Parkin)

When Steve Donoghue was struggling to make a start to his career, **Danny Maher** (1881–1916) was winning races in the United States. At the turn of the century he came to England, and in a career cut short by tuberculosis, he won three Derbys, two St Legers, two 2000 Guineas, a 1000 Guineas and an Oaks, as well as becoming the only American to take the jockey's Championship until **Steve Cauthen** (see p60) won it over seventy years later. In complete contrast, **Johnny Longden** (1907) was born in Wakefield, Yorkshire, but emigrated to the States, where he rode his first winner in 1927, and became the only Englishman ever to head the American jockey's table with 236 wins in 1938.

Until the arrival of **Bill Shoemaker** (1931) (see p51), Longden was the world's most successful jockey. He overtook Gordon Richards' total of 4,870 wins in 1956, and when he retired in 1966 his score had risen to 6,032, his triumphs including the Triple Crown with Count Fleet in 1943 and the Washington International of 1961. He set another record when he became the only man to ride and train Kentucky Derby winners when he saddled Majestic Prince to win the race in 1969.

'Well done!' Walter Swinburn (GB) winning the King George VI & Queen Elizabeth Diamond Stakes at Ascot 1981, on the ill-fated Shergar (Bernard Parkin)

Eddie Arcaro (USA) – 4,799 winners, and the only jockey to win the US Triple Crown twice (Naples Daily News, Florida, USA)

Eddie Arcaro (1916) won more money in his time than any other jockey (and was shrewd enough to invest his share wisely too). He had wonderful hands, switched his whip like a conjurer, and was credited with being the pioneer of the 'acey-deucey' style of riding, with the inside (left) stirrup longer than the outside (right), a style suited to the tight left-handed American tracks. He was also one of the more articulate jockeys who did much to elevate the status and prestige of his profession. He won two Triple Crowns, on Whirlaway in 1941 and on Citation, in his opinion the greatest horse he ever rode, in 1948, and his major victories included five Kentucky Derbys, six Preakness Stakes and six Belmonts. No greater accolade can be given than the words of the great Shoemaker: 'He was the greatest rider I ever saw, he was really terrific.'

The record for the number of wins in a year is held by **Chris McCarron** (1955), who won 546 races in his very first year, 1974, and who headed the lists for races won again in 1975 and 1980 and for prize money in 1980, 1981 and 1984. Another sort of record is held by **Chris Antley** (1966) who in 1987 won four races in one afternoon at Aqueduct, followed by five at the evening meeting at The Meadowlands, making nine wins in the day.

But the greatest prize money winner of all time is one of several Central American jockeys who have successfully invaded the northern tracks. Panamanian **Laffit Pincay**

(1946), rode for two years in his native country, won on his first ride in the States and won his first million in prize money the next year. In 1984 he topped the ten million mark in the season, and the next year set an all-time record with over $13m. His career total is now heading for $130m, and his big wins have included the Kentucky Derby, the Belmont Stakes three times in succession, the Arlington Million and the Washington International; and 1987 he won seven races in a day at Santa Anita.

In 1972 the brilliant Brigadier Gerard won all his races in England except one, the Benson & Hedges Gold Cup at York, and the horse that beat him, Roberto, was ridden by another Panamanian jockey. When Lester Piggott preferred Rheingold to his Derby winner Roberto, trainer Vincent O'Brien obtained the services of **Braulio Baeza** (1940), who proceeded to make all the running on a course that was totally strange to him and to shatter the course record in the process. But Baeza was used to breaking records; back in Panama in 1959 he had won a quarter of all the races run in that country, and when he moved to the States he won just about every major stakes race there too, retiring in 1975 with a total of 3,140 winners.

Panama has produced another very successful rider in **Jorge Velasquez** (1946), who, after beating even Baeza's achievements at home, then went to the top in the States, where he became only the fourth jockey to pass the $100m mark in prize money. But it is another Central American State, Puerto Rico, that has produced one of the most successful yet controversial jockeys riding today. **Angel Cordero** (1942) induces a love-hate relationship with American racegoers. He has won the Kentucky Derby three times, the Preakness twice and the Belmont, the Washington International and the Arlington Million once each, and has eleven times exceeded $5m in prize money in a season, his career earnings being second only to Laffit Pincay. But the list of his achievements is almost counterbalanced by the list of his suspensions, for in his determination to win he has been apt to disregard all else.

An American who has taken his skills to Europe is **Cash Asmussen** (1962). After being Champion in France in 1985 and 1986, he rode for Vincent O'Brien in Ireland for two seasons before returning to France where, in 1988, he became the first to ride 200 winners in a season.

Yves Saint-Martin (1941) (see p55) is way out on his own amongst French jockeys, but **Roger Poincelet** (1921–77) had an enviable reputation on both sides of the Channel, riding over 2,500 winners and heading the French jockeys' table nine times. He won twenty major races there, including three Arcs de Triomphe, and in England won the Derby, the 2000 Guineas and the Oaks. **Freddie Head** (1947), son of trainer Alec Head, took the French Championship five times, and has won twenty-two French classics. In 1987, having won the Epsom 1000 Guineas with Miesque, he went on to win the Breeders Cup Turf Mile in 1987 and 1988.

Whether the sport is cricket, rugby football, tennis or yachting, the Australian sportsman is always respected, sometimes feared, when he comes from the Antipodes to challenge the best of the northern hemisphere. The first Australian jockey to do so was **Frank Wootton** (1893–1940), who became Champion on the flat for four years before 1914; and when military service in the war led to an increase in weight, he turned to jumping, and nearly took the Championship there too.

The name of Wagga Wagga may have brought smiles to the paddocks of English

racecourses in the early fifties, but the smiles soon disappeared when the jockey from that prosperous farming community near Sydney won 2,161 winners and four Championships on English racecourses. **Scobie Breasley** (1914), described by Sir Gordon Richards as 'a great artist, a natural horseman, who rides with his head', won most of the major races in his home country before coming to England in 1950, and his victories in Europe included the 1000 and 2000 Guineas, two Epsom Derbys and the Arc de Triomphe. After successes in Australia and Ireland, **Bill Williamson** (1922–79) won both the 1000 Guineas and the Arc de Triomphe twice, and was considered by many to have been unlucky to have been replaced on Roberto for the 1972 Derby by Lester Piggott.

George Moore (1923) was probably the greatest of the Australian jockeys to come to Europe after winning virtually all there was to win at home, where he once rode fifteen winners at a four-day meeting. 'Like Steve Donoghue', said Sir Gordon, 'he's got something the rest of us haven't got.' He was an artist at producing his horses perfectly balanced for a finishing burst, and seemed to possess an uncanny eye for the gap that wasn't really there but which opened up as soon as he went for it. He rode for Prince Aly Khan in France, and took over the top job with Noel Murless on Piggott's departure. After his best season, 1967, in which he won the Epsom Derby and 1000 and 2000 Guineas, as well as Ascot's King George VI and Queen Elizabeth Stakes, he was the subject of disgraceful threats to the lives of himself and his family. Success followed as a trainer in France and Hong Kong. He finally retired to his native country.

Luca Cumani, son of the champion Italian trainer, won nearly a hundred races as an amateur in Italy before coming to Newmarket as assistant to Henry Cecil and then setting up his own successful stable that won the 1988 English/Irish Derby double with Kahyasi. Italy's best known jockey internationally is Sardinian **Gianfranco Dettori** (1941), who tried a number of jobs before he took to race riding at which he quickly shone, becoming Champion four years later. After winning the 1975 English 2000 Guineas on the Italian owned Bolkonski, he won the race again the next year, and the Irish 2000 in 1977, and has dominated the Italian scene ever since. His nineteen-year-old son, **Lanfranco**, now has the top job with Cumani, and his 40-1 win on Chummy's Favourite in Ascot's Diadem Stakes indicated that cries of 'Bravissimo' may well be heard on English courses for some time to come.

Concluding the list of foreign riders who have successfully brought their talents to England is the 1988 Jockey of the Year, South African **Michael Roberts** (1954). Back at home he completely dominated the racing scene, taking the Championship eleven times (once as an apprentice) and being the first to achieve 200 wins in a season. He came to England in 1976, and his association with Alec Stewart's Newmarket stable led to 121 winners in 1988 and third place in the Championship behind Pat Eddery and Willie Carson. His popularity in England with owners, trainers and punters is now soundly established.

OPPOSITE

Gianfranco Dettori (Italy), champion of Italy, riding Tolomeo at Newmarket in 1983 for Luca Cumani. Tolomeo was at that time Europe's top money winner (Bernard Parkin)

FRED ARCHER

Of the handful of jockeys who have so completely dominated the racing scene that their selection for the accolade of 'Great' is beyond dispute, Fred Archer in many respects stands supreme. His achievements during seventeen seasons of racing were remarkable by any standards; they were especially so when the difficulties of travelling up and down the country in the middle of the nineteenth century are taken into account – poor roads, no cars, no motorways, indifferent rail travel, no aeroplanes or helicopters, not even a telephone.

Two years after Fred had entered this world, his father William had won the 1859 Grand National on Little Charlie, so racing was an important influence on him from his earliest days. He started riding not long after he could walk, and it soon became apparent that he had inherited a natural aptitude for getting on with horses, an aptitude that was later to blossom into genius. In 1868, at the age of eleven, he was apprenticed to Matthew Dawson at Newmarket, and in the following year he brought home his first winner at Bangor – over fences – and the records show that Maid of Trent, the first of nearly 3,000 winners, carried a mere 4st 11lb (30kg)!

Fred's first win on the flat came in 1870, the season bringing him just two wins from fifteen rides, and the next year he recorded his first big win on the lightly handicapped Salvanos in the Cesarewitch. Unfortunately the huge sum of money that his connections made from that gamble disappeared when Salvanos ran unplaced in the Cambridgeshire. In the same year Fred had his only brush with the stewards when he was suspended for a couple of weeks for 'misconduct at the start' at Newmarket, but the season ended with a respectable tally of twenty-five wins from 136 rides.

At the end of his apprenticeship Dawson retained Fred as his lightweight jockey. He had already shown that he possessed the will to win, and now he spent much of his spare time studying form. At the racecourse he watched every runner carefully, and when he dismounted after a race he could tell an owner or trainer not only exactly how his own horse had run, but also how all the others had run too. Unlike some other brilliant jockeys, he was articulate as well as perceptive. He also earned a reputation for extreme punctuality; he was usually first into the parade ring, first to mount and first to arrive at the start. In those days there was no draw and Fred usually made sure of getting the position he wanted, and although he was from now on careful not to incur the starter's wrath, woe betide any young upstart who tried to pinch the inside berth!

His first season as a fully fledged jockey at the age of sixteen earned him second place in the Championship with 110 wins from 397 mounts. He was even now a superb judge of pace, and he excelled in a finish, but he rode in spurs, used a long whip, and was beginning to earn a reputation for treating his horses with undue severity. But if this was

Fred Archer (GB): 2,784 winners and twenty-one Classic victories in seventeen seasons before his death at the age of twenty-nine (Bernard Parkin)

true, he was also hard on himself, for he was tall for a jockey (5ft 8½in; 1.7m) and was already starting to have problems with his weight that were to plague him throughout his career and which were to lead to his tragic end.

In 1874 he received a modest retainer from Lord Falmouth, whose first jockey at the time was George Fordham, and thus began a duel that was to continue over the next decade. In almost everything Fordham and Archer were opposites; Archer was tall and elegant, Fordham was short and stubby; Fred was extremely intelligent, George was perhaps more cunning. In a match Fordham usually came out on top, while in the rough and tumble of a big race Archer was the master.

Fred was now, at the age of eighteen, an indefatigable traveller, driven on by two forces; his intense desire to win, and the persistent demands of his parents for money. Money itself had no particular fascination for him, but he wanted success for the security that it would bring. Unfortunately, even this early in his career he was a compulsive gambler – in those days jockeys were free to bet as they wished. He was by now much in demand, and on one occasion when two owners both wanted his services for their horses in the same match – matches were a feature of racing in the nineteenth century – each one tracked him down on the gallops in the early morning, a case of the early bird getting the worm!

In 1876 he led the jockeys' table with 207 winners, 132 ahead of the runner-up, Harry Constable, and he had earned enough money to set his father up as landlord of the Andoversford Hotel near Cheltenham, which he made his base for the hunting which he enjoyed in the winter months. It was at this time that the great partnership of owner, trainer and jockey that was to dominate English racing over the next decade was formed. Lord Falmouth's first jockey had up to now been George Fordham, but he became incapacitated for a time due to drink, and Fred took his place. With Mat Dawson as trainer, they won the Derby and the St Leger with Silvio in 1877, and the Oaks and St Leger in the following year, and in that season won over £38,000 in prize money for Lord Falmouth.

The year was marred, however, by the death of Fred's elder brother William after a fall in a hurdle race at Cheltenham, and by his own continuing weight problems. His normal winter weight was around 11st (70kg), and to the disadvantage of his height was added a problem with his feet, which were so weak that he was unable to shed weight by running. He therefore had to rely solely on starvation, Turkish baths and on a drastic purgative which became known as 'Archer's mixture'. His daily intake of food was certainly not enough to sustain the frame of a growing teenager; breakfast consisted of a teaspoon of castor oil and half an orange, lunch of a small sardine and half a glass of champagne, and at the end of the day a meagre supper.

Now aged twenty-one, he had already been Champion for five seasons and was approaching his 1,000th winner. Highly intelligent, and driven on by extreme ambition, he was something of a Jekyll and Hyde character; absolutely unpretentious and always well mannered off the course, in a race he was utterly ruthless, and would not hesitate to put another jockey over the rails if he felt threatened. On one occasion in a tight finish at Doncaster he drew blood on the left shoulder of the favourite with his right spur. His explanation was that with a weak ankle he could not control his spur! Nevertheless, he was never disliked by his fellow jockeys, with the exception of Fordham, and they admired his skill and respected his determination. His treatment of his horses had mellowed, however, and he now removed the rowels from his spurs.

The year 1879 started almost incredibly well, with seven wins at the Newmarket Craven Meeting, followed by successes in the City and Suburban Handicap, the Great Metropolitan, the 2000 and the 1000 Guineas, the Oaks, the Prince of Wales's Stakes at Ascot and the Yorkshire Oaks. The next year, too, started full of promise, for the Duke of Westminster gave him a retainer for 1880, and with patrons of the calibre of the Dukes of Westminster, Portland and Beaufort, the Earl of Rosebery and Lord Hastings, it seemed that he could hardly fail to retain the Championship.

But on 1 May he was riding work on a difficult colt called Muley Edris, on whom he had previously had occasion to use his whip somewhat severely. Fred dismounted in order to move some dolls, and the colt went for him. He seized him by the left arm, lifted him and carried him for a few strides, then dropped him, knelt on his chest and began to savage him. The outcome might well have finished Fred's riding career for good and all, but at that moment the horse's hind legs slipped and he almost fell over, and as help arrived he galloped away. With the Derby only three weeks away, here he was with his arm torn and his muscles wrenched and unable to ride. The wounds refused to heal, and, to make matters worse he started to put on weight and became acutely depressed.

Lord Falmouth's doctor seemed unable to help, and eventually it was a local bone setter (from the Andoversford area) who put him on the road to recovery.

He was of course determined to ride Bend Or in the Derby, but the Duke of Westminster had other problems besides the question of his jockey's fitness to ride. Bend Or was unable to run before the Derby because of sore shins, but because of his two-year-old form he was nevertheless made favourite. The shins did not improve, so they resorted to massaging them with brandy; (history does not relate whether it was four-star cognac or cooking brandy, but it seems to have done the trick). Meanwhile his jockey had had to lose a stone in weight, as a result of which he had become weak, nervous and irritable, and his damaged arm was virtually useless and would certainly be of no help in a tight finish.

However, Fred did ride, and managed to get the position he wanted at the start. Coming down the hill towards Tattenham Corner Bend Or was not very well balanced – perhaps he was feeling his shins – but Fred hugged the rails so tightly that he had to lift his left leg in order to clear them; there were those who thought he had actually put his inside leg over the rails in order to keep his position! As they entered the straight Robert the Devil went into a lead which he proceeded to increase. A hundred yards from the post Fred made what might have been a fatal mistake; he went for his whip and dropped it. But Robert the Devil's jockey made a worse one; at the critical moment, instead of driving his horse on past the post he looked round, and Robert faltered. Seizing his opportunity, Fred drove Bend Or forwards with his legs and the two horses crossed the line together.

After what must have seemed an eternity, Bend Or was given the verdict by a head, and what could have been blamed on a lack of judgement on the part of owner and trainer in putting an unfit rider on the favourite was in fact hailed as a superlative piece of horsemanship on the part of the jockey. However, Fred may have been home, but he was not yet dry, for a somewhat ludicrous objection was lodged on the grounds that the winner's breeding had been incorrectly stated on entry. This was overruled, but the narrowness of the margin between triumph and disaster was emphasised when it was found that Bend Or had spread a plate during the race. Despite having to miss a considerable number of winning rides because of his arm, Fred still retained the Championship (for the seventh time).

The year 1881 was perhaps the zenith of Fred's career. At the age of twenty-four, Dawson took him into partnership, though he still treated Fred like any other lad, expecting him to attend evening stables and to treat owners with the same deference as before. Fred won the City and Suburban on Bend Or and the Derby on the American colt Iriquois, and then took part in a match between Bend Or and Robert the Devil, whose owner hoped to avenge his Derby defeat of the previous year. In a superb piece of riding, Fred coaxed Bend Or home to win by a neck.

Another example of Fred's artistry came in the Manchester Cup over 1 mile and 6 furlongs. Valour, owned jointly by Fred and Captain Machell, only really stayed a mile, but the long-distance races of those days amounted to little more than a preliminary canter followed by a sharp sprint for the finish, and the skill lay in deciding when to go. Fred decided to ride two races; first he set off at a good pace, and the rest of the field let him go. After a mile he gave Valour a breather while they caught up; then he set Valour alight again and won by a neck from Sir John Astley's Peter, who lost his owner a substantial wager.

Peter was a difficult ride, and in the Queen's Vase at Ascot he napped when ridden by his stable jockey on the first day. In the Royal Hunt Cup with Fred in the saddle he dropped the bit and half-a-mile from home they were at the back of the field. Instead of hitting him, Fred coaxed Peter back into action, and won the race by a couple of lengths. But in those days horses were expected to work much harder than they do today, and Peter was also entered in the Hardwick Stakes on the Friday. Fred obtained permission to go to the start by cantering right round the course in the reverse direction; suitably disorientated, Peter won again. But there was a limit to what even Fred could do, and later in the Goodwood Cup not even he could persuade the horse to race.

Fred was now, at the age of twenty-four, a rich man. He lived modestly, apart from his gambling, and his only real problem concerned his weight. And his happiness seemed about to be made complete with his engagement to marry Mat Dawson's niece Helen Rose, for whom he set about building a substantial residence at Newmarket. With his involvement with the running of the stable he could no longer afford the time to hunt in Leicestershire, so he and a few friends started the Newmarket Drag.

The 1882 season began well, and included a win in the French Grand Prix, for which he had negotiated a huge fee. In England he was popular with the punters and respected by his fellow jockeys, but in France the jockeys were jealous of his success, while the public were annoyed when he won on an outsider and furious if he failed to win on a favourite. But at home he won six out of seven races at Lewes, and then became involved in a wrangle for his services for the St Leger, which he handled in a way that did his reputation no good with his owners.

To make matters worse, it was suggested that Fred had stopped a horse at York and Goodwood in order to prepare for a betting coup in the St Leger, and although the stewards held an inquiry and found that there was no case to answer, the rumours continued, which spoiled an otherwise extremely successful season, with a tally of 210 winners.

On 31 January 1883 the racing fraternity flocked to Newmarket for Fred and Helen's wedding, with an ox roast, balloons and fireworks, and after a honeymoon at Torquay they settled in to Falmouth House, so called in honour of its primary owner. This was a far cry from his frugal bachelor quarters, with its own Turkish bath, his many gold and silver trophies, and paintings and portraits of his favourite horses. Fred, worried about a spate of burglaries in Newmarket, looked out a silver mounted revolver that had been given to him by a grateful owner, and placed it in a drawer beside his bed.

At last Fred seemed relaxed and happy. He received a huge retainer from the Duchess of Montrose, and won the 2000 Guineas for Lord Falmouth on Gaillard, who was made favourite for the Derby. But Gaillard was always difficult to handle before a race, and when permission was given for him to miss the parade, rumours of a betting coup were rife. For once Fred was unable to secure his customary inside berth at Tattenham Corner, and Gaillard was third to St Blaise and Highland Chief. Rumours and accusations abounded; did Fred stop Gaillard? In fact it was highly unlikely that Fred, with his indomitable will to win, especially in the Derby, would have done so, but subsequent events did nothing to damp the speculation.

First, Fred was beaten by a whisker in the Grand Prix de Paris on St Blaise when the French jockeys hemmed him in. Then at Ascot on the first day he won the Prince of Wales's Stakes on Gaillard from Ossian, who next day beat Fred on St Blaise; Gaillard then won the St James's Palace Stakes on the Thursday and his third race of the meeting on Friday, all somewhat confusing to the punters. It is difficult to see how horses run as frequently as they were in those days could be expected to maintain their true form every time out, but Fred was considerably hurt by the insinuations.

Meanwhile at Newmarket a two-year-old colt put up for sale with its leg dressed to look like a blemish had been snapped up by Mat Dawson for the Duke of Portland. When his new owner first saw him in a trial he was not at all impressed, but when offers were made for him he thought that perhaps others knew something that he did not, and refused to sell. The colt proved difficult to handle and in the stable he required a muzzle and two lads to hold him while one groomed him. But he turned out to be one of the quickest horses that Fred had ever ridden. St Simon won his first race at Derby by eight lengths, and was then matched against the Duke of Westminster's colt Duke of Richmond – all these dukes must have been somewhat confusing! The Duke of Portland overheard the Duke of Westminster's trainer John Porter telling his jockey Tom Cannon to jump off at the start, so Fred was told to do the same. He led by twenty lengths after a couple of furlongs, then gave St Simon a breather, and won.

The year 1884 did not start happily. Fred's brother Charles had his permit to train withdrawn, Helen was pregnant but far from well, and their firstborn son died within a few hours of birth. When St Simon came up from his winter's rest he seemed idle in his work, so Dawson told Fred to wake him up. Fred donned his spurs, and St Simon took off across Newmarket Heath, scattering strings of horses, and finally pulling up on the edge of the town. Lord Falmouth had decided to sell up, and Fred, having been Champion for eleven seasons, was again the subject of rumours, this time of a jockey's 'ring' controlled by himself and Charlie Wood. He thought of switching to riding over fences, even of having a go at the Grand National. To make matters worse, Fred chose the wrong horse for the Derby, and his Championship was threatened by Wood, who rode St Simon to four wins from four starts. (St Simon, who had not been entered for the Derby, retired to stud unbeaten, but since he was also virtually unchallenged it was impossible to estimate his worth, and he is chiefly remembered as a great sire.)

At the end of the season, which had brought 241 winners, Helen gave birth to a daughter, and all seemed well. But a few days later Helen was dead, and Fred felt that his world had come to an end. Eventually his friends persuaded him to take a trip to America, where he was fêted as a hero, but when he returned in March 1885 he weighed 9st 10lb (62kg). He wasted drastically, won the Lincoln on Paradox, a difficult horse who would not race in front, and prepared for the Derby on Melton, a brilliant colt with doubtful legs. In the Derby he was content to let Paradox make the running, and sure enough as soon as he was clear in the straight he dropped the bit. Melton crept gradually closer, but Fred sat still. Then, with fifty yards to go, he pounced, and Melton won by a short head. So grateful was his owner, Lord Hastings, that his present to Fred amounted to £4,525, a tidy sum in 1885!

That year he won four classics, and from 667 rides had a total of 246 winners, a record that was to stand until Gordon Richards broke it forty-eight years later! But by the end of the year he was far from well, and strain was beginning to tell. Apart from his weight problem, and the constant travel in search of winners, he had no secretary, and on top of helping to run the partnership he had to make all his engagements by telegram, letter or personal contact, and carry them in his head.

Nevertheless, he was still very much the Champion, and in 1886 he won his fifth Derby and the St Leger on Ormonde, the French Grand Prix on Minting, and gave the Prince of Wales his first winner on the flat. But now he was losing races that he should have won, and he was headed in the Championship by Wood. In a desperate effort to do the weight on St Mirin in the Cambridgeshire, which he had never won, he ate nothing for three days before the race, spent his time in the Turkish bath, and consequently lost the race, and a sizable bet, by a short head. He still brought home five winners in a day at the beginning of November, but at Lewes he was beaten on an odds-on favourite, and returned home to bed in high fever.

The doctors diagnosed a severe chill coupled with fever and typhoid. On the morning of 8 November they visited him again, and after they had left Fred sent his nurse away. While his sister, Mrs Coleman, was looking out of the window he took the revolver from his bedside drawer. His sister looked round, and a short struggle ensued during which he shot himself, aged twenty-nine years.

His record, set over a mere seventeen seasons, speaks for itself. Five Derbys, six St Legers, four Oaks, four 2000 Guineas and two 1000 Guineas; seven seasons in which he brought home over 200 winners; a grand total of 2,748 winners from 8,004 rides.

STEVE DONOGHUE

Two years before Fred Archer cut short his own brilliant career, the town of Warrington, in Lancashire, saw the arrival into a miserable home dominated by an unsympathetic father of the boy who was to dominate the racing scene in the years immediately before and after World War I.

If Steve Donoghue's home life was unhappy, and if he found school difficult and uninteresting, nevertheless his first recorded encounter with a quadruped showed that he had no lack of two qualities that were to stand him in good stead throughout his career as a jockey – power of observation and intelligence. One day at the circus, spectators were challenged to survive three circuits of the sawdust ring astride a donkey whose buck was such that he might not have been out of place at a rodeo in the Far West! No one lasted the course, whereupon the resident clown leapt upon the unforgiving brute's back and showed how it should be done. Most of the audience found it hysterically funny, but it was not lost on Steve that the clown had mounted the donkey facing backwards; leaping into the ring he did the same, and won the challenge.

It was not long before he was to display another quality – determination. Anxious to get away from home, where he was frequently thrashed at the slightest excuse, he wrote to the Kingsclere trainer John Porter to ask for employment, but received the answer that there were no vacancies. Intelligent enough to reason that Porter would be at Chester races, Steve hitchhiked to the Roodeye, discovered who the trainer was, and accosted him in person. Impressed by the young boy's determination, Porter told him to return next day with his father if he was really serious. Another thrashing might have been the only outcome, but perhaps father saw a heaven-sent opportunity of having the boy taken off his hands, and the upshot was that young Steve found himself with his few possessions travelling back with the horses to Kingsclere.

The stable lads' quarters were like heaven after his Warrington home, but he nevertheless felt homesick and returned there. But he now knew that he wanted to work with horses, and we find him next with Dobson Peacock at Middleham, where he learned to ride. This time, however, he had left home without his father's permission and under a false name, which created difficulties, to put it mildly, as the census of 1901 loomed. So he left and took a job driving a horse and cart in Manchester, but it was not long before he found his way to Newmarket, where he obtained work as a stable lad with Alfred Saddler at Freemason's Lodge. Here his evident ability would have earned him an apprenticeship, but he still could not risk his father's wrath, and seeing an advertisement for a job in Chantilly, he applied and was accepted.

So 1903 found Steve in France, without a word of the language, with an English trainer who was shortly to become bankrupt. However, at least he was now riding work, and the French practice of timing gallops by the furlong, much as they do in America, developed another valuable attribute – judgement of pace. In 1904, on his first ride in public, he was third in a race at the Paris course of Angoutème, and winners followed at Aix-les-Bains and Hyères the following year, but it looked as though he would be doomed to the minor courses of France for the foreseeable future.

His break came in 1906 from an unexpected direction. He heard that his brother George was in difficulty at The Curragh, and so he came to Ireland, where he found happiness for the first time in his life. He was taken on as stable jockey to Philip Behan, and rode his first winner in Ireland in a maiden plate at Phoenix Park. More wins followed, including one at an interesting but unusual (but typically Irish) meeting at Skerries Strand, where part of the course ran along the beach. Having ridden in the first race without success, Steve rode the same horse again in the last. By now the tide was well in, and by taking the lead and kicking sea water into the faces of his pursuers he won fairly comfortably. More significant, though, was his first big win, in the Irish Cesarewitch at The Curragh.

In 1908 Steve married the trainer's daughter Brigid. The following year he won his first race in England at Liverpool, and headed the list of winning jockeys in Ireland, and at last he was on his way to the top. In 1910 he received a retainer from Atty Perse at Stockbridge, and rode Charles O'Malley into a creditable third place in his first Epsom Derby. But his upward climb was not all smooth. Illness, in the form of typhoid and a liver complaint, plagued him that year, and a horrible fall at Windsor did nothing for his progress in 1911, though he did win a hurdle race at Birmingham!

But sooner or later a potentially great rider meets up with a great horse, and in 1913 Steve was given the ride on an odd looking grey colt over which someone seemed to have spilled the paint pot; the two-year-old certainly caught the eye, but possibly not for the right reasons! But ''andsome is as 'andsome does' was never truer than in this case, and an apparently astonishing performance at home preceded his first win in a maiden two-year-old race at the Newmarket Craven meeting in April, and he went on to win the Coventry Stakes at Royal Ascot. His name was The Tetrarch.

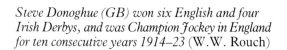

Steve Donoghue (GB) won six English and four Irish Derbys, and was Champion Jockey in England for ten consecutive years 1914–23 (W.W. Rouch)

The Derby of 1913 is remembered not for the horse that won, nor for Steve's mount, Bachelor Wedding, but for the incident at Tattenham Corner when a suffragette ran out onto the course in front of the runners, bringing down HM King George V's runner and ending her own life in the process. Bachelor Wedding, however, went on to win the Irish Derby at the Curragh for Steve, who also rode a winner for the King at Lingfield.

It was unfortunate for two of the very greatest jockeys, Steve Donoghue and Gordon Richards, that world wars affected both of their careers. At the outbreak of World War I Steve, in his thirty-second year, was just about taking over from Danny Maher as the leading jockey of the time. Racing continued on a much reduced scale during the war, and from 1916 onwards it was confined to Newmarket. In 1915 Steve tried to enlist but failed his medical, and it was some consolation to him that he won both the 2000 and the 1000 Guineas and the substitute Derby at Newmarket (on Mr Solly Joel's Pommern), and the Chester Cup on the course where his story really began sixteen years previously.

A 1916–17 winter trip to South Africa to ride for Solly Joel provided a single winner on his last ride, but the summer brought his second Derby victory on Gay Crusader. The year 1918 was, for Steve, one to remember in more ways than one. At the Derby meeting he rode eight winners, and at Royal Ascot he was presented by the King with a gold mounted whip on which were engraved the names of all the royal winners that he had ridden. He also broke his wrist in a fall at York, refused to have the operation that his doctor advised, and rode another winner in a manner which gave a new twist to the phrase 'single-handed'!

The early twenties, with English society trying to recapture the gaiety of the pre-war years, and racing flourishing once again, found Steve at the height of his powers. Three consecutive Derbys set a record that has yet to be broken: Humorist in 1921 (sadly the horse died of consumption a month later), Captain Cuttle in 1922, and Papyrus in 1923. In the same year (1923) Papyrus crossed the Atlantic, no easy journey in those days, to take on the best three-year-old in the States in a match at Belmont Park. The American challenger, Zev, won by four lengths, but the rigours of the voyage and conditions utterly strange to Papyrus – the dirt track was hard and dusty during the pre-race training period but turned to mud shortly before the race – made it difficult to compare the real merit of the two horses. Later Steve successfully sued the *New York Herald* for suggesting that he had not tried in the race, winning substantial damages and costs and receiving a public apology.

This period must be considered the zenith of Steve's career, with three consecutive Derbys and eight consecutive championships. But he was now forty years of age, he was no longer as strong as he was, and his ambition to ride winners at any cost led him to accept outside rides at the expense of his loyalty to trainers who retained him. This in turn led to his losing good rides and to his accepting poor ones. But the public still adored him, some punters simply backing 'Steve's horse' wherever and whatever he was riding, and speculation about the Derby was less concerned with the merits of the horses engaged than with Steve's intended mount, a situation that unfortunately sometimes led to his involvement in plots to deceive the public.

He was now living with Lady Torrington at Elston House, Shrewton, and the expense of helping to maintain this residence, coupled with his love of parties and his gambling, put undue strain on his resources. He went to Deauville with Jimmy White, incurred

Steve Donoghue (GB) winning the fourth of his six Derbys, and his second of three in succession, shown here with Captain Cuttle in 1922 (Sport & General)

huge losses at the Casino, and was involved in court proceedings, and as he left the paddock for the start of the 1925 Derby a writ was thrust into his hands – surely a unique method of service! But he had already won the 2000 Guineas on Manna, and now came a Derby victory which even interfered with business in the House of Commons. A junior MP was stationed by the tape machine, and when the news came in he rushed into the Chamber to put the Supplementary Question: 'Is this house aware that Manna has won the Derby?'

He then went to Paris to ride in the Grand Prix, in which several horses were brought down on a bend. Steve suffered concussion and a dislocated and broken shoulder, but he was to suffer even more when the doctors tried unsuccessfully to reset the shoulder without an anaesthetic; poor Steve was allergic to chloroform. But the esteem in which he was held is indicated by the list of visitors to his hospital, including representatives of the President of France, the Aga Khan and Baron de Rothschild. But France seemed unlucky for him, for at Deauville in August he was thrown on the way to the start.

The following year, 1926, was not a happy one. He had lost the Championship to Gordon Richards in the previous year, and he was now starting to lose races that he should have won. He had no classic win, no ride in the Derby, and with only sixty-six winners he could only manage seventh place in the Championship behind Gordon Richards. In the Lincoln he had finished last, while his son Pat, who had already savoured the moment of beating his father at Bath the previous season, won on a 100-1 outsider. But father came back to win the City and Suburban Handicap and the Irish Derby, and although many tried to persuade him to retire, he could neither afford to do so nor could he bring himself to shoulder the responsibilities of being a trainer.

Soon, however, a great horse was to come to his rescue. The 1928 Champion Hurdle at Cheltenham was won by a gelding who was never to jump a fence again, and whose career had started somewhat inauspiciously when he failed to reach his reserve at the Ballsbridge Sales in Dublin. As he cheered home the winner with his trainer, Ivor Anthony, Steve was emphatic that the horse would win on the flat, and so began his association with the immortal Brown Jack. And at this moment he needed rescuing, for he was subject to a Receiving Order which required him to pay 50 per cent of his earnings to the Official Receiver while his financial affairs were sorted out. And in 1929 bankruptcy proceedings were started.

This was perhaps not the moment to plunge into a secret second marriage, not to Lady Torrington, nor even to a rich heiress, but to an American dancer named Ethel Finn. The marriage was not to last for long, and probably because of it Lady Torrington, who had made a will leaving her property to Steve in trust for life, revoked it and left him nothing. (She committed suicide two years later in a state of bankruptcy.)

But on the opening day at Royal Ascot in 1929, Steve and Brown Jack were second in the Ascot Stakes, and then on the final day won the Queen Alexandra Stakes, the longest flat race in the calendar, a feat that they were to repeat over the next five years! And when they won this race in 1934 for the sixth year running, Steve was fifty and the horse was ten. Since he had been gelded when he had seemed to have no future on the racecourse, Brown Jack continued racing long after his contemporaries were enjoying themselves at stud, but it was nevertheless a considerable feat to be beating horses half his age in so testing a race.

Meanwhile Steve had broken a leg in a fall at Nottingham in 1930, when amongst his 'get well' telegrams had been those from King George V and Lord Derby, had won the 1931 Derby for Tom Walls on April the Fifth, and had suffered the indignity of being caught in the starting tapes at the Royal Ascot meeting of 1933. But the year ended on an even more ominous note; on the last day of the season he was beaten by Gordon Richards, and the cries of 'Come on Steve' were drowned by those of 'Come on Gordon'. Gordon, who had taken the Championship from Steve back in 1925, was on the crest of a wave, having just surpassed Fred Archer's total of 246 wins in a season, eventually setting a new record of 259.

Shortly after Brown Jack's final success at Ascot in 1934, Steve flew to Paris to watch the Grand Prix, and at a celebration party at the Hotel King George V on the eve of the race picked up a chance ride on Admiral Drake, on whom he then proceeded to win the race. Steve's last chance to partner Brown Jack came the night before he won his fourth Irish Derby, when he rode the old horse into the ring at the International Horse Show at Olympia to raise funds for a hospital.

Though his career had been taking a downhill path over the last few seasons, Steve finally hung up his boots on a good note. In 1937 he won the 1000 Guineas and the Oaks for Sir Victor Sassoon on Exhibitionist, and the Irish Derby on Phideas, and at last Sir Victor was able to persuade him to retire and start training. His fellow jockeys gave him a farewell dinner and a silver trophy at the Piccadilly Hotel, and the following April a dinner for 400 was organised at the Dorchester in order to raise funds to enable Steve to equip his new stable.

So in 1938 he started training at Blewbury in Berkshire, but he was not content just to give orders and then watch what was happening from the sidelines; in a gallop he would follow behind the horses being schooled, and afterwards he would know more about their performances than the lads who had ridden them. In his first season as a trainer he had several wins, enough to show that he had the ability to succeed in this new branch of his profession.

His first Epsom winner came in 1939, as did the war. He had over fifty horses in his stable, but the difficulties of carrying on in wartime began to get him down. He became involved in a tiresome wrangle over Ethel's maintenance (they had parted some years previously), and his younger son was shot down and killed with the RAF over the North Sea. Steve himself did not live to see the end of the war. He died at the age of sixty on 23 March 1945, and was buried in his birthplace, Warrington.

His record, especially in the classics, had been impressive: six Derbys, two Oaks, two St Legers, three 2000 Guineas, a 1000 guineas, as well as classic wins in Ireland and France; ten successive Championships from 1914 to 1923. What then had been the secret of his success?

Two qualities above all seem to stand out: hands, and sympathy with the horses he rode. He taught his son Pat, '. . . The importance of gentleness of touch and voice towards the horse, of treating the reins as though they were made of silken thread, and of communication to the horse of trust and confidence.' His sympathy with horses was demonstrated time and again when he succeeded with difficult horses with whom others had failed.

But though he mastered his horses, his own affairs he could not manage, and a combination of great extravagance and extreme generosity led to bankruptcy. In 1934 his personal lifestyle was impressive; he lived at the Albany, just off Piccadilly, employed a chauffeur/valet, had his food sent round from Fortnum and Mason, and wore the best hand-tailored clothes. But his income could not support such outgoings,

OPPOSITE

Lester Piggott (GB) with Cash Asmussen (USA) and Cutting Blade, winner of the Windsor Castle Stakes, 1986 – Lester's first Royal Ascot winner as a trainer (Bernard Parkin)

Steve Cauthen (USA) winning the Ribblesdale Stakes on Alydaress, Royal Ascot, 1989 (Bernard Parkin)

Pat Eddery (Ireland) winning the King George V Stakes, Royal Ascot, 1989, on Carlingford
(Bernard Parkin)

Steve Donoghue (GB) on his second Derby winner, Gay Crusader (W.W. Rouch)

and he resorted to borrowing money which he could not repay, a situation which was made worse by his gambling losses.

At the same time his generosity knew no bounds. After the 1925 Derby he gave a party for 800 children from his old school in Warrington, and he helped the school on many other occasions. When he was leaving the course after coming nearly last in another Derby, he was accosted by a party of gipsies who had backed his horse because of their faith in his jockey. With tears in his eyes, he put his hands in his pockets and gave them all his spare cash.

But let the final words be those of the jockey who succeeded him as Champion. Speaking on Steve's retirement, Gordon Richards said, 'No jockey and few men in our time have enjoyed the popularity of Steve Donoghue. But believe me, however popular he may have been with the public, he was still more popular among us in the weighing room, for he helped the least, the last and the poorest of us.'

Sir Gordon Richards (GB) on his 1930 St Leger winner, Singapore (W.W. Rouch)

SIR GORDON RICHARDS

Whether jockeys are born or made will for ever be a subject for discussion if not argument. Some great jockeys undeniably have racing in their blood; one who did not was the son of a Shropshire mineworker whose only connection with horses was through the ponies that hauled the coal from the coalface down the mine, and it was with these that one of the greatest jockeys of all time made his first acquaintance with horses.

Born in Oakengates in 1904, Gordon Richards developed in his early days two characteristics that were to become hallmarks of his race riding in later life. The strength of his legs was built up by walking four miles to and from school each day – it was only a mile from home, but his mother insisted that he return home for lunch! And riding the pit ponies bareback across the fields improved his sense of balance. At school he was brighter than average, but after employment in a warehouse he realised that what he really wanted was a job with horses. When he saw an advertisement in the local paper he answered it, and thus started his career with Martin Hartigan, who trained for the financier Jimmy White at Foxhill in Wiltshire.

So in 1919, at the age of fifteen, Gordon set off with his father to walk the two-and-a-half miles to the station. A very different life awaited him at his destination, where he was met by Jimmy White's chauffeur and driven to the establishment where he was to be paid the princely sum of five shillings (25p) a week. A frequent visitor to Foxhill was Steve Donoghue, whose characteristic riding style of upright stance and long reins Gordon was to copy, and it was not long before Hartigan realised that in his young apprentice he had a rider with two considerable attributes – strong legs and sympathetic hands.

Gordon's first ride in public came in 1920, and the following year he found himself walking the five-year-old Gay Lord five miles to Shrivenham station en route for Leicester. There, after another three-mile walk to the racecourse, he won the Apprentice Plate, watched by his hero Steve Donoghue, and then a double at Lewes confirmed his promise.

Later that year Hartigan moved to Ogbourne, near Marlborough, in an area that was to become Gordon's home for the rest of his life. Soon the winners began to come; five in each of his first two seasons, nineteen in his third, and in 1924 came his first ride in the Derby. But it was perhaps a foretaste of what lay ahead in this particular race, for he finished almost last in torrential rain. But as some consolation he won the Stewards Handicap on Derby day, and later in the year, in which he scored sixty-one winners, he had the thrill of riding for HM King George V at Goodwood.

In 1925 Gordon was retained by Captain Thomas Hogg, with Hartigan having second call on his services, and his 118 winners included hat-tricks at Worcester, Haydock and

Wolverhampton, and a four-timer at Alexandra Palace, and in only his sixth season he became Champion Jockey. But Fate now took a hand, and appendicitis, pleurisy and tuberculosis did their best to hinder a promising career. But on a quiet walk prescribed by his doctor he was charged by a bull, and his quick reaction convinced him if not his medical advisers that he was fit enough to start riding again!

He was Champion again in 1927 with 164 wins from 792 rides, but the man who was to become a byword for integrity also had his first brush with the stewards. Sadly his mother died from asthma, whereupon Gordon showed his generosity, sense of duty and loyalty by taking over responsibility for his family. That winter Captain Hogg took Gordon to St Moritz, where he was to spend many a winter month, and in the spring he secretly married Margery, whose father worked in the GWR railway workshops in Swindon. (He had planned to keep the wedding secret until he had ridden 100 winners, and duly made the announcement in the unsaddling enclosure on reaching his century; unfortunately the result of the race was reversed, so he was still on 99!)

So the winners continued to roll in; 139 in 1929, the Oaks and the St Leger in 1930, though he lost the Championship by one winner to Freddy Fox. Then in 1931 began his long association with the greatest trainer of his time, Fred Darling, at Beckhampton. But if one season had to be picked out as his greatest, 1933 might well be the choice. The Chester Cup on Dick Turpin gave him particular pleasure, and he had scored 100 winners by the end of June. At York he won five races out of six – but was booed by the crowd during a farcical two-horse race when both his trainer and Michael Beary's had given the same instructions – to settle in behind! But such was Gordon's relentless progress that Fred Archer's record of 264 winners in a season looked fallible at last.

The press followed Gordon everywhere, and the bookmakers refused odds of more than 3-1 against any horse that he rode. (At Birmingham a moderate animal with no form at all was backed in a selling plate to win £20,000 with Gordon in the saddle, and after it had run true to form was sold for eighteen guineas!) In October he won the last race at Nottingham, went through the card of six races at Chepstow the next day, and won the first five on the second day – twelve consecutive wins. By the middle of the month, with twenty-nine days racing to go he was only thirteen short of his target, which was finally achieved in a selling plate at Liverpool on 8 November.

The congratulatory telegrams poured in, amongst them one from the King which arrived at the course within an hour of his breaking the record. His Majesty also sent him a silver cigarette case and a pair of racing pigeons from the Sandringham loft. Gordon had started pigeon racing back in 1930, and won his first race in 1934.

By 1935 Gordon could have had the pick of all the horses in training, but in spite of offers from the Aga Khan and from the royal stable he remained loyal to Fred Darling and Martin Hartigan. However, in 1936 it looked as though a Derby win might be on the cards at last on the Aga Khan's Taj Akbar. Gordon won the Chester Cup on him, and in the week before the Derby showed that he was in top form by riding eight consecutive winners at Bath and Salisbury. But in the big race they were beaten into second place by Charlie Smirke and the stable's other runner, Mahmoud.

The St Leger in 1937 on Lord Glanely's Chumleigh was followed by the 2000 Guineas in 1938 on Mr. H. E. Morrish's Pasch, and yet another Derby second in 1939. Then came the war. Turned down by the RAF on medical grounds, Gordon continued to ride during the restricted wartime racing programme, and did not emerge entirely unscathed. He signed on as an air raid warden, was concussed in a motor accident in the blackout, broke a leg when kicked at the start of a race at Salisbury, and was lucky to escape injury when his car was dive bombed by a lone German aircraft.

In 1942 Gordon passed the total of 2,748 winners set by Fred Archer, though he had taken twenty-one years to achieve what Archer had managed in sixteen, and in 1945 he rode his 3,000th winner. That winter he was able to return to his beloved St Moritz, and in 1946 his partnership with Mr A. J. Dewar's Tudor Minstrel, whom many considered the best two-year-old they had ever seen, raised hopes of Derby success in 1947. But though they won the 2000 Guineas, giving Gordon his eleventh classic win, the Derby turned out to be his twenty-second failure in that race.

By now Fred Darling had retired and Noel Murless had taken over at Beckhampton, which was now owned by Herbert Blagrave. The year 1948 brought broken ribs in a fall at Brighton, but also a period in which he won 36 races from 68 starts, a winning percentage of 53! Two years later he achieved his 4,000th winner on his forty-sixth birthday, but also experienced an unhappy day at Bath, where he was disqualified for interference after riding the winner, and then beaten by a fourteen-year-old by the name of Lester Piggott, who was to beat him three times at Folkestone a week later.

The press were now beginning to compare the man who had dominated racing for the past two-and-a-half decades with this precocious new rising star who was eventually to succeed him as Champion, but in fact Gordon's finest hour was yet to come. One morning when riding a gallop at Newmarket on a promising two-year-old he was passed by a big ungainly chestnut called Pinza, owned by Sir Victor Sassoon. Together they won at the St Leger meeting, and, though beaten at Ascot, Gordon's hopes for the Derby were kindled yet again.

Coronation year, Gordon's fiftieth, started well, with six wins in the first week of racing and a win on Pinza at Newmarket. Then, in the Queen's Coronation Honours List, he received the first knighthood ever bestowed upon a jockey. As Derby day dawned the hearts of racegoers were torn between a desire for a royal win in coronation year, and a genuine wish to see Sir Gordon triumph at last. And triumph he did, as Pinza brought him the one trophy that had eluded him for twenty-nine seasons.

His first action after winning the Derby was typical: he gave £50 to his valet, £10 to every other valet on the course, and £5 to every Epsom gateman. The Marlborough Post Office was overwhelmed by congratulatory telegrams, and Sir Gordon was much in demand at functions all over the country. Oakengates, his birthplace, wanted to erect a statue of their hero, but he suggested putting the money into a veterinary hospital instead.

After Pinza had beaten the Queen's Aureole in the Derby, the Duke of Edinburgh had said to him, 'Well, I suppose you're going to retire now', but Her Majesty had intervened, 'Oh no he's not, he's going to win the Derby for me next year on Landau.' But, two months before he was due to ride Landau in the Derby of 1954, a fall at Salisbury put him out of action and he had to miss the big race. He came back to win again at Sandown and at Royal Ascot, where he rode in a race full of incident after which Lester Piggott had his licence to ride withdrawn for his riding of the Derby winner, Never say Die.

More wins followed, including two for the Queen on Landau, and it would have been a wonderful end to a great career if Sir Gordon, who had seriously begun to consider retirement, had been able to depart on the crest of the wave. But when mounting the Queen's Abergeldie in the paddock at Sandown, the filly reared over backwards on top of him, bringing to an end what was arguably the most illustrious riding career in the history of racing. In thirty-five seasons he had won 4,870 races from 21,834 rides, and had been Champion twenty-six times.

But figures by no means tell the whole story, for Sir Gordon by his conduct had set himself head and shoulders above anyone else in his profession. Contemporary owners, trainers and fellow jockeys held him in high esteem. HM King George V wanted Gordon to ride for him because he was 'Absolutely straight and always did his best to win'. Lord Rosebery described him as 'The greatest jockey I have ever seen. Of course every jockey wins races that he ought to have lost, but Gordon has lost far fewer races that he ought to have won than any other jockey.'

Both Fred Darling and Noel Murless, undoubtedly among the greatest trainers that English racing has ever seen, praised him for his utter integrity, his reliability, and his complete dedication to the task in hand, whether it was a schooling gallop at home, a selling plate, or a classic race. Perhaps even more telling was the judgement of another great jockey. Steve Donoghue's advice to a punter was, 'If you must back a horse, and you don't know, back Gordon Richards; you will always get a good run for your money.'

But unlike Steve Donoghue, Gordon Richards displayed considerable financial acumen in the conduct of his affairs. Unlike some others, this was coupled with generosity, and he always tried to see that those in need of help benefited from his success. And this was not only true after his success had made him a rich man; as an apprentice he had once asked Martin Hartigan to let him have £200 of the money being saved out of his wages until the end of his apprenticeship, not for himself but so that he could help his parents. And riches never robbed him of humility; though he earned three times the salary of the Prime Minister, he still used the same lodging when riding at Newmarket as he had done as an apprentice. And after the award of his knighthood, he asked that he should continue to be listed on race cards as 'G. Richards'.

Two questions remain. What was the secret of his phenomenal success? And why did success in the Derby elude him for so long? The answer to the second may well lie in the fact that he always showed loyalty to those who retained him, and would not ride a fancied horse in the Derby for someone else if his own stable had a runner. And as regards the first, it seems that in the opinion of his contemporaries two factors contributed above all others to his success on the racecourse: balance and strength. He had his horse balanced at the start, kept him balanced throughout the race, and had the strength, especially in his legs, to keep a horse straight and to drive him to the finish.

When Sir Gordon retired as a jockey in 1954, his place with Noel Murless was taken by Lester Piggott. The stewards of the Jockey Club paid him the unique honour as a jockey of inviting him to dine with them, and when he finally retired after fifteen happy years as a trainer they gave him the ultimate accolade of honorary membership of the Jockey Club. On 10 November 1986 Sir Gordon died at the age of eighty-two, leaving behind him memories of a great horseman and of a great English gentleman, who walked with royalty yet never lost the common touch.

Sir Gordon Richards (GB), 'First Knight of the Turf', and twenty-six times Champion, with Lady Beaverbrook, to whom he was racing manager (Bernard Parkin)

Lester Piggott (GB) displaying his individual style on Miramar Reef, Royal Ascot 1984 (Bernard Parkin)

always a much sought after vacancy awaiting him, and this time it was back at Newmarket, where Henry Cecil's Warren Place stable was now the most successful in England.

At Epsom in 1981 Lester's career was nearly brought to an end when the five-year-old sprinter Winsor Boy panicked in the starting stalls and dived under the front gate, leaving his jockey with a nearly severed ear and other injuries. A week in hospital left him fairly weak, but he returned to win the 1000 Guineas on Fairy Footsteps, and by the end of the season he had regained the Championship after a break of nine years – Willie Carson had taken the title from him back in 1972, and had in turn been deposed by Pat Eddery.

The following year brought another Championship, and in 1983 Lester won his ninth Derby on Teenoso when Steve Cauthen, his regular jockey, was claimed elsewhere. He then shot an 'own goal' when he declined to ride Daniel Wildenstein's All Along in the Arc de Triomphe as planned, preferring a known soft-ground performer. Not only did he miss winning rides in the Arc and the Washington International, opportunities eagerly snapped up by Walter Swinburn, but Wildestein declined to employ Piggott again. This of course left Henry Cecil in a difficult position, and led to the break up of yet another winning partnership, with Lester's place being taken by Steve Cauthen.

In 1984 Lester's main ambition, apart of course from winning another Derby (in which he was fifth on Alphabatim), was to break the record of twenty-seven classic wins. This he achieved in brilliant fashion in the Oaks on Circus Plume, and he went on to win his twenty-eighth classic in the St Leger on Commanche Run. And at the end of the year he announced his intention to retire to start a new career as trainer. But first he was to win a final classic, the 1985 2000 Guineas on Shadeed for Michael Stoute.

Lester's record as a race rider speaks for itself: nine Derbys, eight St Legers and a total of twenty-nine classics in England; five Irish Derbys, three Arcs de Triomphe and three Washington Internationals; 4,349 wins from 19,809 rides (22 per cent); Champion eleven times. His greatest strengths were his temperament, ideal for the big occasion, which brought out the best in him, and his single-mindedness, his utter determination to win; his greatest handicap, his determination to win at all costs, which led in his early days to the wrath of the stewards, and later to the break up of three great racing partnerships. But Lester was such an outstanding jockey that each setback was followed by a new opportunity.

The public loved Sir Gordon, regarding him with genuine affection; their relationship with Lester was more one of respect, knowing that, as with Steve Donoghue, they would always get a good run for their money. Lester lacked the charisma, too, of Fred Archer, and the oft-told remark by Jack Leach, writing in the *Observer*, will go down in history: 'When he was a kid and won the Derby on Never Say Die I watched his face when he was being led in. It looked like a well-kept grave. Except for a few isolated occasions, it has looked like that ever since.'

Lester himself once said, 'I do not smile easily in public . . . racing is a serious business.' But he is surely not without a sense of humour. After an extraordinary episode when he dropped his whip and leant over and snatched the whip from the hands of another jockey, (he used the term 'borrowed'), he is reported to have said, 'After all, I did ask him.' (The stewards, needless to say, were not amused.)

Lester was a shrewd investor, and was preoccupied with saving the results of his success from the clutches of the tax man. And to understand what followed it is necessary to bear in mind both the peculiarities of the way in which success on the racecourse in England is rewarded, and the burden of the British tax system at the time when Lester's earnings were at their height.

A jockey's earnings are made up of the retaining fees that he may receive from one or more owners; of riding fees, on a set scale for winning and unplaced rides; and of his percentage of prize money won. Over and above these fees are the customary 'presents' from satisfied owners. All these earnings are taxable, but while the various fees and winning percentages are controlled by the authorities and are clear cut, owners' presents are not, and often take the form of cash. Next, in the sixties and seventies someone on Lester's level of earnings with additional investment income could be taxed at a maximum rate of 98 per cent, and in one particular year when higher rate taxes, previously collected in arrears, became due in the same year as tax on the rest of the income, it was possible, in spite of huge earnings, to have a negative net income! And on top of these taxes on income, since the early seventies there has been the added imposition of Value Added Tax, levied on a jockey's 'services'.

Such a tax climate inevitably generated schemes for tax avoidance, generally regarded as legal, and for tax evasion, which is not. And when it became known that Lester's tax affairs were being investigated by the Inland Revenue, not a few successful men slept uneasily! In 1988 Lester was convicted of tax fraud and sentenced to three years' imprisonment. There were many who thought this sentence harsh enough. But worse was to follow: in the *London Gazette* of 5 June 1988 there appeared the following announcement: 'The Queen has directed that the appointment dated 1st July 1975 of Lester Keith Piggott to be an Officer of the Civil Division of the Most Excellent Order of the British Empire shall be cancelled and annulled, and that his name shall be erased from the register of the said order.'

Meanwhile the conduct of his training establishment was in the capable hands of his wife Susan, assisted by his daughter Maureen, who had earlier been a successful three day event rider. But to compound Lester's misfortune, in 1988 Susan nearly lost her life in a horrific accident when supervising work at Newmarket, and Maureen had to take on full responsibility for the running of the establishment, obtaining a temporary licence, and bringing home her first winner at Yarmouth in September. Later the same month the Jockey Club brought a ray of light to Lester's cell when they announced that they would not bar him from resuming his career as a trainer on his release from prison. And when Lester was released on parole on completion of one year of his three year sentence, television viewers were treated to a broader smile than most racegoers had seen in the heyday of his racing career!

Back in his comfortable home behind his training establishment, Lester, whose phenomenal success was due to his natural ability and flair coupled with sheer determination and hard work, reflected on the problems of young jockeys today.

A lad coming in to racing today must above all really want to do it; after all there are easier ways of making a living! And he must work hard at it. One of the problems today is that instead of a three-year apprenticeship, a lad can leave after one year, so few trainers are prepared to spend time teaching someone who may leave as soon as he becomes useful. And now a lad with the minimum of experience can earn only £20 a week less than someone who has been in stables all his life.

And how did today's stars compare with those of the past?

It's very difficult to compare the past with today; the conditions are so different. Fred Archer, for example, had probably only two or three others in most of his races. Today conditions change so quickly. But Eddery, Carson, Cauthen, Pincay, Cordero, Shoemaker, Saint-Martin, they would have been stars at any time.

Lester's views on the state of the sport today reflect his concern for those without whom there would be no racing at all.

I think there ought to be much better prize money for the lesser races; it's so difficult to win a race, and an owner who has a win should receive enough to pay his training fees for the season. The minimum first prize ought to be £10,000. I think, too, that there ought to be more centralised racing, with about a dozen courses. We should concentrate our resources on these. Other courses could still race if they could make it pay, but would not receive help. And certainly racing should be treated more favourably with regard to tax.

To the racing public, Lester appeared as the supreme artist in the saddle; one on whom they would wager their last fiver in the knowledge that no one would try harder to come back first past the post. If at the same time he appeared somewhat remote, this is entirely understandable, for if you are slightly hard of hearing, and if speaking in public is not your forte you are hardly likely to relish being interviewed on radio or appearing on television, or indeed speaking at all to strangers, especially reporters.

But to those who know him well, and especially to his family, Lester is someone different. In public his understandably defensive attitude inevitably produced that rather sombre expression that became so well known on the pages of the sporting press; at home and among friends his face is often wreathed in smiles, and his sense of humour is readily apparent.

It would be surprising if Lester became as successful a trainer as he was a jockey, (and he has said that Susan will continue to hold the stable licence), for it is difficult to pass on the elements of genius to others. But one of the reasons for his success was his almost uncanny judgement of a horse's capabilities and potential, and if he can acquire the sort of horse that he liked to ride the stable will surely keep the name of Piggott on the front pages of the racing press.

But whatever the future may hold, Lester Piggott has a strong claim to have been the greatest flat race jockey the world has ever seen.

WILLIAM SHOEMAKER

The only auspicious part of Bill Shoemaker's arrival on this planet in 1931 was the fact that he weighed in at a mere 2½lb (1.1kg) which augured well for a career as a jockey. The doctor attending his mother at the family home at Fabens, Texas, told her that he was unlikely to last the night. But his resourceful grandmother wrapped him up and laid him on the open oven door. This makeshift incubator saved for the racing world one of the greatest jockeys of all time.

Eddie Arcaro, who dominated the American racing scene before Shoemaker made his mark, said of him: 'Regardless of the particular sport, Bill Shoemaker, by his accomplishments, must be considered one of the outstanding athletes in the history of sport. I doubt we'll ever see another race rider having his special combination of talents. He has it all and has done it all.' And this assessment was made many years ago. Perhaps the most astonishing aspect of this story is that Shoemaker was still riding in 1990!

Young Shoemaker arrived during the years of the Depression, and the family were forced to move round looking for work. He spent seven years on his grandfather's cattle ranch near Abilene, where he started riding in order to collect the mail from the mailbox, and one day he nearly drowned when he fell into a huge cattle drinking trough because he was too small to clamber out. Eventually he rejoined his father in California, where his schooldays were memorable more for his prowess in the boxing and wrestling rings than for any academic achievement, and he obtained his first job on a Thoroughbred ranch while the family imagined he was still at school.

He learned his horsemanship in a hard school breaking yearlings, and he was thrown so often that it was open to question as to who was being broken. In 1949 at the age of seventeen he rode in his first race at the Golden Gates track in the mud, and in such conditions jockeys usually armed themselves with two pairs of goggles. Shoe forgot his second pair, so at the half-way mark he was virtually blind. In the third race he was due to ride a horse called Shafton V, who had won the previous week at odds of 4-5 with an experienced jockey. With the unknown Shoemaker declared to ride, the odds went out to 9-1, and the stewards called George Reeves, the trainer, to explain why he had put a green rider on a fancied horse. To his credit Reeves refused to budge, and Shoe duly brought home his first winner.

In his second week Bill scored seven firsts, and ended the season as the top apprentice with 219 wins, taking second place in the Jockeys' Championship. In the following year (1950) he tied for the Championship with 388 winners, bettering a record that had stood for over forty years. His first big win in a $100,000 stakes race came in 1951 for trainer Warren Stute on Great Circle in the Santa Anita Maturity, and in the following year he set a new record with 485 wins from some 1,600 rides, a success rate of over 30 per cent.

It was at this time that Eddie Arcaro suggested to trainer Rex Ellsworth that he should engage the services of the twenty-four-year-old Shoemaker, and so he won a small race on the great Swaps. Johnny Longden then won the Santa Anita Derby on him, but Ellsworth was now determined that Shoemaker should have the ride in the Kentucky Derby. In the week before the big race, they won over 7 furlongs, and, as is sometimes done on American tracks, Bill worked the horse on over a mile, clocking the phenomenal time of 1 minute 36.4 seconds (37.3mph). In the Derby they beat Arcaro on the favourite Nashua, and at Hollywood Park (California) Swaps set the official world record for the mile at 1 minute 40.4 seconds (35.85mph). Matches are more of a feature of the American racing scene than they are in Europe, and a match was arranged between Swaps and Nashua. On the morning of the contest there were doubts about the soundness of Swaps, but Ellsworth decided to run him without telling his jockey. Nashua won, and Swaps was afterwards found to have an infected foot.

In the 1957 Kentucky Derby, Bill incurred his only disciplinary penalty when he misjudged the position of the finish and stood up in his stirrups well before the line. However, he made up for this lapse by winning the second leg of the Triple Crown, the Belmont Stakes, on Gallant Man, also setting the 1½ mile record at 2 minutes 26.6 seconds (36.83mph). In the following year, Bill won 300 races, passed a total of 3,000 winners, and won nearly $3m in prize money.

The 1959 Kentucky Derby was an interesting race in more ways than one. Shoemaker had won an earlier race on Sword Dancer, and hoped to ride him in the Derby, but after winning the Blue Grass Stakes at Keeneland on Tony Lee he was claimed to ride that horse instead. On the left-handed American tracks Tony Lee tended to run out to the right, and on the final bend this is what he did, bumping Bill Boland and Sword Dancer in the process. Boland thought that Shoemaker had done this on purpose, and so retaliated; but the ensuing knock put Tony Lee back on a straight line, causing him to change legs, and he went through to win. (One cannot help wondering what the English Jockey Club stewards would have made of this one.) The year ended with a win in the Preakness, the third leg of the Triple Crown, and with Shoemaker's election to the Jockey's Hall of Fame at Pimlico.

The 4,000th winner was passed in 1961, the 5,000th three years later, and in 1965 Bill won his third Kentucky Derby. But Fate has a habit of intervening when things are going too well. In previous years he had had some lucky escapes. On one occasion a mare called Dutch Wife was in the lead when, at a gap in the rails where horses crossed the track, she ducked out, hit a post and killed herself; Bill ended up on her belly between her legs, which could have been dangerous had she survived but which in fact cushioned his fall and saved him from injury. On another, a fall when schooling left him with a broken back which was not discovered until he was X-rayed some years later.

Then at Santa Anita in 1968 an apprentice tried to go for a gap that wasn't there, and in the ensuing pile-up Bill suffered a broken leg that was to keep him out of the saddle for a year. And, after three wins on his first day back in 1969, a filly came over backwards in the paddock before the Derby and a broken pelvis and internal injuries put him out for a further three months. For a while he thought this might be the end of his racing career, but he rebounded to win three races again on his first day back in the saddle.

The records continued to tumble: 6,000 winners passed in 1970, 46 stakes races won

Willie Shoemaker (USA) and Peter Scudamore (GB) contested a match at Cheltenham in June 1989. The records show that Scudamore won. Shoemaker has had more winners than any other jockey in the world – 8,833 at the final count (Bernard Parkin)

in 1971 (setting a record), and 577 winners in 1972, beating Eddie Arcaro's record. By 1976 he had passed the 7,000 mark, and the time had come to stop chasing records and to be more selective in his choice of rides, to go for quality rather than quantity. In 1977 he won his seventh Santa Anita Derby on Habitony, and the next year he nearly pulled off the English Derby when he came second to Greville Starkey and Shirley Heights with Hawaiian Sound, a considerable achievement taking into account the difference between the more or less standard American circuits and the twisting, undulating Epsom track.

In 1980 he teamed up with the horse that he considers the greatest that he ever rode, and took Spectacular Bid through his four-year-old season unbeaten, winning the race formerly known as the Santa Anita Maturity, and the Santa Anita Handicap and the

Woodward Stakes. In 1981 he topped the 8,000 winner mark, and became the first rider to win a race worth $1m in the inaugural running of the Arlington Million.

Now well into his fifties but with little thought of retiring – and with his undiminished capability and the backing of the great trainer Charlie Whittingham there was little reason to retire – he continued to rewrite the record books. In 1985 his total winnings passed the $100m mark (on Lord of War in the Santa Anita Handicap), and the following year he became the oldest rider to win the Kentucky Derby, when at fifty-four he won it for the fourth time with Ferdinand, on whom he went on to win the $3m Breeders Cup Classic in 1987, the year in which he also won his eighth Santa Anita Derby with Temperate Sil.

In 1988, at the age of fifty-eight, he rode his smallest number of winners since 1968, the year in which he broke his leg, but his horses still won over $4m, bringing his career total to nearly $122m from a staggering total of 8,780 wins from over 40,000 rides, a winning percentage of nearly 22 per cent. If the average distance of races is taken to be three-quarters of a mile, that amounts to some 30,000 miles, or approximately one-and-a-quarter times round the earth, bringing home prize money for his owners at the rate of over $4,000 per mile.

Finally in 1989, having been at the top of his profession for forty years, he decided to make a farewell tour that would take him all around the world. His European tour brought him wins in Zürich (Switzerland), Epsom and Warwick (England), Madrid (Spain), Hamburg (Germany), and Stockholm (Sweden), and at Cheltenham in June he took part in a unique engagement, a match versus Champion Steeplechase Jockey Peter Scudamore – the records show that Scudamore won. His last race, appropriately named 'The Legend's Last Ride', was in February 1990 on the track where he had triumphed so often. An incredible 63,000 racegoers turned out to cheer him home at Santa Anita, California, and though he was unable to retire on a winner, his career total of 8,833 wins, nearly three thousand more than any other jockey, looks virtually unbeatable. Why has he been so phenomenally successful?

First, there have been two partnerships that have complemented his own talents. Although jockeys in the States are not retained by trainers as they are in England, his unofficial partnership with Charlie Whittingham, one of the great trainers of the world, brought him a host of winners; and his engagement of Harry Silbert as his agent back in 1949 ensured that the potential winners kept coming right through till 1986.

But more important has been his own natural ability. Weighing in at only 98lb (44kg), and only 4ft 11in (1.5m) in height, he realised early on that persuasion was going to be a more powerful weapon than force, and he developed a quiet style that had the effect of relaxing the horses he rode in the early stages of a race and of galvanising them into action towards the finish. And throughout his long career he has only once been disciplined, and that was for misjudgement and not for contravening the rules of racing, when he mistook the position of the finish in the Kentucky Derby of 1957. His integrity, unflappability and good sportsmanship have·endeared him to racegoers around the world.

Now that he has finally hung up his boots, he can look back on forty years of race riding during which he has set standards of integrity and performance that are unlikely ever to be matched. As Eddie Arcaro said, there will never be another like him.

YVES SAINT-MARTIN

Over three decades there was one jockey who was universally respected on both sides of the Channel and of the Atlantic. A Chevalier de l'Ordre National du Mérite in his home country, he was described by Brough Scott as 'a prince among jockeys of any era', and he was a fine ambassador for his country both in England and in America.

Yves Saint-Martin was born in 1941 near Bordeaux where his father was in the prison service, and since he entered this world at not much more than a kilogram in weight, there was every chance that he might turn out to be a jockey. He was fortunate enough to be apprenticed to a great trainer, not only of horses, but also of jockeys, François Mathet, who had himself been an extremely successful amateur rider. He started training immediately after World War II, and ran his stable with the military precision of a former cavalry officer.

Saint-Martin remembers little of his first ride, which ended in the ambulance, but he rode his first winner at seventeen at Le Tremblay, and three years later he won his first British classic, the 1962 Oaks, on Monade. And if the English thought that this was just a 'one-off' performance by the twenty-year-old Frenchman, they certainly took notice when he returned to win the King George VI and Queen Elizabeth Stakes at Ascot with Match. And the Americans, too, acknowledged that here was a rising star of considerable potential when he and Match snatched the Washington International from the best they could put against them.

The following year the Mathet–Saint-Martin team won the Epsom Derby with Relko, and in 1965 Yves won the first of his nine French Derbys (the Prix du Jockey Club,) and he was to win his last twenty-two years later for M. de Royer-Dupré, for whom he rode regularly after the death of François Mathet in 1983. In 1970 he won it on Sassafras, with whom he scored the first of his four victories in the Arc de Triomphe later in the year. His second Arc came in 1974 on Daniel Wildenstein's Allez France, who won thirteen of her twenty-one races, and was probably one of the greatest fillies seen on French racecourses.

It was no mean achievement for a foreign jockey to win every English classic. In addition to the Oaks of 1962 and the Derby of 1963, Yves won the 1000 Guineas of 1971 on Altesse Royale for Noel Murless and in 1976 on Flying Water for Angel Penna, the Argentinian trainer who was outstandingly successful in three continents, South America, North America and Europe. The 2000 Guineas he won in 1974 on Nonoalco, and the St Leger in 1976 on Crow, and for good measure he also won the Champion Stakes three times, the King George VI and Queen Elizabeth Stakes twice, and the Newmarket July Cup.

In Ireland he won the Derby for Peter Walwyn in 1974 with English Prince, and twenty-two years after his triumph in the Washington International he crossed the

Yves Saint-Martin (France), won every English Classic. Here on Strawberry Road, Ascot 1985 (Bernard Parkin)

Atlantic again in 1984 to win the first running of the Breeders Cup Turf with Lashkari. Two years later he won the Breeders Cup Mile with Last Tycoon. In 1983 he had had a horrific fall at Chantilly which nearly ended his career, but the following year he bounced back to win the French Derby and the Arc, as well as the Breeders Cup Turf.

When he retired in 1987 at the age of forty-six, he had won 3,313 races, including twenty-nine French and seven English classics, and had won the Cravat d'Or, the French jockeys' championship, fifteen times. Few jockeys have stamped their authority on racing beyond the confines of their own country as has Yves Saint-Martin.

PATRICK EDDERY

The Champion Jockey of 1989 was was born in Kildare in 1952, and since both his father and his maternal grandfather were jockeys, it is perhaps not too surprising that he claims to have been riding ponies at the age of four, and racehorses at eight. But his initiation into the world of racing was not particularly impressive, for during his apprenticeship in Ireland he had just one ride that came in last, and he rode in seventy races before he had a winner. But his break came at the age of seventeen in 1969, after he had moved to that great trainer of horses and jockeys, Frenchie Nicholson. The horse that got him off the mark was Alvaro, on whom he recorded eight consecutive wins, and the following year he brought home five winners from seven rides at Haydock. In 1971 he was leading apprentice with seventy-one winners.

When Peter Walwyn was looking for a jockey, he approached Frenchie Nicholson and obtained Pat's services, and during the eight years that he rode for Peter he rode eight hundred winners, was Champion four times, and established a great partnership with the horse he regards as the best he has ridden to date. With Grundy, he won the 1975 Epsom and Irish Derbys, the Irish 2000 Guineas and the King George VI and Queen Elizabeth Stakes at Ascot. He had already in 1974 won his first classic, the Oaks on Polygamy, a race that he was to win again in 1979 with Scintillate for Jeremy Tree. He won his first Championship, too, in 1974, and reigned supreme until he was dethroned in 1978 by Willie Carson.

Perhaps 'dethroned' is not quite the right expression, because, as far as the championship was concerned, he virtually went into temporary exile in the land of his birth. But few jockeys, and certainly very few Irishmen, could have turned down the opportunity of taking over from Lester Piggott as first jockey to Vincent O'Brien, and certainly not when the third partner in the team was Robert Sangster. But if Pat's absence in Ireland gave others a chance at the Championship in England, he found ample compensation in the number of high class winners that he rode for the O'Brien stable, and he took the Irish Championship in 1982.

His winners during this period included three in the Arc de Triomphe, Detroit, trained in France for Robert Sangster in 1980, Rainbow Quest for Jeremy Tree in 1985, and Dancing Brave for Guy Harwood in 1986; his second Epsom Derby in 1982 on Golden Fleece; and the 2000 Guineas of 1983 and 1984 on Lomond and El Gran Senor, on whom he also won the Irish Derby of the same year. He won the Irish Derby again in 1985 with Law Society, and the Champion Stakes and the Breeders Cup Turf in New York with Pebbles.

But 1986 was surely a vintage year. In Ireland he won the Oaks and the St Leger, and at Royal Ascot, where O'Brien was without a runner, he rode in all twenty-four races and won six of them. Then, after Dancing Brave had narrowly failed to win the Derby, Pat took over the ride and won both the King George VI and Queen Elizabeth Stakes and the Arc de Triomphe. In a season in which he had also ridden six winners from twelve consecutive rides in a day, three at Nottingham in the afternoon, and three at Windsor in the evening, he also regained the English Championship.

At the end of 1986 he received another offer that he could not refuse, and returned to England to ride for Dancing Brave's owner, Prince Khalid Bin Abdullah of Saudi Arabia. The Prince is typical of all that is best in the Arab involvement in British racing, and this is exemplified by his honorary membership of the Jockey Club, a rare distinction for a foreigner. He owns studs in Berkshire, Ireland and Kentucky, and has several trainers in England, among them Guy Harwood, Jeremy Tree and Barry Hills, and in France André Fabre.

Riding for the Prince, Pat won his fifth Championship in 1987 in a close race with Steve Cauthen, and won his fourth Arc on Trempolino, becoming the only jockey to have won three in succession. In 1988 he achieved a century of winners in 101 days, and finished the season fifty-three ahead of Willie Carson. The year 1989 brought his seventh Championship, and one particular meeting that he likes to remember: at Royal Ascot he rode eight winners, equalling the record set by Lester Piggott.

Riding as he does for the first Arab to invest heavily in British racing, Pat feels that the Arab involvement is good for the sport. 'They spend a lot of money here, they provide a lot of jobs, and they do stand their stallions here. I find them very good to work for and easy to deal with. And in any case before the Arabs our racing was dominated by Robert Sangster.'

On the state of the sport in England, he considers racing to be well organised and well run, and the stewarding to be very good, but shares the general anxiety regarding the low level of prize money. 'We have the best racing in the world, but our prize money is far too low; in America the prize money is phenomenal, and so much money goes back into racing. The bookmakers take everything out of racing in England, and the government takes everything out of racing in France! Owners are paying millions for horses to win peanuts.'

Pat does, however, see difficulties in the education of young jockeys. 'It's hard for a lad today; we only have a one-year apprenticeship, and that's nowhere near long enough. But having got to a stable a lad must work hard and respect the trainer. If I started again I would go to a small trainer, because the big stables have their own retained jockeys, and it's no good just getting the occasional ride, you've got to ride in plenty of races to get the experience.'

Pat's wife Carolyn is the daughter of the great jockey Manny Mercer, and they live with their two daughters on one of the two stud farms that Pat owns near Aylesbury, and his brother-in-law Terry Ellis act as his manager and books his rides. Travel takes up much of Pat's time, though much less since he acquired a twin-engined plane and the services of a full time pilot. His winter schedule is a busy one, with visits to Hong Kong and Japan, returning in time for Christmas with his family. He then takes a family holiday before thinking about the next season.

Competitive in all he does, Pat will make the likes of Willie Carson, Steve Cauthen and the younger jockeys fight hard to take the Championship from him in the near future.

*Pat Eddery (Ireland) with
trainer Luca Cumani* (Bernard Parkin)

'I have a bit of a weight problem, because
the lightest I can do is 8st 4lb (nearly
53kg), and it's difficult to lose weight
during the cold weather. Maybe I'll have
a go on the all-weather tracks in February.
I haven't ridden on them yet, though I've
ridden in Hong Kong and on dirt in the
States. We shan't know what they're really
like until the bad weather comes. In
America they use a chemical to prevent
freezing, and it doesn't half sting your face.
But I like the American courses, they're
sharp but well banked, though you need a
bit of luck to win there. Their stalls are
completely different to ours; while we sit
down and try to relax our horses, they stand
up in the stalls and set their horses up for
a quick start.'

STEVE CAUTHEN

'1976: Leading apprentice jockey in USA.' – '1977: Sportsman of the Year.' – '1978: Honored at Sport of Kings Convention.' – '1979: Wins with first mount in England.' – '1980: Receives William Hill Golden Spurs Award.' – '1983: England's Jockey of the Year.' – '1984: England's Champion Jockey of 1984.' – '1985: First rider to top jockey lists in America and England.' '1987: Named Jockey of the Year by *Pacemaker International*.' These are just a selection of the headlines from *The Blood Horse*, one of the leading American racing weeklies, and published in Kentucky, where Steve Cauthen was born in 1960.

Steve's parents, Ronald (Tex) and Myra Cauthen run a stud in Kentucky, at Walton, and have been involved in racing for most of their lives. But when they first placed their young son on a horse, literally before he could walk, little did they know what they were starting. Like most Kentucky boys, Steve grew up with horses, and by the age of twelve he knew that he wanted to be a jockey. But whereas Lester Piggott rode his first winner at that age, the minimum age for a jockey in the States was sixteen. Steve, however, put the next four years to good use, riding work, getting to know the racehorse, learning how to handle half-a-ton of high spirited and often wayward horseflesh, and above all studying, both on the racecourse and through films, the different styles and actions of the leading jockeys, from the starting stalls right through to the finish of a race.

His first ride in public came shortly after his sixteenth birthday, and though it was on a rank outsider who finished way down the field, Steve impressed his trainer with the sympathetic way in which he rode the horse. His second ride was similar, and then on 16 May came his first win. Two days later he first entered the record books; he became the first jockey to ride a hat-trick of winners within a week of taking out his licence. On 19 May he lost his 10lb (4.5kg) allowance. By the end of the season he had beaten the existing record of 120 first season winners by three.

No English jockey could have done what Cauthen did in the autumn of 1976, because racing in America is organised on a different basis from that in England. In the States racing may take place at one course for several weeks, after which the circuit switches elsewhere. So at Arlington, Chicago, Steve rode in 164 races and won 64 of them. All the time he was learning, and his strike rate of 24 per cent wins was impressive. At Aqueduct, New York, he won twenty-nine races in three weeks, including six in a row. When he returned to Kentucky eight months after his first ride he had won $1/4m in prize money and had earned himself $90,000. Not a bad start!

The 1977 season started as the previous one had ended, with twenty-three wins in a week, including two runs of five winners, and in April he had six consecutive winners (for the second time) at Aqueduct. But for a flat race jockey, as even the great Shoemaker discovered, there are dangers as well as triumphs, and in May Steve was involved in a pile-up at Belmont which left him with a broken right arm, two broken fingers and a rib, concussion and twenty-five stitches in his face and arms.

This proved, however, to be little more than a temporary setback, and on his return to the saddle he resumed his winning ways. Soon he lost the rest of his allowance, but this in no way lessened the calls for his services, and after winning the Washington International and riding six winners in a day for the third time at Belmont, he achieved the hitherto unprecedented total of $6m in prize money – and the record he broke was his own, when he passed the $5m mark earlier in the year.

Just as the magic words 'The Triple Crown' will cause owners, trainers and jockeys in England to modify their plans in the hope of winning the three major races confined to three-year-olds, the 2000 Guineas, the Derby and the St Leger, so in the States the lure of the Kentucky Derby and the Preakness and Belmont Stakes tempts the owners of promising three-year-olds there.

The colt that was to give Steve his first Triple Crown was Affirmed. He won three two-year-old races on him in 1977, two of these wins being over another great horse, Alydar, who beat him on another occasion, and an intriguing battle for the Triple Crown seemed in prospect for 1978. Affirmed won his first four races of the new season, including the Santa Anita Derby (without Steve in the saddle, since he had been disciplined for careless riding,) and all looked set for a great race when he and Alydar met for the Kentucky Derby. In fact Affirmed won relatively easily after Alydar had bumped another horse.

But in the Preakness two weeks later both horses (and their jockeys) knew that they had been in a race when Affirmed just got home by a neck, and it would have been no disgrace to Steve if he had lost by that margin. By the time of the Belmont Affirmed was starting to feel the effects of six wins in the season, and after Alydar seemed to have the race within his grasp, it took all of Steve's artistry and determination to drive him home by a head.

Even the best jockeys have lean periods, and 1979 started inauspiciously when after losing two races Steve lost the ride on Affirmed to Laffit Pincay. (American racing differs from English in another respect in that jockeys do not usually have retainers, and trainers are therefore free to engage the in-form jockey of the moment.) Then the jockey who had already set an unprecedented string of records had 110 rides without a single win. It is much more difficult to break back when trainers are looking elsewhere, and although a rider of Steve's talent and determination would surely have made a comeback sooner or later, his opportunity came from an unexpected direction.

Robert Sangster was heir to a football pools fortune and had made racing a successful business too, and his partnership with Irish trainer Vincent O'Brien and Lester Piggott had dominated the English racing scene as would none other until the arrival of the Al Maktoum family. But he needed another jockey for his horses in training with Barry Hills in England, and, no stranger to the American racing scene, he had been impressed by Steve's performance on his home ground.

Steve was now sufficiently wealthy, at the age of eighteen, never to have to work again if he didn't want to, and certainly even Sangster couldn't offer the prospect of earnings to match those he had enjoyed in the States. But here was a challenge that Steve thought

Steve Cauthen (USA) on his 1985 2000 Guineas winner Oh So Sharp, Ascot 1985 (Bernard Parkin)

worth taking, and coming when it did, there seemed little to lose in giving it a try. In April 1979 the 'Six Million Dollar Kid' arrived in England.

While O'Brien trained Sangster's horses in Ireland, Barry Hills looked after his string in England, and, having himself started at the bottom of the business, he was sufficiently impressed by the young American's attitude to work to endeavour to provide Steve with a reasonable chance of a win on his English debut. Steve siezed the chance with both hands, and steered the 7-4 chance Marquee Universal to a one-and-a-half length victory in the rain and mud at Salisbury.

Not a bad start, and nine wins on nine different tracks – and very different they were from those of the American circuit – earned him the Wilkinson Sword Trophy at the end of his first month in England. And then on his nineteenth birthday he celebrated with three wins in Bremen, Germany.

One of his unplaced rides on his first outing at Salisbury had been on Tap on Wood in the 2000 Guineas Trial, and his sympathetic handling of the colt resulted in Steve being given the ride in the classic itself. In spite of his owner, Tony Shead's optimism, Tap on Wood wasn't considered as more than a long shot for a place, and when the unbeaten Kris, trained by Henry Cecil and ridden by the veteran Joe Mercer, took the lead the result seemed a formality. Not, however, to young Cauthen, who astounded everybody by urging Tap on Wood past Kris for a half-length victory in his first English classic.

In September Steve rode his 1,000th winner, strangely enough on Robert Sangster's Thousandfold, and he ended the season with 52 English and 15 foreign wins. In 1980 he had 61 winners, and 87 in 1981. The next season he passed the magic century total and he repeated this in 1983. Then in 1984 his big chance came when Lester Piggott lost the Wildenstein rides and eventually parted from Henry Cecil. Steve had already started to pick up the Wildenstein engagements and, much to Barry Hills' disappointment, Cecil signed him up for 1985. But at the end of the 1984 season, Steve won the Championship for the first time. His score of 130 was helped by the misfortunes of other jockeys – apart from Piggott's situation, Pat Eddery, who had replaced Piggott with Vincent O'Brien, was spending more time in Ireland, and Willie Carson was sidelined by injury – but nevertheless Steve had achieved what no other American had managed to do since Danny Maher in 1913.

Steve will always be grateful to Barry Hills for the start he gave him in English racing, but with Cecil's powerful stable behind him he established himself firmly in the front rank of jockeys. His Championship of 1985 with just five short of two hundred winners included his first Epsom Derby and an English Triple Crown to add to his American one. Oh So Sharp snatched the 1000 Guineas from Bella Colora and Lester Piggott by a short head, and in the Oaks she trounced the opposition. But it takes an outstanding filly to beat the colts in the St Leger, and only two fillies had managed to win their Triple Crown in this century. Oh So Sharp duly did so.

The Derby was interesting in several ways. Slip Anchor started favourite after his Derby Trial win at Lingfield; he led the field from start to finish; he won by seven lengths easing up; his time beat Shergar's record by eight seconds; he gave trainer, jockey and owner (Lord Howard de Walden) their first Epsom Derby; and Steve became the first jockey to win both the Kentucky and Epsom Derbys.

The year 1986 was a (relatively) lean one, if a season that produced 149 winners could be so described! But having now won all five English classics in seven years, he was without a classic win, and he yielded the Championship to Pat Eddery. But in 1987 he bounced back, and but for a sinus operation on Reference Point he might well have taken his third Triple Crown. The brilliant colt missed the 2000 Guineas because of the operation, but after victory in the Mecca Dante Stakes he gave Steve his second Derby and his second St Leger, and he also won Ascot's King George VI and Queen Elizabeth Diamond Stakes.

In 1988 Steve won both the English and Irish Oaks with Diminuendo, but when he had scored 104 winners he suffered a horrific fall at Goodwood which kept him out of the saddle for the rest of the season.

'I don't actually remember much about it,' he says, 'but I've seen the race video and talked to other jockeys who rode in the race. The filly Preziosa was taking a terrific hold, and eventually she clipped the heels of the horse in front and down she came, rolling right over me.' Steve was lucky to recover in time for the 1989 season.

In 1989 Steve resumed his winning ways. With Old Vic he won the French and Irish Derbys, and when the St Leger was transferred from Doncaster to Ayr because of subsidence on the Yorkshire course he won that with Michelozzo. He ended the season with 163 wins and second place in the Championship behind Pat Eddery on 171.

When Steve arrived in England in 1979, the legend of the young prodigy had preceded him. His arrival could easily have aroused resentment among English jockeys, for whom it has never been easy to break into the American racing scene; and all the more so when he was immediately successful and was clearly going to deprive some of them of mounts on which they might win. But he was well aware of the danger.

I never went into the weighing room as 'the Million Dollar Kid' but just as another jockey with a job to do and a lot to learn about English racing. I had to learn how to handle horses on different tracks, and to find the best ground on each. And I learned that a change in the weather could mean a change in tactics, not only making it necessary to take a different route but also affecting one's decision as to whether to hold a horse up or let him run on. But of course I was very lucky to be given rides on good horses by Barry Hills right from the start.

Apart from admitting extreme dedication and a will to win, Steve is fairly reticent about the reasons for his startling success, but his skilful and sympathetic handling of horses has earned him the respect of owners and trainers and of the racing public. So too has his extraordinary ability to read a race in which he is riding, and to modify his tactics accordingly. Maybe this is partly due to the fact that in the States so much attention is paid during training to the stopwatch. At any rate he is a superb judge of pace, and in one respect he has already had a profound effect on English racing; races in which he is riding are now likely to be run at a true pace, for if they are not his fellow jockeys are likely to see little more of him than his backside!

Both his fellow jockeys and the racing public like him for his modesty – he is quick to pass on praise to the trainer and the stable staff after a win – and for his generosity; in the country of his, even if temporary, adoption, he is always ready to give his time and his money to charity.

Steve rides in England because he likes the scene, the life and the people. But the backwardness of English racing in many respects amazes him.

Racing in England has everything going for it, great races, good horses, and the great advantage of the involvement of the royal family, and it should be the best in the world. But the facilities on English racecourses, for all those involved right down to the stable lads, are antiquated, and the prize money is peanuts! The authorities are way behind the times, and the sport makes plenty of money, but far too little comes back into racing. I also think the domination of the sport by the Arabs is a problem, because they frighten off the small owner. They are very competitive, and good luck to them, but it's difficult for someone to buy a horse for, say £60,000, when the Arabs are paying hundreds of thousands.

Steve Cauthen (USA) with Reference Point after victory in the 1987 King George VI & Queen Elizabeth Diamond Stakes at Ascot (Bernard Parkin)

So what improvements would he like to see introduced?

I would like to see the facilities improved, even if this means more centralised racing. And the prize money ought to go up, because this would mean more money not only for owners but also for trainers, jockeys and stable lads.

And talking of stable lads, what would be his advice to a young jockey starting out today?

It's a pity that the old apprentice system has gone, because although some trainers abused it as a means of getting cheap labour, others were particularly good at making young jockeys. It's still true of some trainers today, and I would advise a young jockey to go to one of these. It's no good starting in one of the big stables because they will have their retained jockeys, and the young lad may not get a ride for years.

Steve lives in the modest but comfortable gate lodge at Stechworth Stud, three miles from Newmarket, and does much of his travelling to race meetings by air. 'You just can't plan a journey by road; sometimes it can take two hours, sometimes four.' He rides quite often in France during the summer, and will ride in the States when English horses go over for one of the prestige races such as the Arlington Million or the Breeders Cup series. And he likes to ride in Hong Kong as a means of getting back into shape for the start of the season in England. But as for the all-weather tracks, 'I'm all for it, though it doesn't interest me personally because I like to recharge my batteries during the winter.'

As part of the recharging process, Steve particularly likes shooting, but his interests are broadly based: tennis, golf, snooker, music and dancing, all have a part in his life.

Steve is now firmly part of the English racing scene, and is likely to be challenging for the Championship for many seasons to come. But he is not only undeniably a great horseman; he is also a fine ambassador for his own country.

OPPOSITE
Willie Shoemaker (USA) before winning the Bessborough Stakes, Royal Ascot, 1984, on Robert Sangster's Sikorski (Bernard Parkin)

Yves Saint-Martin (France) on his 1976 Newmarket 1000 Guineas winner, Flying Water, at Longchamp (Bernard Parkin)

Part II

NATIONAL HUNT RACING

O F ALL EQUESTRIAN SPORTS, none can match the sheer thrill and excitement of riding a Thoroughbred horse over fences at up to 30 miles per hour; none can match the risk either, for on a rough average the National Hunt jockey can expect to hit the ground about once in every ten rides. Although falls on the flat, when they occur, may have horrific consequences because of the speed at which a rider is fired into the ground, and because of the closer bunching during races, there is usually little that the flat race jockey can do to avoid them. The rider over fences can influence the jumping of his horse, but even the best cannot avoid the crunching fall when it comes.

The very best do on the whole seem to stretch the races to falls ratio, partly of course because they tend to ride the better horses. But it's the old chicken-and-egg situation in a different guise; you can't get the best rides until you've ridden a lot, and if you ride a lot of moderate horses the falls are bound to come more often. On the other hand the very best may also be chasing the Championship, in which case, while they will not wish to risk their chances by taking rides on 'no hopers' in novice chases, they may well accept engagements that they would not otherwise take. Those who consistently beat the ratio owe something to their position as established jockeys, something to luck, but probably more to their own skill and horsemanship.

The sport of steeplechasing is generally regarded as having been born in Ireland in 1752, when two gentlemen of the names of Blake and O'Callaghan rode against each other from Buttevant church to St Leger church in County Cork, a distance of 4½ miles (7.25km). The first recorded meeting in England is supposed to have taken place near Market Harborough in Leicestershire just before the turn of the century, and the first regular course to have been laid out at Bedford a decade later. Racing began at Aintree in 1829, and the race that was to become the Grand National was inaugurated ten years after that. Cheltenham held its first meeting in 1831, and the origins of the National Hunt Committee, amalgamated with the Jockey Club in 1968, go back to 1866.

But though the Grand National has been running for 150 years, and the National Hunt Meeting has been at Cheltenham since 1911, the Golden Age of National Hunt racing may be said to date from the revival of racing after World War I, with the inauguration of the Cheltenham Gold Cup in 1924 and the Champion Hurdle three years later.

OPPOSITE
John Francome (GB) on Brown Chamberlin, leading Borough Hill Lad, Cheltenham, 1984 (Charles Parkin)

The home of national hunt racing – Cheltenham, England (Bernard Parkin)

Although steeplechasing may be regarded as the poor relation of flat racing because, though the risks are greater, the rewards are very much smaller, it draws a devoted section of racegoers for three main reasons. First, it has its roots in the countryside, via point-to-pointing and hunting; second, followers of National Hunt racing are more able to identify their equine heroes – the Golden Millers, the Arkles and the Desert Orchids will draw the crowds to Newbury on a wet afternoon in November in a way that the stars of the flat, most of whom disappear to stud as soon as they have hit the top, never could. Third, and perhaps most significant of all, though there are few who can take on the moguls of the flat and hope to win a pattern race, let alone a classic, it is perfectly possible for the small owner and trainer to carry off substantial prizes over fences. And finally, there is still a considerable amateur involvement, which at least means that many of those who administer the sport at the top will have gained some understanding of the problems and the pressures that face the professional steeplechase jockey.

Many of the leading riders of the nineteenth century were associated with the Grand National, and one of the earliest was **George Stevens** (1833–71), who won it in 1856, 1863, 1864, 1869 and 1870, the last two on the same horse, The Colonel. No other rider has approached this feat, and it was sad that Stevens, who reputedly rode in fifteen Nationals without falling, was killed at the age of thirty-eight in a fall when his horse shied while hacking.

From the turn of the century the English Jockeys' table gives a fair indication of those who dominated their profession. **F. Mason**, Champion six times from 1900 to 1908, also won the National in 1905. **F. B. Rees** took the title in 1920, 1921, 1923 and 1924, and in 1926/27, and won the first Cheltenham Gold Cup on Red Splash in 1924. **W. Stott** was Champion for five seasons in succession, and piloted Golden Miller to the second of his five Gold Cup wins in 1933. 'The Miller's' pilot in his next two Cheltenham victories was the outstanding rider of the immediate pre-war period, **Gerry Wilson** (1904–69), Champion for the six seasons from 1932/33 to 1937/38 and again in 1940/41. Only two weeks after the 1934 Gold Cup he rode Golden Miller to win the Grand National in record time, and just before winning the Gold Cup again in 1935 he won the Champion Hurdle on Lion Courage.

The career of **Fred Rimell** (1913–81) blossomed before the war, when he was Champion for the last two seasons, was interrupted for six years, and resumed with the first two post-war championships, during which he won the 1945 Champion Hurdle on Brains Trust, trained by Gerry Wilson. Rimell was a real horseman, having combined riding work for his father with hunting when he whipped in to the Croome Hunt in Worcestershire during the mid-thirties. He won thirty-four races on the flat before weight caused him to switch to fences, and he was regarded as the best of his time in a tight finish. He twice rode five winners in a day, at Windsor and Cheltenham.

Most people think that Lester Piggott made history when he 'borrowed' the whip from another jockey during the course of the Arc de Triomphe; Fred Rimell pre-dated this by several years on a horse that was jumping to the right in the National Hunt Handicap Chase on Cheltenham's left-handed course. He knew that Poor Flame ought to win, but in trying to keep him straight he lost his whip. He was a lazy horse so Fred leant across to the jockey lying upsides, on a horse that was clearly not going to be involved in the finish, and with a brusque 'You don't want that, do you!', seized his whip and won by a head. He did however reward the donor afterwards!

In 1957 Fred married Mercy Cockburn, and started training whilst still riding, with the advantage that owners sent horses for him to train and ride, and he built up one of the most successful training stables in England, which Mercy took over and carried on successfully until her retirement in 1988. As a trainer, Fred headed the table four times, and won four Grand Nationals, two Cheltenham Gold Cups and two Champion Hurdles, and there is little doubt that, but for the interruption of the war, he would have been as great a jockey as the best of his successors.

In the decade after World War II Ireland produced some superb horsemen, and none better than **Bryan Marshall** (1916), another whose career was interrupted by the war, in which he served in the 5th Royal Inniskilling Dragoon Guards in north-west Europe. He learned his horsemanship out hunting over the Tipperary banks and the Limerick walls on a pony, and at the instigation of Major Dermot McCalmont he was apprenticed to Atty Perse and at the age of twelve rode his first winner on the flat. After a season whipping in to the Kilkenny hounds he went on a trip to the United States with Gerald Balding, where he broke a leg schooling. He rode his first winner over fences in Ireland – and finished second and fourth on the same horse one day at Punchestown.

Bryan's first win over fences in England was on the outsider in a three horse race at Carlisle in 1937 – the other two fell. But as the winners began to come the war

Champion national hunt jockey Peter Scudamore (GB) presents the Wilfred Sherman Trophy for the Champion Flat Race Jockey of 1987 to Steve Cauthen (USA) at Cheltenham (Bernard Parkin)

intervened, though he did make his acquaintance with Aintree from the saddle while on leave in 1940. Wounded the day he landed with his regiment as a captain in Normandy, he returned a month later to see the campaign through to the end of the war, when he showed that he was no mean show jumper before returning to England in 1946 to resume his career.

Before the end of the 1945/46 season he had ridden twenty-two winners, and after a chance win on Fulke Walwyn's Leap Man at Cheltenham he rode regularly for Walwyn and was runner-up to **Jack Dowdeswell** in the Championship of 1946/47 and Champion the following season. His crowning achievement was to ride two successive Grand National winners for Vincent O'Brien, Early Mist in 1953 and Royal Tan in 1954. A great judge of pace and immensely strong in a finish, he would probably have been Champion for longer had he not, in common with many of those whose careers were interrupted by six years of war, only been able to ride the top weights.

The next four seasons belonged to another great Irish horseman, **Tim Molony** (1919), who also learned his trade over the banks, though in his case he raced over them – and the penalty for a mistake at racing pace is liable to be infinitely worse than over brush fences. Champion from 1948/49 to 1951/52 and again in 1954/55, his 900 winners included three successive Champion Hurdles for Willie Stephenson with Sir Ken, and in 1953 he added the Gold Cup to make the double on Vincent O'Brien's Knock Hard. Meanwhile on to the scene had come the greatest jockey of the fifties, **Fred Winter** (1926) (see p82), but after taking the Championship in the 1952/53 season Fred was deposed due to injury by one of those whose misfortune it is to be remembered more for a disaster than for his achievements.

Dick Francis (1920) is of course better known now as a bestselling author of crime novels set against a racing background, but he was also the Champion National Hunt Jockey of 1954/55. That he was a consummate horseman is not surprising, for not only were his father and grandfather successful National Hunt jockeys, but his father later managed the Holyport stables of W. J. Smith, where the Queen and Princess Margaret learned to ride, and it was Dick's job to school the ponies for the royal clients.

After a wartime career as a fighter and bomber pilot, he started riding as an amateur for George Owen in Cheshire, and it was not long before his success led the stewards to advise him that he must either turn professional or confine his activities to hunter chases. In 1949 he was second (to Russian Hero) in the Grand National on Lord Bicester's Roimond, and in 1952, riding for Peter Cazalet and Frank Cundell he took the Championship with seventy-six winners. In 1956 he came to Aintree for his eighth National with every hope of winning it for National Hunt Racing's most popular patron, HM Queen Elizabeth the Queen Mother. And as Devon Loch led over the last fence it seemed that a dream was coming true.

What happened next has never been satisfactorily explained, but only forty yards from the post, as the huge crowd was already starting to cheer a royal winner, Devon Loch's coordination deserted him, he fell to the ground, and **Dave Dick** swept by on ESB to give Fred Rimell his first National as a trainer. But if he was robbed of the greatest prize in steeplechasing, Dick Francis soon began to collect the prizes elsewhere, and the Champion Jockey became American Crime Writer of the Year and took the Edgar Allan Poe Mystery Award, to which many others have been added since.

Stan Mellor MBE (1937) was another who benefited from the expertise of George Owen. After experience in show jumping with ponies, he rode as an amateur before turning professional in 1954. He won the Championship in 1959/60 and again for the next two seasons, retiring in 1972 with a record of 1034 wins which was to stand until broken by John Francome fourteen years later. With the grey Stalbridge Colonist he was one of the few to beat both Mill House (by half a length at Kempton), and Arkle, from whom he was receiving 35lb (15.8kg) in the Hennessy Cognac Gold Cup of 1966. He is now a successful trainer both on the flat and over jumps, and produced the unpronounceable Lean Ar Aghaidh to thrill spectators of the 1987 Grand National, in which he made most of the running in the hands to Guy Landau to finish third and then to win the Whitbread Gold Cup at Sandown three weeks later.

He was deposed by **Josh Gifford** (1941) who, after winning over fifty races as an apprentice on the flat, headed the table in 1962/63 and 1963/64. He then broke his thigh in a fall at Nottingham, and broke it again in a car accident the following summer, being out of action for fifteen months during which the Championship was seized by Terry Biddlecombe. He then bounced back to retake the crown in 1966/67, and with 122 winners beat the record set by Fred Winter fourteen years earlier. He and trainer Ryan Price made a formidable team, which won four of the first five runnings of the Schweppes Gold Trophy.

In 1967 he had a great chance of winning the Grand National for Price on the 15-2 favourite Honey End. They led over Bechers the second time round until the whole field was baulked by a loose horse at the next fence, allowing the outsider Foinavon to go through and win. When Josh retired from the saddle in 1970 he took over as trainer of Price's jumpers, and in 1981 achieved the fairy tale victory of Aldaniti and **Bob Champion** in the National. Both horse and rider had come back from injury and illness against all the odds, a story that became a box office success as a film.

Terry Biddlecombe was to enliven weighing rooms up and down the country from the moment that he won his first race as an amateur in 1958/59 until his retirement sixteen years later. After twenty-two wins as an amateur he turned professional in 1959/60, and four seasons later he went as first jockey to Fred Rimell, forming one of the great partnerships of National Hunt racing. The next season he took advantage of Josh Gifford's injury to take the Championship with 114 winners, retaining it the following season with 102. Josh came back for two seasons, and then Terry shared it again in 1968/69 with **Bob Davies**, (who won it outright in 1969/70 and 1971/72.)

In 1967 Woodland Venture's preparation for Cheltenham had been fraught with difficulty; he fell at Kempton on Boxing Day (in Arkle's last race), and then developed ringworm, but in the Gold Cup he stormed home to give Rimell and Biddlecombe their first win in the race. Terry never won the National, but in 1970 a fall deprived him of the ride on the winner Gay Trip, whom Pat Taaffe rode in his absence. His tally of over 900 winners was only gained at the cost of a terrifying list of injuries; a hundred concussions; six broken shoulder blades, five wrists, three thumbs, two fingers, two ribs, two ankles, two vertebrae, a leg, a collar bone and several damaged kidneys.

But Terry, for all his cavalier attitude both on and off the course, was no mere daredevil; he possessed superb judgement of pace and lightning reactions, and his horses were perfectly balanced in the approach to a fence and quickly rebalanced afterwards. But he was also utterly fearless, and if there was the slightest chance of a win he took it. One of the most popular characters ever to sit on a racehorse, he was honoured on his retirement in 1974 with an appearance with Eamonn Andrews on the television programme 'This Is Your Life'. Since then he has enlivened the scene for television viewers at the Cheltenham National Hunt Festival with his pithy comments on his successors.

Ten days before the 1973 Cheltenham Gold Cup **Ron Barry** broke his collar bone. Most jockeys wouldn't have contemplated riding in the race (and wouldn't today have been allowed to do so), but Ron's major worry was how to get The Dikler to the post. He

OPPOSITE
Stan Mellor, MBE (GB) on one of his 1,034 winners, Park Ranger, at Cheltenham 1968 (Bernard Parkin)

Josh Gifford (GB), Champion four times and now one of the most successful trainers, winning on Aryaman at Ludlow in 1961 (Bernard Parkin)

was allowed to go down early, and then had no option but to let this confirmed puller run his own race, beating **Richard Pitman** and Pendil by a short head. The weighing room gossip has it that he bought a case of champagne for his fellow jockeys and that he arrived at Uttoxeter the next day for four rides fuelled entirely with the golden liquid, made all the running to win the first, and had to be propped up on the scales to weigh in!

Another weighing room anecdote about the Champion of 1972/73 and 1973/74 concerns a race at Newcastle in 1977, when Jonjo O'Neill on the hard puller Hidden Value asked Ron to set a decent pace on Forest King. Half way round Hidden Value pulled up alongside, and Jonjo shouted to Ron who responded by catching hold of Hidden Value's bridle. But after this had happened three times he shouted back, 'I'm fed up with all this "Ron, Ron, Ron" ', and gave Jonjo's horse a slap on the backside. Hidden Value shot into a ten length lead and then blew up leaving Forest King to win comfortably. It's not surprising to learn that after riding his final mount, Final

Argument, to victory at Ayr in 1983, Ron was carried out of the weighing room by his fellow jockeys.

Apart from **Tommy Stack**, who was Champion in 1974/75 and again in 1976/77, and who rode Red Rum to his third and final victory in the Grand National of 1977, the period from the mid-seventies to the present day belongs to three of the very greatest National Hunt jockeys – **Jonjo O'Neill** (1952) (see p96), **John Francome** (1952) (see p90) and **Peter Scudamore** (1958) (see p104).

But of course there have been many top-class jockeys who have never won the English Championship, and not a few of them from Ireland. **Aubrey Brabazon** has the unique record of having scored hat-tricks both in the Cheltenham Gold Cup, with Cottage Rake in 1948, 1949 and 1950, and in the Champion Hurdle, in 1949, 1950 and 1951 with Hatton's Grace – and all for Vincent O'Brien. **Martin Molony** (1925), younger brother of Tim, excelled both on the flat and over fences, and had his career, which included three Irish Grand Nationals and the Cheltenham Gold Cup as well as two Irish Cesarewich's on triple Champion Hurdler Hatton's Grace, not been cut short by a fractured skull, he would have been the equal of any jockey of his day.

One of the greatest horsemen to come out of Ireland was **Pat Taaffe** (1930), associated for ever with the great Arkle, whom he rode to a hat-trick of Cheltenham Gold Cup wins

Terry Biddlecombe (GB) with HM Queen Elizabeth The Queen Mother after dismounting from her third placed Game Spirit, Cheltenham Gold Cup, 1974 (Bernard Parkin)

in 1964, 1965 and 1966. Born to racing – his father trained Mr What to win the 1958 Grand National, and he himself show jumped in Dublin as a boy – he rode his first winner as an amateur at the age of seventeen. 'Invited' by the stewards to turn professional in 1949, he began the long and successful partnership with trainer Tom Dreaper that was to bring home, in addition to Arkle's three Gold Cups, another Gold Cup with Fort Leney in 1968 and most of the major steeplechasing prizes in England and Ireland.

A shade under 6ft in height, he was a natural horseman who was something of a National specialist; he won two at Aintree, on Quare Times for Vincent O'Brien in 1955 and on Gay Trip (deputising for Terry Biddlecombe) for Fred Rimell in 1970, as well as six Irish Grand Nationals. His mantle was inherited by **Tommy Carberry**, who with L'Escargot won the Cheltenham Gold Cup in 1970 and 1971 and the Grand National of 1975, as well as a third Gold Cup on Ten Up in 1975.

Several leading riders are remembered mainly for their Champion Hurdle victories; **Jimmy Uttley**, winner of a hat-trick on Persian War in 1968, 1969 and 1970, **Paul Kelleway**, winner on Bula in 1971 and 1972, **Paddy Broderick**, partner of Night Nurse in 1976 and 1977, and **Steve Smith-Eccles**, three times winner on See You Then in 1985, 1986 and 1987. But the field today, dominated as it is by Peter Scudamore, contains several who will be doing their utmost to unseat him in the near future – **Brendan Powell** and **Richard Dunwoody**, who is considered to be the best jockey riding over fences today, are but two examples.

Pat Taaffe (Ireland) and Arkle, one of the greatest steeplechasing partnerships of all time (Bernard Parkin)

Brendan Powell (Ireland) landing over Becher's Brook on his way to victory in the 1988 Seagram Grand National on Rhyme 'n Reason (Bernard Parkin)

Because of its origins, its association with hunting, the weights carried and the inclusion in the calendar of plenty of races especially for them, the amateurs have always played a notable part in National Hunt racing. Many of the top professional riders started out as amateurs, and with that experience behind them they had a much better start than the lad who must work his way up through the stable, as John Francome did.

In the first sixty years of the Grand National, twenty-nine were won by amateurs; of the last eighty-six Nationals, they have only won thirteen. But among these last are some pretty illustrious names: **Jack Anthony**, who won it in 1911 on Glenside, 1915 on Ally Soper (when the war-time race was run at Gatwick), and in 1920 on Troytown; **Fulke Walwyn**, on Reynoldstown for his second victory in 1936; two Americans, **Tommy Smith**, victor in 1965 on Jay Trump, who had not only won the Maryland Hunt Cup over fixed timber twice previously, but won it again after winning the National, and who nearly won the Grand Steeplechase de Paris as well; **Charlie Fenwick**, on Ben Nevis in 1980; and, most recently, one of the most popular wins that summed up the spirit of National Hunt racing, that of **Dick Saunders** in 1982 on Grittar, owned and trained by the Leicestershire hunting farmer (and Cottesmore Hunt Chairman) Frank Gilman.

One of the most popular partnerships was that of **Simon Sherwood** and the grey Desert Orchid, and when they won the 1989 Cheltenham Gold Cup the cheers rivalled those heard when the ex-Champion Hurdler Dawn Run won it with Jonjo O'Neill in 1986. Simon, who started out as an amateur, rode mainly for his brother Oliver, and though he never had as many rides, and consequently not as many winners, as some of his contemporaries, he was a consummate horseman.

LEFT: *Richard Dunwoody (GB) on his 1986 Seagram Grand National winner West Tip, Cheltenham 1988* (Bernard Parkin)

ABOVE: *Simon Sherwood (GB) on his way to winning the 1989 Tote Cheltenham Gold Cup on the most popular steeplechaser since Arkle, Desert Orchid* (Bernard Parkin)

FRED WINTER, CBE

In the entire history of National Hunt racing, one man seems to stand head and shoulders above all others. For his outstanding success both as a jockey and as a trainer, and for the respect in which he is held by everyone connected with the sport, Fred Winter must surely be regarded as one of the truly great horsemen of the world.

Born in 1926, the son of a first-class jockey and trainer, Fred rode his first winner on the flat at the age of thirteen, when he beat, among others, Gordon Richards and Harry Wragg in a £100 race at Salisbury in 1940. He was then apprenticed to Harry Jellis at Newmarket, but in 1941 only two more winners came from eighty rides, and increasing weight was clearly going to limit his chances of a successful career on the flat. The war was now in its fourth year, and Fred joined the Air Training Corps, took a job in a factory repairing damaged planes, and hoped to join the RAF. In fact he ended up by joining the Parachute Regiment, and was subsequently commissioned into the West Kent Regiment with whom he served in Palestine.

By the time that he was demobilised in 1948 he had already won his first hurdle race at Kempton, and had decided on his future career. But his first two seasons gave little clue to the triumphs that were to come, for on his fifth ride he dislocated his shoulder, and early in the 1948/49 season he broke his back in a Novice Hurdle at Wye, was off for a year, and nearly gave up. But in the following season he had his first winner for Ryan Price, at Newton Abbot on Boxing Day, thus starting an association that was to last for virtually the whole of his riding career. With eighteen winners from 131 rides, Fred was now on his way.

The 1950/51 season brought a double at Haydock for Lord Rosebery, and his first ride in the Grand National. His fellow jockeys bet him that he would not survive Bechers first time round, and his confidence was scarcely improved when eleven horses fell at the first. He and Glen Fire parted company at the Canal Turn, but at least he won his bet! By the end of the season he had had thirty-eight winners from 221 rides, and had fallen eighteen times with no worse injury than a broken finger. More important, he finished fifth in the Jockeys Championship behind such famous names as Tim Molony, Bryan Marshall, Arthur Thompson and Martin Molony.

The first day of the 1951/52 season brought a broken collar bone, but he was soon back in the saddle with a treble at Plumpton. Not long afterwards, however, after eleven falls from a dozen rides there, he vowed never to ride over fences at Plumpton again. By January Fred had amassed fifty winners, and in the Cheltenham Gold Cup he had a foretaste of a more famous occasion a decade later; as he jumped the water on Shaef, the bridle was knocked off his head by another horse, and only the reins kept the bit in his mouth. It was quite a feat not only to finish the course but to be second to Mont Tremblant!

It was at this time that Fred struck up a partnership with a great horse – the Contessa di Sant' Elia's Halloween. His previous owner, Captain Dick Smalley, had won point-to-points and amateur chases with him, but so far no professional rider seemed to have found the key to staying on board. So, when asked to ride him, Fred went to Smalley for advice. The advice, 'Sit still and do nothing,' proved effective, for first time out together they won over 4 miles 1 furlong at Hurst Park, and they went on to win many races, including Kempton's King George VI chase in 1952 and 1954. The season ended with eighty-five winners in spite of a cracked arm and another broken collar bone, and second place in the championship behind Tim Molony.

Statistically, Fred's best season was 1952/53; his greatest number of rides (470), and falls (41), but also of winners (121), a record that was to stand until Josh Gifford broke it fourteen years later. It was also the season in which an accident to Dave Dick led to Fred's involvement with owner Dorothy Paget and trainer Fulke Walwyn. Lanveoc Poulmic was a half brother to Mont Tremblant and though a brilliant jumper was extremely difficult to sit on over a fence. Fred, however, soon came to terms with him, and together they won five races that season. The sixth might well have ended Fred's career; hot favourite at Kempton on Boxing Day, Lanveoc Poulmic hit the last fence so hard that even Fred had no chance of staying in the saddle. But he found himself in the predicament that is every jockey's nightmare: his leg was trapped in the stirrup, and as the horse moved on only Fred's presence of mind saved him. Reaching for the bridle, in itself no mean feat from that position, he pulled the horse's head round so tightly that he came to a standstill, until a spectator came to his assistance.

On that same day at Kempton, Fred won the King George VI Chase on Halloween, having already won two important races on him earlier in the season. It was indeed a brilliant season, and 'Winner-a-Day Winter' was the title accorded to him by his fans. His 100th winner came at Sandown on Air Wedding in a three mile chase after he had disappointed the punters by being unplaced on the favourite in the Imperial Cup, and perhaps his proudest moment to date was when both the Queen and the Queen Mother came down from the Royal Box to congratulate him in the paddock. At Fontwell in May came that 121st winner, Gribun, trained by Ryan Price.

On the same day Fred won on a horse called Cent Francs, but when Ryan Price bought him fate took a hand, and on the first day of the next season Cent Francs fell at the first fence, and Fred suffered a badly broken leg that was to keep him out of the saddle for the rest of the season. However, Fate, or whoever arranges these things, provided more than adequate compensation when Fred went to Liverpool to watch the Grand National. He did see Bryan Marshall win it on Royal Tan, but far more important was his first sighting of Diana Pearson.

His courtship was abruptly terminated when Diana left on a world tour, but Fred showed determination, and the following April they became engaged. Meanwhile Fred had resumed his partnership with Halloween, and after finishing second in the Grand Sefton Trial at Hurst Park under a huge weight they won four in a row, including the King George VI Chase for the second time. Victory in the Champion Hurdle at Cheltenham on Claire Soleil and his engagement to Diana rounded off a great season, which was also important for the start of his association with a horse that was to enable him to realise every jockey's ambition of winning the Grand National.

At 17 hands, Sundew was nothing like Halloween, but then one of Fred's greatest strengths was his ability to size up and come to terms with horses of all shapes and sizes – and temperaments. In his first Grand National, ridden by Paddy Doyle, Sundew had fallen at the 26th fence, and then, less than three weeks later, had been second in the Welsh Grand National at Chepstow with Fred, giving nearly two stone to the winner. In December they fell at Newbury, but won a 3½ mile chase at Hurst Park before beating the 1955 Grand National winner Quare Times in Haydock's Grand National Trial. Arriving at Aintree in good shape, Sundew was going well throughout the first circuit, but was brought down by a loose horse at Becher's second time round in the race that was won by Dave Dick on ESB when the Queen Mother's Devon Loch, ridden by Dick Francis, inexplicably fell to the ground on the run-in from the last fence.

In the 1956 King George VI Chase the brilliant but erratic Galloway Braes fell, breaking his own leg and concussing his jockey. Today Fred would have been compulsorily out of the saddle for a set period, but in those days there were no such restrictions, and the next day at Newbury he scored a double! The Cheltenham meeting was disappointing; the Champion Hurdle favourite Claire Soleil was unplaced and Fred rode not a single winner. And so to Aintree with Sundew. Although he had won the Grand International Chase at Sandown, his record at Aintree was hardly inspiring; he had fallen in his two previous Grand Nationals, and in the Grand Sefton Chase in November he had jumped appallingly – at the fence after Becher's Fred had found himself with both his legs on the same side of the saddle, with the Canal Turn next!

Grand National day did not start well, for Fred was beaten on the favourite in the Coronation Hurdle. But Fred's preoccupation had all along been with winning the National, and he had taken advice from such experts as Pat Taaffe and Dudley Williams. Following the shortest and clearest route towards the inside, Sundew won by eight lengths from Wyndburgh. Sadly this was Sundew's last triumph. His owners, against Fred's advice, decided to run him three weeks later in the Whitbread Gold Cup at Sandown, where he was pulled up. After two more indifferent performances, he was involved in a pile-up at the Haydock water jump ridden by another jockey, broke his shoulder, and had to be put down.

Having won the 1956/57 Championship from Michael Scudamore with eighty winners, Fred won that of 1957/58 from Tim Brookshaw with eighty-two, and after he had won a long-distance hurdle at Sandown for Fulke Walwyn, the trainer pronounced him the greatest jockey he had ever seen – praise indeed from the man who had guided Reynoldstown to victory in the 1936 National. Though the season brought no major wins, it produced Fred's 500th winner (on Taxidermist at Ludlow,) and Cheltenham 1959 will long be remembered for his five wins; Flame Gun won the Cotswold Chase, Fare Time the Champion Hurdle, and Top Twenty the Grand Annual Challenge Cup, all these on the first day of the meeting. The second day yielded no winners, but the gallant Top Twenty was sent out again to be second in the Champion Chase. On the final day Claire Soleil won the Spa Hurdle, while Gallery Goddess rounded off the meeting with success in the Grand Annual Challenge Cup.

Once again Fred seemed set for the Championship, but a fall in a novice chase at Leicester in April left him with a fractured skull, and the title went to Tim Brookshaw. Probably his best season was 1960/61, when he won the feature race on each of

Fred Winter (GB) won two Grand Nationals as a jockey and two as a trainer, and is seen here on his 1962 winner, Kilmore (W.W. Rouch)

Cheltenham's three days and on the next two at Hurst Park, including the Champion Hurdle on Eborneezer and the Gold Cup on Saffron Tartan. Earlier he had won the King George VI Chase on Saffron Tartan, and in both these big races the runner-up had been Dave Dick, who after being beaten on Pas Seul in the Gold Cup said, 'I've no doubt now that Fred is the best I ever saw, and there won't be another like him.'

Meanwhile there had arrived in Ryan Price's yard an eleven-year-old horse called Kilmore that had scored eleven wins from fifty-four starts in Ireland and who was to be aimed at the Grand National. But when Fred saw him finish unplaced under Gay Kindersley in the Kim Muir Memorial Challenge Cup after the Champion Hurdle he was not impressed. However, he rode him for the first time in the National, and when they came fifth he realised that he had a promising prospect for the following year.

The prospects for 1961/62 looked good, with retainers from Ryan Price and Fulke Walwyn and the ride on Saffron Tartan for Don Butchers, and indeed his first five rides for Walwyn produced four winners and a second! But then Saffron Tartan broke down in November, and a run of thirty-two losing rides was followed by a broken collar bone, which meant that the ride on Mandarin in Newbury's Hennessy Gold Cup went to the Irish ace Willie Robinson, who will always be remembered for his association with Mill House and his duels with Pat Taaffe and Arkle. Mandarin duly won, and Fred wondered if he might not be 'jocked off'. But he was soon back in form with four wins at Kempton, including a splendid performance on Mandarin, and his hopes for Cheltenham were high.

A run of five losers was followed by a win in the County Handicap Hurdle, and in the Gold Cup he rode one of the best races of his career. Pas Seul was the ante-post favourite at 15-8 on (though he went right out to 9-4 against before the start), and there was plenty of support for the experienced Fortria. A bad mistake at the open ditch, which Dave Dick did well to survive, put paid to Pas Seul's chances, and it seemed as though Pat Taaffe had the race at his mercy on Fortria. But at the crucial point at the top of the hill four furlongs from home Fred saw a gap on the rails, pushed Mandarin through, and won by a length.

And so to Aintree with Kilmore once again. Since his fifth place in the previous National, Kilmore had hardly distinguished himself, with falls in the Becher Chase at Aintree in November and at Lingfield only ten days before the National. (He had also been unplaced in the Hennessy ridden by Josh Gifford.) Fred realised that Kilmore was another horse on whom one should virtually 'sit still and do nothing', and in the National this is what he did, taking 'the Winter route' towards the inside, and only going to the front as they approached the last fence. His second National victory must rank as another of Fred's greatest rides.

He was now in his thirty-seventh year, and with obviously limited prospects ahead over fences, he applied for and received a licence to ride on the flat. But he quickly realised that this was a different game altogether, and in any case his attention was now riveted on the Grand Steeplechase de Paris. Little did he know that he was to be the hero of one of the most amazing episodes in the history of racing!

His arrival at Auteuil with a severe stomach upset was hardly auspicious, and if ever a course demanded a jockey in full control it was Auteuil, with its twisting four mile figure-of-eight course and its variety of fences which included a bullfinch, a 6ft high privet hedge which continental horses are used to brushing through but at which their English cousins tend to jump too high, thus losing ground. Mandarin, being somewhat keen and difficult to restrain, had a rubber covered bit to protect his mouth, and as the fourteen runners approached the bullfinch the bit broke. So here was Fred, travelling at speed on a horse without breaks or steering, and with twenty-one fences and over 3½ miles still to go!

If the French jockeys had treated Fred Winter as their forebears had once treated Fred Archer, Mandarin would have played little further part in the race. The next four fences were in a straight line, but then came a bend to the left. By this time Fred had discovered that 'neck-reining' allied to the use of his legs brought a modicum of control, and the Frenchmen actually helped them round the bend. Fred's main fear was that Mandarin would pull himself clear of the others, but a mistake at the water dropped him back so that he once more had a lead. Even so, it required all Fred's strength and horsemanship to keep him on course. Then coming to the last fence Mandarin faltered – he had in fact broken down – but Fred continued to drive him on and it looked as though a miracle was about to take place. Then, half way up the long run in, the French horse Lumino challenged strongly, and as the two crossed the line it was Lumino who went ahead. Had the gallant little Mandarin held on for long enough?

Both horse and rider headed back to the unsaddling enclosure completely exhausted, and as they waited for the result of the photograph, they looked a sorry sight. Then came the moment of triumph as they were pronounced the winners. Not only the huge British contingent, but also thousands of Frenchmen, cheered the result of one of the most extraordinary races of all time. For Fred, however, the day was far from over. Booked to ride Beaver in the next race, the Champion Four Year Old Hurdle, he had to be dressed by Stan Mellor and helped out to the paddock. He then proceeded to win another of France's major trophies!

A few weeks later, Fred rode his first winner in Ireland, and at the start of the 1962/63 season he won a hurdle race at Belmont Park, New York. The season at home suffered the worst weather for many years and many meetings were lost through snow and frost. Fred was out of luck at Cheltenham, but on Grand National day at Aintree he won both divisions of the Liverpool Hurdle. In the National itself Fred was repeating the tactics that had been so successful the year before, when at the water a falling horse kicked Kilmore, and they did well to complete the course in sixth place.

Fred Winter, CBE (GB), four times Champion Jockey, eight times Champion Trainer, winning on Malacca, Ludlow 1961 (Bernard Parkin)

In April Fred rode eight winners in a week in the Westcountry, and then suffered a punctured lung in a fall at Chepstow, though this was only diagnosed three days later. After an operation and during the ensuing convalescence Fred decided that the time had come to retire – not because of injury, but because in his own words, 'I was being beaten when I should not have been beaten.' His career was crowned by his appointment in HM The Queen's Birthday Honours List as Commander of the Order of the British Empire, and a few days later he was invited to lunch with the Queen and Prince Philip at Buckingham Palace.

In fact two factors conspired to keep Fred in the saddle for one more season: first, although he had decided to train he had not yet found a suitable establishment; second, Kilmore, who would be fourteen when the next National came round, was showing no sign of his age whatever. How wonderful it would be to bow out with a third Grand National victory!

In the meantime he won a race at Leicester which, whilst in no way approaching his Auteuil feat, certainly provided much light entertainment for the racegoers. Four runners went to the start, but David Nicholson fell at the first, and the other two went at the open ditch at number five. The loose horses gave Fred's mount, Carry On, a lead until they wisely veered off to the stables whereupon he deposited Fred into the water jump. Undeterred, Fred remounted, but Carry On hardly lived up to his name, for he refused at the next open ditch, and at the second attempt executed a spectacular somersault, at which point Fred decided the moment had come to retire. Meanwhile Nicholson had remounted, returned to the scene of his fall, and restarted, but after two more fences he pulled up. The other two had also been reunited with their mounts and had returned to the fifth fence to restart. Seeing this, Ryan Price ran out to Fred as he was walking back to the stables, presumably only too glad that the farce was over, and instructed him to wait for the other two to catch him up, get a lead over the ditch, and carry on. With a lead which Fred was careful to preserve until the last fence, Carry On duly won!

A week later Fred gave a magnificent display of riding when bringing What a Myth home to victory at Sandown, and in January he won five races from six rides at Sandown and Windsor, and in February four from five rides at Newbury. But before the National disaster was to strike Ryan Price's stable. When Rosyth won the Schweppes Gold Trophy at Liverpool for the second time after running unplaced in five out of six races in between these two victories, the stewards refused to accept Ryan Price's explanation and withdrew his licence to train. Then at Aintree Kilmore fell at the 21st just as Fred felt that he was about to achieve that final ambition.

His final meeting at Cheltenham brought no winners on the course on which he had won over sixty races including three Champion Hurdles and two Gold Cups, but he received a presentation from the Cheltenham Steeplechase Company and Life Membership of the Club. Beaverbrook Newspapers gave him a statuette of a horse and rider, and the Variety Club of Great Britain gave him a farewell lunch at the Savoy.

The statistics of Fred's seventeen season career speak for themselves – 929 wins from 4,298 starts, a winning percentage of nearly twenty-two, and along the way 319 falls, with a fractured spine and skull, a broken leg, broken collar bones, a punctured lung and several other injuries as well. To what did he owe his success?

His tactical judgement of a race was supreme and he was quick to spot an opening and to go for it; his shrewdness in choosing the inside route when others dared not do so; his courage when driving a horse at the last fence at the end of a gruelling race; and his great power and strength in a finish; all these contributed to his success. Because of the risks they share, jump jockeys are inclined to be a more friendly bunch than their counterparts on the flat. But like Sir Gordon Richards on the flat, Fred was liked and respected by his fellow jockeys because he was a man of absolute integrity. Once, early in his career, he had been instructed not to win; his reply was to advise the owner to back his horse, for he would do his best to see that it did.

It is strange to discover that Fred did not actually much like jumping fences, which he regarded purely as obstacles between the start and finish. Perhaps for this reason he was, in Ryan Price's words, 'The most useless schooling jockey in the world.' And in his own words, 'The only thing I really enjoyed in racing was winning.' But Ryan Price also said of him, 'He rode me at least a hundred winners that no one else in the world would have won on,' and 'He raised the standard of National Hunt jockeyship higher than it has ever been, and I don't mean just by his riding, but by his conduct both on and off the course.' And that great trainer Peter Cazalet at the Variety Club lunch summed it all up. 'Thank you, Fred, for your splendid example to all young jockeys. Few individuals stand out in leadership as you do, and during the last ten years you have stood out alone.'

What a note upon which to end! But this was by no means the end, merely the start of a glittering new career. The story of Fred Winter the trainer is as exciting as the story of the jockey, and has as many highs and lows. The transition from the one career to the other is by no means easy, and many high-class performers in the saddle have failed to make it. The reason is not difficult to see: the jockey is an artist, a brave and skilled individual performer, who, though part of a team, is not its leader; the successful trainer must be a leader, an organiser, and an administrator, as well as an expert horseman in the general sense. Fred was admirably equipped to make the transition.

In his first two seasons as a trainer he won two Grand Nationals, with the American Maryland Hunt Cup winner Jay Trump in 1964 and with Anglo in 1965. Champion Trainer eight times, he won four Champion Hurdles and a Cheltenham Gold Cup, and proved that his eye for a jockey was as keen as his eye for a horse – Richard Pitman won him a Champion Hurdle, John Francome rode for him for his entire career and won him the Gold Cup, and Peter Scudamore brought home the 1988 Champion Hurdle with Celtic Shot.

In 1987 one of the world's greatest horsemen, who had survived over 300 falls as a jockey, fractured his skull in a fall in his own home, and was forced to retire as a trainer in 1988. It is doubtful if anyone will stamp his authority on the sport as surely as Fred Winter has done.

JOHN FRANCOME, MBE

Irishman Eddie Harty was, we believe, the only man to have won the Grand National and ridden in the three day event at the Olympic Games; Sir Harry Llewellyn the only rider to have been second in the Grand National and to win an Olympic Gold medal for show jumping; John Francome may be the only man to have won the Cheltenham Gold Cup and a team gold medal for show jumping – in the Junior European Championships.

Born at Swindon, where his father worked on the railway, John Francome was another outstanding horseman from a family with no horsey background. And like some others his first taste of the thrills of riding was gained on the back of a donkey at the seaside. He acquired his first experience of horses by helping the milkman in return for riding home on his horse, and at the age of six his father bought him his first pony, but couldn't afford a saddle as well. But herein probably lay the secret of his future success, for he developed the balance and grip that enabled him to sit on a horse without recourse to holding on by the reins.

Hunting with the VWH in the winter, gymkhanas and Pony Club camp in the summer, and a few lessons from Mrs Molly Sievewright and Dick Stilwell, backed up by a keen observation and a determination to succeed, led to success in show jumping. John's father bought him a Grade 'A' horse called Red Paul on which he not only competed in the Jumping Derby and won the Young Riders Championship at Hickstead but also helped the British Team to win the Junior European Championships at St Moritz in 1970. But when he left school, without any obvious qualifications, he was shrewd enough to sense that he was unlikely to make his fortune show jumping, and he decided to become a jockey.

John's father had done odd jobs for Fred Winter at Uplands, Lambourn, so he contacted the trainer, and in the autumn of 1969 John found himself under a first-class stableman and teacher, head lad Brian Delaney. He worked hard in the yard in order to get noticed – the only way to get schooling rides – and he did odd jobs so as to be able to trade his moped for a car. Meanwhile Red Paul was at Richard Pitman's yard, and John took time off to ride him in his last season as a Junior, at the end of which he was sold to Debbie Johnsey, who was to take fourth place in the individual show jumping at the Montreal Olympics with Moxy.

In December 1970 John rode a winner on his first ride in public, on Multigrey at Worcester, but his second ride, and his first for Fred Winter, brought nothing more than a broken wrist. Then his weight began to increase, the weight-reducing pills started to bring on cramp, and he almost decided to give up the battle. But he realised that the only sound way to lose weight was to eat less, and he decided to diet. In his second season he was able to get rides from Ken Cundell as well as from his own stable, and when

Richard Pitman took over from Paul Kelleway as first jockey to Fred Winter he started passing on rides that he could not take.

In his second season John's eighteen wins included his first important one on Free Thinker in the Free Handicap Hurdle at Chepstow, and his third season brought his tally to twenty, but also a broken arm at Worcester which necessitated a steel plate. In 1973/74 he started his climb up the jockey's table, but broke the same arm again, which this time involved a bone graft from his hip. But eleven of his thirty wins had been for outside stables, and during the summer Fred Rimell offered him the post of first jockey. After talking the matter over with Fred Winter he decided to stay where he was, but took a second retainer with Captain Richard Head, for whom he rode eighty winners in the next five seasons, including the 1977 Mildmay Chase and the 1980 Topham Trophy on Uncle Bing and the 1975 Panama Cigar Final and the 1979 Welsh Champion Chase on Border Incident, two of the best jumpers he rode.

The year 1975 brought John his first win at the Cheltenham Festival Meeting on Flame Gun in the National Hunt Chase. In his warm-up race for Cheltenham at Doncaster Flame Gun was going well approaching what John believed (in thick fog) to be the third last fence. But having won his three previous races on the horse it was with some consternation that John realised that he was in fact about to jump the last – with far too much ground to make up to win. Never at a loss for a solution to a tricky problem, he told Richard Head that his horse had made a bad mistake on the far side, a claim that, thanks to the fog, could not be disputed! And his conscience was eased by the probability that, had Flame Gun won at Doncaster, his penalty might have precluded a win at Cheltenham.

That season ended with seventy wins, and third place in the Championship behind Tommy Stack and Graham Thorner. It also recorded John's first clash with the Jockey Club stewards at Portman Square, over an incident at Plumpton. (Though he was extremely successful there, he thought no more of Plumpton than had his trainer Fred Winter: 'If the world had a backside Plumpton would be in the middle of it' summed up his feelings for the course.) In the race his mount, Boy Desmond, had been badly hampered when the horse in front had broken down and had been pulled out sharply to avoid jumping the next hurdle. Accused of leaving Boy Desmond, who finished fourth, with too much to do, he suggested to the local stewards that they call in the rider of the other horse. This they did, but he was unaware that he had impeded anybody, so his evidence was unhelpful, and at Portman Square John received a seven day suspension.

In 1975 Richard Pitman retired, and John took over as first jockey at Uplands, and although such great horses as Bula, Pendil, Lanzarote, Crisp and Killiney were on their way out, he still won good races on the first three, and with ninety-six wins he took the Jockey's Championship for the first time at the end of the 1975/76 season.

He had also been involved in an incident even more embarrassing, since there was no fog, than that involving Flame Gun. Coming into the straight at Huntingdon on second favourite Floating Pound, on whom he had won the Embassy Chase Final three weeks earlier, he jumped what he thought was the last fence and pulled out to avoid the open ditch parallel to the finishing line, making sure that he kept close enough to the wing to make Andy Turnell go outside him. His laughter when he saw Andy forced into taking the fence was quickly stifled when he realised that he had himself failed to jump the last!

It says much for both his trainer, Fred Winter, and his sporting owners, Mr and Mrs Boucher, that they all realised that nothing they could say or do would match their jockey's own embarrassment at his lapse, and even the stewards were surprisingly lenient with just a £75 fine. (It did moreover cost Winter his 100th winner at the end of the season.)

In 1976 John married Miriam, whom he had met when she was a trainer's secretary, and who has since combined the duties of a busy jockey's wife with a successful career of her own as a model.

The year 1979 brought another Championship with ninety-five winners, and then 1980/81 started a run of five consecutive seasons with over a hundred winners. The following year typified the ups and downs of the struggle for the Championship; by Christmas John led the table by twenty-five from Peter Scudamore. Then at Newbury in March he was concussed when Virgin Soldier was brought down by a horse ridden by Sam Morshead, Mercy Rimell's first jockey. Virgin Soldier rolled on Sam, whose rides were then taken by Scudamore, who found himself with a lead of twenty with five weeks of the season to go, only to break his arm at Southwell. John then started telephoning trainers in earnest, until he had to win ten races in twice as many days, then six in fourteen, finally one in a week. Bank Holiday Monday with four fancied mounts provided nothing, but on 1 June he drew level with Peter's total – and decided, as he had earlier promised, to share the Championship with him.

By June 1984 John had passed Stan Mellor's record of 1,034 winners, and had also won the first Rail Freight World Jockeys' Championship. The following November he beat Josh Gifford's record for the fastest fifty winners by a day, helped by thirty-five in only eight weeks from the stable of John Jenkins. The Hennessy Gold Cup and the King George VI Chase on Burrough Hill Lad boosted his hopes of beating Jonjo O'Neill's 149 winners in a season, but he had already told Fred Winter that this season would be his last, and when The Reject deposited him at Chepstow's open ditch and trampled all over him he decided to call it a day, with 101 winners and his seventh Championship.

His scorn for stewards was barely concealed, feeling as he did that they combined the tasks of lawmakers, policemen and judges, without understanding the pressures and dangers of the jockey's profession. Apart from several minor brushes with these gentlemen, there was what became known as the Banks Affair. For a jockey to become friends with a bookmaker may be perfectly harmless, but it only takes a few fancied horses to run below form before the inevitable gossip leads to suspicion that there is some skulduggery afoot. And the horse that brought the matter to a head happened to be called Stopped!

Favourite for Sandown's Imperial Cup, Stopped was a hard puller who had to be settled at the back of the field in the early stages, and on this occasion John failed to find a clear way through a mass of tiring horses at the last bend and came in third. The case ended up at Portman Square, with John fined a hefty £750 and suspended for six weeks, and John Banks fined £2,500 and banned from all racecourses for three years – not for stopping horses, but for 'damaging the interests of racing' by passing and accepting confidential information concerning horses in training. And when later in his career Francome found that his telephone had been tapped by the tabloid press, it came home to him that fame and success have their price.

*John Francome (GB) –
seven Championships and
1,138 winners – off duty
but obviously on form
(Bernard Parkin)*

Although he was not perhaps as unlucky as some in the matter of injuries, he nevertheless lost some 460 days racing, and his views on falls are interesting.

Horses fall for all sorts of reasons but tiredness and ignorance are the main causes. Intelligent horses with good jockeys rarely make a mistake, let alone fall, but the combination of the two doesn't occur very often. For every natural jumper there are a dozen with hardly any coordination at all, and the brainless jockeys outnumber the intelligent ones by about the same ratio. A lot of horses don't fall so much as the jockeys on top wrestle them to the ground. You can count the good riders on the fingers of one hand, and it's the same in show jumping and eventing. Now if you look at Peter Scudamore, he hardly ever has a fall, while some of the most experienced jockeys are simply on a wing and a prayer.

So often the secrets of a jockey's success lie in his early upbringing, and John's bareback riding stood him in good stead; if he could sit on a pony with no saddle at all, he was that much better equipped to stay with a chaser hitting the top of a fence at 25mph. And his show jumping experience helped to develop that judgement of stride which made racegoers observe that horses seemed to arrive wrong at fences with Francome less often than with other jockeys.

A total of 1,138 winners bear witness to his skills, and over half of these were for Fred Winter. Much of John's success was due to the relationship between these two, based on the mutual respect that each had for the other, and helped by the fact that Fred never forgot from his own riding days the problems, pressures and risks that a jockey must face. That John, an outspoken and forceful character himself, spent the entire sixteen years of his riding career at Uplands speaks for itself.

At his home in Lambourn he spoke about the secrets of success.

It's something you're born with, a feel for what the horse is doing underneath you, knowing what it's thinking, what it's going to do, and what it's capable of doing. I rode a lot of horses that I sat on for the first time in the paddock, and by the time you get down to the start you can tell what they're going to do. Very occasionally, if I was riding a three-year-old that had never run over hurdles before, or a novice chaser, I used to pop them over a hurdle or a fence on the way to the start. I know you shouldn't do it, but I don't think it's a bad thing; they do it abroad. I remember Peter Scudamore going to France and his horse turned upside down at the practice hurdle.

John's advice to a young jockey is to get himself into a large yard with plenty of good horses.

Then when you do get an opportunity you may get the chance of winning a race. In a small yard either they haven't got good horses or if they do have something they fancy, they try to get an experienced outside jockey. Then you must work hard and show you're keen. And when you start getting a few rides, get on the phone to other trainers – the worst thing they can say is 'No'. And I don't know why more lads don't go on a sales course in the summer; after all, if you want to sell washing machines or refrigerators they'll send you on a course to learn how to sell yourself, and that's what a lot of lads just don't know how to do. It's not a bit of use having all the talent in the world if you're not going to get to use it. Riding is only one small part of being a successful jockey.

Then a young jockey must work at it; when I began I could ride because I'd done a lot of show jumping, but I couldn't ride a finish to save my life. I'd never ridden on the flat, but I really worked at it, and it wasn't until my last two or three seasons that I could really ride a finish. I also think there should be more opportunities for young jockeys; there ought to be more bumpers' (National Hunt flat races), and if a trainer takes out a licence for a lad to ride, he should, provided he is not injured, be guaranteed a minimum number of rides during the season.

But of course owners would prefer the services of John Francome!

Agreed, but if a lad is working hard he should be given opportunities; it's no good just giving him one or two rides in a season, he'll never get the hang of it.

As one would expect from someone whose views on his profession are pretty definite, he has fairly strong ideas on what ought to be done for the improvement of racing.

The first thing I would do would be to upgrade the medical and veterinary facilities at racecourses, and I'd do it within a week! There have been dramatic improvements recently, but there's still an awful lot to be done. The voluntary first aid services do a wonderful job, but it shouldn't be left to a voluntary service, and there should be up-to-date veterinary facilities as well.

The actual organisation of racing seems to be getting more up- to-date, though I think they're probably a hundred years behind everything else. Certainly the Jockey Club seem to be three steps behind the bookmakers; selling 40 per cent of SIS (Satellite Information Service) was almost as unthinking an act as when they missed the chance of a Tote monopoly back in the sixties. They certainly should have been looking to buy one of the big chains of bookmakers.

And I'd bring in a rule that you can only hit a horse four times; after that you get fined £150 or something like that. As long as they allow an indefinite rule, there are bound to be different interpretations as to what is excessive use.

There would still be the problem of differentiating between jockeys who hit a horse and those who merely waved their whips.

If you can't see the difference, then you shouldn't be stewarding. I also think that racecourses must realise that they are in the entertainment business, and must lay on other things to bring in the crowds. I think it might mean more centralised racing, which in some ways would be good, because an awful lot of time is now spent by jockeys and trainers in travelling round the country; on the other hand if you live in the Westcountry, for example, it's better to be able to go racing at Newton Abbot.

John can look back on some wonderful memories. His best horse?

On his day, Sea Pigeon without a doubt; when he won the Champion Hurdle he was just cantering. After all, he was good enough to run in the Derby as a three-year-old, and he was one of the few top class flat horses that took well to hurdling.

Now retired as a jockey, his most cherished memory is of the day he rode three winners in an afternoon at the Cheltenham festival – Dering Rose, Sea Pigeon and Friendly Alliance. He now looks forward to a second career as a trainer, but, surprisingly enough, not over fences but on the flat. 'One thing I don't miss is coming into the yard and being told that so and so can't run because he's got a leg – it's like running a horse hospital with National Hunt horses!'

An entirely new establishment on the outskirts of Lambourn is planned, planning permission having finally been granted, and a couple of years should see him in business. Meanwhile he is putting his experience to good use, writing, enlivening TV racing commentaries with his knowledgeable and pithy observations, and running a tipping and racing results service.

Seven times Champion National Hunt Jockey, a Cheltenham Gold Cup, a Champion Hurdle, two King George VI and two Hennessy Gold Cups and a Tote Gold trophy are testimony to his skill as a rider.

JONJO O'NEILL

To some the essence of National Hunt racing is summed up in the word 'Aintree'; for others the word is 'Cheltenham', and certainly Aintree's Grand National has a very different appeal from the Cheltenham Gold Cup. The National, with its 4½ miles, (7.25km), thirty-two daunting obstacles, and the rough and tumble of a huge field is the jumping world's most famous race, and these characteristics, combined with the fact that it is a handicap, make it also the most unpredictable, with the fascinating possibility of an unfancied winner. The Gold Cup, on the other hand, with its 3 miles (4.8km) over regulation fences and a stiff uphill finish, is the true Blue Riband of National Hunt racing, the supreme test of speed, stamina, jumping, jockeyship and training.

The National produces more drama, and many a tear has been shed in the unsaddling enclosure. But in March 1986 the scene at Cheltenham after the Gold Cup was every bit as emotional as anything witnessed at Aintree. The first horse (and a mare too) to win both the Champion Hurdle and the Gold Cup, ridden by the grinning Irishman who had fought his way back from injuries severe enough to look like costing him his right leg, returned to the unsaddling enclosure to cheers such as even Aintree could not match.

Probably the most popular, certainly one of the bravest, and arguably one of the greatest jump jockeys, Jonjo O'Neill was born in Castletownroche in County Cork in 1952 into a family whose only connection with horses had been the failure of his uncle to make the grade as an apprentice jockey. He always wanted to be a jockey, so father made him cycle the seven miles to and from school each day rather than take the bus in order to toughen him up for this toughest of tough careers. His first fall at the age of six from his father's hunter (bareback) did nothing to dim his enthusiasm, and eventually father bought him an unbroken pony called Dolly. Jonjo broke her in and hunted her with the Duhallow as a two-year-old, often giving a lead to his elders and betters!

Jonjo's first taste of victory came in a donkey race, but in 1969, aged sixteen, after a short period with Dan Reid in Mallow, he was apprenticed to Michael Connolly at The Curragh, where he quickly earned a reputation for wanting to run before he could walk, and also for complete lack of fear. His first win on the flat came in September 1970 at The Curragh, and a chance ride at Navan, his first in a steeplechase, also provided a winner. With a hurdle race victory under his belt too, he was able in 1972 to obtain a job with Gordon Richards in Cumbria, the county that has remained his home ever since.

Jonjo's first visit to what was to become the scene of his greatest triumphs involved leading the Whitbread Gold Cup winner Titus Oates in the parade for the Cheltenham Gold Cup. Two days later he won his first race in England on Katie J at Uttoxeter, only to be relegated to second place on an objection. And with just this one result from six rides he returned to Castletownroche at the end of the season.

On his return to Greystoke he immediately clocked up four winners in a row, but suffered a setback in the Mackeson Gold Cup at Cheltenham in November when he slapped Proud Stone down the shoulder when up with the leaders approaching the last fence; aiming for a bold jump, he got such a reaction that he was shot into orbit; one bruised jockey, one loose horse, one disgruntled owner! Nevertheless, he ended the season with thirty-eight winners and the Junior Jockey's Championship.

He was now on his way, and the next four seasons yielded a respectable tally of 207 winners in all, including a Castleford Chase at Wetherby and a Topham trophy at Aintree on Clear Cut. Then came 1977/78, a season to remember. By the end of December he had won seventy-six races, and in the next five weeks he took his tally to ninety-six, and had scored wins on three great horses – Alverton, Night Nurse and Sea Pigeon. A week later he had set a new record for the fastest 100 winners, beating that set by Fred Winter back in 1953.

His win on Alverton, however, had not been particularly auspicious. In a two-horse race at Teesside they completely misjudged the seventh fence; Jonjo was unshipped, and Alverton came down on his knees, bringing down Colin Hawkins on Kruganko. Both jockeys managed to hang on to the reins, but Jonjo was quickest back in the saddle and won the race. His victory on Night Nurse he owed to Paddy Broderick's concussion in a Boxing Day fall, and it was Night Nurse that he beat on Sea Pigeon in his second of two Scottish Champion Hurdle victories at Ayr.

Then in April he had an outstanding meeting at Perth. On the first day he had ridden Father Delaney for his 124th win, one short of the record for a season set by Ron Barry five years earlier. On the second day he won the first two hurdle races on Besciamella and Majetta Crescent, and Ron Barry was the first to congratulate him on setting a new record. The handicap chase he won on Crofton Hall, and the novice chase on Father Delaney again, and finally he won the sixth race on the unfancied Tiger Fleet.

On the last day of the season Lothian Brig gave Jonjo his 149th winner at Stratford, and with his eyes firmly set on the century and a half, he flew to Market Rasen to ride Pleasure Seeker in the first race of the evening meeting. But he could not leave until his fellow passenger Tim Thomson-Jones had ridden in the 4.50 at Stratford, they were held up in traffic on the way to the airport, and in the end he had to watch Pleasure Seeker win his race from the air on the approach to Market Rasen's Airstrip! His record of 149 was to stand until it was broken by Peter Scudamore in 1989, and he won for no less than forty-two different trainers. Forty-five of these wins were for Peter Easterby, with whom he had a wonderful working relationship; he had no retainer, and if Jonjo found a better horse to ride, then Peter would find another race for his horse. Much of Jonjo's success was due to this mutual confidence, and Easterby seldom gave him any instructions but always gave him the necessary information about his horse.

The year 1979 brought the mixture of triumph and disaster that even the most successful jump jockeys have to endure. The Cheltenham Gold Cup was run in a blizzard, and as the field rounded the top of the final hill, Jonjo on Alverton could dimly see that Tommy Carberry and Tied Cottage, twenty lengths clear, were going only too well. He shouted to Philip Blacker on Royal Mail that they had better get going or they would never catch him, but still there was no sign of Tied Cottage coming back to them. Royal Mail began to tire, and gradually the gap narrowed. Those standing at the last fence will never forget the jump that Jonjo conjured out of a tired horse. Taking off a stride early, Alverton sailed past Tied Cottage in the air, the Irish horse stumbled and fell, and Jonjo won his first Gold Cup.

To run the Gold Cup winner sixteen days later in the Grand National is a serious decision; it was not taken lightly, and it was only taken because Alverton recovered quickly from his Cheltenham effort, seemed in fighting form, and occupied a position in the handicap that he would never occupy again. With 10st 13lb (69.4kg) he had a real chance of winning, and as they approached Becher's for the second time Jonjo really thought his dream would come true, for Alverton's jumping had been impeccable apart from a slight error two before Becher's. But for some reason he failed to measure the most fearsome obstacle in racing that he had jumped so well on the first circuit, crashed through the fence, and died on hitting the ground beyond the huge ditch.

On the previous day Jonjo had scored a thrilling victory on Night Nurse when beating Dramatist in the Sean Graham Trophy Chase over the Mildmay course. Night Nurse's regular rider had been Paddy Broderick, with whom he had won the 1976 and 1977 Champion Hurdles, and Paddy's great ambition had been to ride him to victory in the Cheltenham Gold Cup. But at Kempton on Boxing Day 1977 when he asked Night Nurse for a 'long one' going to the last, they had hit the top of the hurdle and somersaulted, bringing to an end Paddy's long and illustrious career. From his first ride on Night Nurse, when he won the William Hill Yorkshire Hurdle at Doncaster in 1978 from Andy Turnell on Bird's Nest, Jonjo realised that here was an exceptional jumper, brilliant but economical, and with quick acceleration away from a fence which often gained lengths on his rivals.

Two days before Alverton's Gold Cup, Jonjo had felt he should have won the Champion Hurdle on Sea Pigeon. Beaten three-quarters of a length by Monksfield, he blamed himself for making his effort too early, though to be fair it must be said that his trainer's instructions had been 'not to leave it too late'. Sea Pigeon had finished the 1973 Derby in a respectable seventh place, after which he had been gelded. In all he won 16 races from 45 starts on the flat, and 21 from 40 over jumps. With Jonjo in the saddle he won 11 out of 24 hurdle races and 4 out of 7 on the flat. These successes included two wins, a second and a third in the Scottish Champion Hurdle, a win, a second and a fourth in the Cheltenham championship, and a Welsh Champion Hurdle. (Sea Pigeon had also been second to Monksfield in the 1978 Champion Hurdle when ridden by Frank Berry, and won his third Champion Hurdle in 1981 under John Francome, when on both occasions Jonjo was out of action.)

On the flat, their greatest success was in winning the Tote-Ebor handicap at York in 1979. A week earlier Jonjo had broken three toes in his left foot, but, keen to have a go at the likes of Piggott, Carson and Cauthen, he scraped through the medical examination by presenting his right foot for inspection; the Irish entry in his medical book had failed to specify which foot had been injured! Sea Pigeon ran a brilliant race, but was caught on the line. Those minutes while they waited for the judge's verdict were not the happiest; the Yorkshire crowd would willingly have lynched the Irish jockey if their favourite, trained by Peter Easterby a few miles away, had had the race snatched from him. The cheers that greeted his win were only marred for Jonjo by a summons before the stewards and a warning as to his riding in future.

Jonjo O'Neill (Ireland) (right) gives Richard Dunwoody (GB) (left) a send off at his wedding in July 1988 (Bernard Parkin)

In January 1982 their win in the Bradstone Mandarin Handicap Chase at Newbury gave Jonjo 'the greatest thrill I've ever had on a horse'. At Doncaster in February they beat the 1978 Cheltenham Gold Cup winner Midnight Court in the Pennine Chase, and the prospects looked good for Cheltenham. But in the Gold Cup Night Nurse, kept to the inside in search of better going, hated being hemmed in, and was pulled up at the second last.

The following December (1982) Michael Dickinson asked Jonjo to ride Wayward Lad in the King George VI Chase at Kempton on Boxing Day. Although Dickinson's Cheltenham Gold Cup winner Silver Buck was favourite, Jonjo thought Wayward Lad could win; but he already had the ride on Night Nurse. In the end he could not bring himself to abandon him, even though he doubted whether, at the age of eleven, Night Nurse could beat Silver Buck, and in the race itself all he saw of Wayward Lad was a distant – 50 lengths – view of his winning in the capable hands of John Francome! But he had no regrets for his loyalty to a great horse, who was then retired from racing.

The year 1982 had also seen the start of Jonjo's association with Ekbalco, who had already had considerable success in the hands of Dave Goulding. The partnership was a brilliant one, winning the Welsh Champion Hurdle twice, though on the second occasion he was disqualified for failing a dope test – penicillin cream had been applied to a saddle sore, from which a prohibited substance had entered his bloodstream – and four other major races. Jonjo rates him in the same bracket as Sea Pigeon and as 'one of the best horses never to win the Cheltenham championship', in which he ran after his preparation had been interrupted by the weather. Sadly it was his bold jumping that ended his career, for in the 1982 Fighting Fifth Hurdle at Newcastle he took off a stride early and fell, and had to be put down after doing the same again in 1983.

The 1983/84 season was the third in which Jonjo scored a century of winners, and by the end of December he had ridden seventy-two. Another dozen wins came his way over the next two months, but so too did the falls; on 10 January at Wetherby he was kicked in the ribs when Swop Shop fell on the flat; on Friday 13 – Black Friday – at Ascot he was badly winded when Torreon broke his back; on 31 January at Leicester Fearless Seal fell on the flat and Jonjo chipped a bone in his elbow; three days later the elbow was damaged again when Flittermere came down at Sedgefield; and after a fall at Huntingdon a week later he had to undergo an operation in Carlisle hospital for a broken cheek bone. The punters began to write him off, but this merely made him more determined, and his reward came at Cheltenham when he won the Champion Hurdle on the mare Dawn Run – from a field that included the young Desert Orchid.

The reception accorded Dawn Run by her Irish fans, including a number who seemed determined to take home 'a piece of the action' in the form of some souvenir that formed an essential part of the kit with which Jonjo had to weigh in, was only matched by that for the veteran lady owner. Mrs Charmian Hill had bought the mare for 5,800 Irish punts at the Ballsbridge Sale as a three-year-old, and had ridden her both in her early days and in her work at Paddy Mullins' stables. Then, at the age of sixty-three, she had ridden her to her first win at Tralee in 1982, on the very day on which she received notice that, owing to her age, her licence to ride would not be renewed!

The trainer's amateur rider son Tony continued with the mare on the winning trail, until Mrs Hill wanted a more experienced, but if possible Irish, jockey for the 1984 Champion Hurdle. Between mid-November and mid-March Jonjo and Dawn Run won four races worth a total of nearly £85,000, including that Champion Hurdle. After winning the French Champion Hurdle at Auteuil with Tony Mullins, she was destined to make her début over fences at the start of the 1984/85 season. Could she become the first Champion Hurdler to win the Gold Cup?

Jonjo is not alone among great jockeys who lack success in the Grand National, and in his eight rides the furthest he got was the Canal Turn second time round in 1977, when he was knocked out of the saddle by another horse. In 1973, his first National, he wore the first colours of Mr Noel le Mare on Glenkiln, whose interest in the race departed at the Chair; the owner's second colours were carried by Red Rum! And in 1983 not even the lure of a £10,000 riding fee plus 10 per cent of the prize money could overcome the jinx when Beacon Time was brought down at the nineteenth.

Jonjo's courage in the face of adversity and injury is legendary. Apart from the usual catalogue of broken collar bones (five – plus one when skating!), ribs, vertebrae, an arm, a wrist, a hand, and a leg, one particular injury stands out. When he had survived a fall

OPPOSITE
Jonjo O'Neill (Ireland) winning the 1980 Welsh Champion Hurdle on Sea Pigeon (Bernard Parkin)

Peter Scudamore (GB) on Sabin du Loir (Bernard Parkin)

Willi Schultheis (Germany), winner of the Hamburg Dressage Derby in 1955–59, 1961, 1965 and 1969, with Doublette

Reiner Klimke (Germany) – Olympic Champion 1984, World Champion 1974, 1982, European Champion 1962, 1967, 1973, 1985 – Ahlerich, Seoul, 1988
(Bob Langrish)

in 1978 he thought he had been especially unlucky when a loose horse came along and trod on his arm, breaking it so badly that it had to be plated. But the second break of his right leg was even more bizarre; at Bangor in December 1980 Simbad crumpled on landing over a hurdle, and skidded along on his belly, giving Jonjo the softest of landings. But as he stepped off he somehow managed to push his right leg between the two hind legs of another horse, rather like pushing one's leg into a pair of blunt scissors travelling at 30mph!

A disastrous attempt to ride again before the wound had healed resulted in an operation in a Swiss hospital where bone was grafted from his hip and a titanium plate inserted into the leg, which nearly had to be amputated, and thirteen months out of the saddle. Most would have called it a day, but not Jonjo, who was to return to even greater triumphs than before, culminating in his Cheltenham Gold Cup win on Dawn Run in 1986.

He acknowledges a great debt to Hugh Barber, orthopaedic surgeon at Carlisle's Cumberland Infirmary, who not only carried out endless repairs to his shattered body, but also understood his need to get back to work 'today, not tomorrow!' In Barber's own words, 'No one else would have continued as a jockey after the suffering and discomfort Jonjo went through with his broken leg the second time.'

If Dawn Run's Cheltenham Gold Cup of 1986 is Jonjo's best memory, he also won't forget an evening in March 1981. 'I was out of the saddle with my broken leg, and was doing a number of radio programmes and chat shows. I was told that I was to join Peter O'Sullivan and Dicky Davies for a quiz programme, but when I entered the studio I nearly died.' He had been inveigled on to 'This Is Your Life'.

When asked about the reasons for his success Jonjo's sense of humour erupted, 'Because I was brilliant, you know!' But more seriously he admitted to much hard work and plenty of dedication. Certainly courage played its part too, though Jonjo isn't sure whether he was fearless or whether fear was overcome in the heat of the moment. Certainly he was never afraid to take the chance of going for a gap. 'Sometimes I paid the penalty, sometimes it paid off handsomely.' His 831 winners prove the point!

As to advice to a young jockey starting out today:

Unless you love the game and love horses, don't do it. It's a twenty-four-hour-a-day job, come rain, hail or snow, and you fall, get kicked, and break bones. Hunting will help, there's a lot of horsemanship involved. I started in a small stable of fifteen horses, and that was too small. Then I moved to a larger one and I nearly got lost, there were eight apprentices all trying to get rides. There's a lot of luck in it, being in the right place at the right time.

Apart from the low level of prize money in England, Jonjo feels that the state of the sport is pretty good. But asked what improvements he would introduce if he were senior steward of the Jockey Club, his sense of humour burst out again. 'First I'm not, second I wouldn't want to be, and third I wouldn't know where to start!'

Having had perhaps more than his fair share of injuries as a rider, no sooner had he retired and made plans to start training than he had another fight on his hands, and his struggle to overcome cancer required all the courage that even he could muster. But overcome it he has, and his infectious grin and great sense of humour are likely to enliven the darkest days of winter for some time to come.

PETER SCUDAMORE

The 1988/89 National Hunt Season in England will be remembered for the thrilling performances of a great horse, Desert Orchid, and for the record breaking partnership of a great trainer, Martin Pipe, and as great a rider over fences as we have ever seen, Peter Scudamore. By the New Year the fastest fifty winners and the fastest century were behind him, and at Warwick in February he broke the record of 149 winners in a season set by Jonjo O'Neill eleven years earlier. Could his luck continue to hold? It could, and it did, for in April he rode into the winner's enclosure for the 200th time that season, and became only the third jockey to ride more than a thousand winners – the other two being Stan Mellor and John Francome. Lucky he certainly has been, but something other than luck must account for his phenomenal success.

Peter was certainly born into racing, for his father Michael, a real horseman as well as an accomplished jockey, won the 1957 Cheltenham Gold Cup on Linwell and the 1959 Grand National on Oxo, and in the year before Peter was born he finished second in the jockey's table to Fred Winter.

So when others of his age were worshipping footballers or cricketers, Peter's heroes were the likes of Fred Winter, Terry Biddlecombe and the great National Hunt jockeys. With first hand experience of the 'downside' of the jump jockey's career, Peter's mother had hoped his ambitions might lie elsewhere, but with the great Pat Taaffe as her son's godfather there wasn't much hope of her wish coming true. And in any case it was she who taught Peter to ride, and who introduced him to the Pony Club. But if she hoped that he would be drawn towards show jumping or eventing, for both of which he showed considerable talent, he himself had other ideas. 'I enjoyed the show jumping and eventing, but they just weren't fast enough for me, I always wanted to race.'

When he left school Peter went to Royston to join that great trainer of both horses and riders, Willie Stephenson, for whom his father rode, and who had employed such good jockeys as Tim Molony and David Nicholson. He rode a couple of times on the flat, and now wishes he'd done more before turning to steeplechasing, riding first as an amateur and then as a professional for David Nicholson, whom he joined for the 1978/79 season.

In 1981/82 Peter had a chance of winning the Championship, when a fractured skull ended his season. Then the following year his first Championship came in circumstances that illustrate the bond which binds that very special breed of sportsman, the National Hunt jockey. The 1982/83 season had been going well, and by Christmas he was as we have already seen, in second position, some twenty-five winners behind John Francome. Then John hit the sort of bad patch that comes up every now and then; he would pick the wrong horse in a race, or even pick the wrong meeting at which to ride; nothing seemed to go right. David Nicholson's horses, on the other hand, all seemed to be in form, and Peter's confidence grew. John won two big races, the Schweppes Hurdle at Newbury and the Sun Alliance Chase at Cheltenham, but was then concussed when brought down at Newbury.

Seven days compulsory rest for John was bad enough, but the irony of the situation lay in the fact that in falling his horse had rolled on Sam Morshead, whose horse had brought John down, and whose rides for Mercy Rimell were then taken by Peter. With five weeks of the season left Peter headed the table by twenty winners. Then he broke his arm in a fall at Southwell. Back in the saddle John made every effort to find those twenty, and when he did so, with three days' racing left, instead of continuing he decided to share the Championship with Peter.

Peter's first outright Championship came in 1985/86, and he retained his crown for the next two years. His most significant wins included the Welsh Grand Nationals of 1985 and 1986 at Chepstow, and at Cheltenham the Triumph Hurdle of 1986, the Queen Mother Champion Chase of 1987 and his most important single win, the Champion Hurdle on Celtic Shot for Fred Winter in 1988. Then came the fantastic season of 1988/89. If a successful novelist, even such a complete master of his craft as Dick Francis, had written a story on the lines of the Pipe–Scudamore steamroller during that winter, his readers would surely have thought that advancing years had perhaps brought about a separation from reality. Even the greatest racing journalist of our time was at a loss to find the words to describe the Scudamore magic. 'How on earth,' wrote John Oaksey in the *Daily Telegraph* when Jonjo's record of 149 winners in a season had been surpassed, 'can you rate a man who has gone that far beyond the bounds of probability?' And that was in February, with four months of the season still to go.

The horse that brought Peter that record was a four-year-old novice hurdler called Anti Matter, certainly not the greatest horse he has ever ridden, and but for an extraordinary coincidence it is unlikely that he would have hit the headlines again until he had won a more prestigious contest. At Towcester's evening meeting in April Peter reached his double century on Gay Moore, the first man ever to do so, and then at Stratford in May he won again on Anti Matter, bringing a record for Martin Pipe; never before, either on the flat or over jumps had a trainer saddled 200 winners in a season.

When the season finally closed, Peter had ridden 221 winners, and the only man likely to break that record in the foreseeable future is Scudamore himself. So what accounts for his astonishing run of success?

He has undoubtedly been lucky. As every true sportsman knows, luck plays its part for better or worse, a fact acknowledged by that other great jumping rider John Francome when he entitled his autobiography *Born Lucky*. In Scudamore's case luck played its part when the warm winter of 1988/89 ensured the most open National Hunt season that there has ever been, with very few days' racing lost to the weather. But luck alone cannot explain how Peter has managed not just to survive without serious injury, though he has seen his share of ambulances and hospital beds, but to beat the established average of a fall in every ten rides.

'A champion among champions' (from left to right): Stan Mellor, John Francombe, Graham Thorner, Peter Scudamore, Ron Barry, Jack Dowdeswell and Bob Davis (Bernard Parkin)

Most of the great jockeys undoubtedly owe much of their success to partnerships with one or more great trainers: on the flat, Richards with Darling, Hartigan and Murless, Piggott with Murless, O'Brien and Cecil, Shoemaker with Whittingham; over fences, Winter with Walwyn, and Francome with Winter. Peter Scudamore owes much to David Nicholson, and to Fred Winter and his successor Charlie Brookes. But though he had already been Champion when he started riding for Martin Pipe, theirs is the partnership that has set the jumping world alight.

Martin is the son of one of the Westcountry's most successful bookmakers. But his father, while pleased at his son's success, may have cause to regret that the Pipe/Scudamore team has probably enabled punters to take considerably more out of his chain of betting shops than they have put in. Martin's approach to training is totally professional, and neither effort nor money are spared to give his horses the best possible chance to win. He is not alone among trainers in this, but he has three other priceless advantages: a remarkable eye for picking horses that can win; a singular knack of placing them in suitable races; and the services of the best National Hunt jockey riding today. In November of the 1989/90 season his success rate was running near to a phenomenal 50 per cent.

Peter for his part is the first to acknowledge his debt to his trainers and owners, and has described Martin as a genius. But his own total dedication and complete professionalism, and his single-minded obsession with riding winners, have played a large part in his success. He also rates the instruction he received from his mother, the help his father gave him, and his early experience before he became a jockey as important factors. And we recently saw evidence of his all-round ability as a horseman when he took part in the challenge match between the three day event riders and the National Hunt jockeys at Gatcombe Park and Aintree in 1989.

On a cold and damp morning in March, Richard Dunwoody, Simon Sherwood, Steve Smith-Eccles, Brendan Powell, Graham McCourt and Peter Scudamore arrived at Gatcombe to ride round the Horse Trials Championship course on horses provided by the eventers. Mark Phillips had only slightly modified some of the more difficult fences, and it really was a challenge, quite different from travelling at a steady, though much faster, pace over regulation steeplechase fences more or less on the level.

'I was a bit nervous beforehand,' said Peter, who rode Ian Stark's relatively inexperienced Mix 'n' Match, and who had arrived too late for the official course walk and practice session, 'but it was a great thrill. We're not used to riding such well mannered and well balanced horses.' Spectators who had arrived to see the thrills and spills were disappointed, for the contest proved that the jockeys were all real horsemen, and Mark Phillips said of Peter Scudamore, 'He is not Champion for nothing. This was the performance of a true craftsman.'

I wondered what it had been like for Peter to let his stirrups down and jump these obstacles.

As far as length of stirrups is concerned fashions change. Today we tend to go with our horses more than they used to, perhaps because the fences are less stiff than they used to be. I think that jump jockeys everywhere, and especially overseas, tend to model their style on their flat race jockeys. In America they ride with their toes in the stirrups; in Australia they all ride very short, and in France they sit up on their horses' necks. Here there was a time when they were influenced by Lester Piggott and they rode very short – Andy Turnell, for example.

But in National Hunt you don't win races unless you get round, and there's a lot of basic horsemanship involved. I think it brings in a bit of the aspects of other equestrian sports. The flat jockeys are better at the actual race riding and in the finish, but we're involved in that too. We don't have to be as accurate as the show jumpers or eventers because we're not pushing for height, we're pushing for speed.

One thing my father taught me was to sit well into a horse. Another was to slip the reins over a fence. One reason why the girls don't go better is that they crouch forward on a horse and don't slip the reins, which is fantastic so long as all goes well, but if a horse makes a mistake or pecks there's no give and they're pulled over his head.

Apart from this useful advice to the fair sex, Peter has some perhaps unexpected advice for the aspiring National Hunt jockey.

First of all go out and jump as many fences as possible, whether it's hunting or show jumping or eventing. Then go to a flat race stable and ride as much as you can on the flat. I don't think many jump jockeys are ready to ride successfully until they're about twenty-one or twenty-two. I certainly wish I had ridden more on the flat. You need the finesse which flat racing adds to basic horsemanship.

Peter's views on the state of the sport today are much in line with those of his contemporaries.

I think National Hunt racing has never been healthier, but we can't stand still, we have to move forward. I'd like to see prize money increased so that an owner who wins one or two races can pay his training fees for the season, and the distribution of prize money needs to be looked at too. The Arabs now dominate the flat, and a lot of owners who can't afford to take them on are turning to National Hunt. And more money has got to be found for those who work in racing, especially the stable staff. There's masses of money going into racing, but it's not coming out at the right end. I'm certainly not a bookmaker basher, Martin Pipe's family are bookmakers and I understand and respect their point of view, but they have been given the opportunity to take a lot of money out of racing through the short-sightedness of those who control the sport.

Peter thinks that the administration of the sport is on a fairly sound basis.

I think the system of amateur stewards is good on the whole. Sometimes we don't agree with their decisions, but we don't always agree with the umpire or the referee in other sports, and they do try to be scrupulously fair. If you have professional stewards, as they do in Australia for example, then if a jockey makes a mistake, then he knows the stewards will be watching him in every race. What I would like to see is a good ex-professional jockey acting as adviser to the stewards, because actual race-riding is something that not a lot of stewards understand. We're not always pleased to see the top jobs in racing going to military men, but at least they know how to organise things properly – the pro's might make a hash of it. Perhaps the balance could be altered slightly.

I'm hopeful that the introduction of all-weather tracks will come off, it's got to, because at the moment when we lose a day's racing the punter still goes to the betting shop and he bets on dog racing, and when horse racing resumes we don't always get him back. But it will be hard on the horses, and we've got to get the right track; they've had trials, but we won't really know yet how jockeys fall on it or what the kick-back will be like till we race on it.

Perhaps with all-weather tracks 200 winners in a season will not seem such a fantastic goal. But as this new venture started in the autumn of 1989, Peter had his sights on another target, John Francome's record of 1,138 winners. On 11 November, with seventy-four winners for the season so far, he needed just one more from four rides at Cheltenham to equal the record, but could only manage one second place. At Worcester on 15 November Regal Ambition, a Martin Pipe odds-on novice hurdler, took him to Francome's total. 'But,' he said afterwards, 'it's the next one I worry about.' And the very next day, his only ride at Towcester, the evens favourite Bar Fly, hardly took off at the last flight of hurdles and gave Peter a crashing fall.

When Peter's fans opened their papers on the morning of Saturday 18 November they were again greeted with the unaccustomed sight of 'Scu' hitting the deck, this time from Espy at the last fence of the Novice Chase at Ascot. But finally, at Ascot that afternoon, Peter won the Kennel Gate Novice Hurdle for Charlie Brookes on Lord Howard de Walden's Arden, and so, with a total of 1,139 winners, he passed into the record books as the most successful National Hunt jockey of all time.

Part III

DRESSAGE

F OR SOME, DRESSAGE IS a mystery; for others it is a source of wonderment. For some it is merely a necessary step in the training of a horse for what they regard as better things; for others it is an expression of the highest form of co-operation between horse and rider. It is in reality the foundation upon which all equestrian sport is based. In its widest sense it starts when a foal is first handled, and it ends only when the mature horse has achieved the highest goal that it is possible for him to attain. Anyone who doubts this can do no better than to ponder the FEI definition of the object of Dressage.

The object of Dressage is the harmonious development of the physique and ability of the horse. As a result it makes the horse calm, supple, loose and flexible, but also confident, attentive and keen, thus achieving perfect understanding with his rider.

The language of horsemanship contains many expressions that are international, and 'Dressage' derives from the French word *dresser*, meaning 'to train' (an animal). Every riding horse requires, therefore, a degree of dressage in order to make him fit for whatever purpose his rider intends, whether he be hack, hunter or competition horse; even the racehorse needs a minimum of training before it is safe to take him onto the gallops or onto the roads in order to reach them.

The successful show jumping rider spends infinitely more time schooling his horse on the flat than he does over jumps, though his version of dressage may not be as correct as that of the horse trials or three day event rider, for whom it is an important part of his discipline. But while dressage (with a small 'd') is a means whereby a rider schools or trains his horse in order to make him a better ride or to enable him to perform better in some other equestrian sport, Dressage (with a capital 'D') long ago developed into an equestrian sport in its own right; no longer merely a means to an end, it became an end in itself, encompassing the whole range of training from basic level right through to the test for the Grand Prix.

As with so much equestrian sport, the origins of dressage lay in the requirements of the horse for war, and it developed in times of peace as a means of diversion or entertainment. The war horse not only had to be obedient, he also had to be light in hand, for his rider as often as not had a weapon of some sort in his right hand and could therefore only control him with his left, and the same would apply to peacetime pageants and carousels, and to martial sports such as jousting. Collection, in the form of shortened paces, was important for preliminary manoeuvering either as a body or individually, and extension, in the form of lengthened paces, was necessary to out-manoeuvre an opponent. Lateral (sideways) movements were particularly important for individual combat, while the physique of the horse had to be developed to enable him to carry the considerable weight of the knight in armour.

Early attempts at achieving lightness in hand and collection depended mainly upon the use of extremely severe and mutually opposing aids, if the use of sharp bits with long cheeks in the horse's mouth and grotesquely sharp spurs against his flanks could be so described. There was little that was 'harmonious' about the horse's development, and even if the rider thought he had achieved a 'perfect understanding' with his horse, the poor animal was unlikely to be 'supple, loose and flexible', and certainly not 'confident', though quite possibly extremely 'attentive' and apparently 'keen'!

The first horseman to attempt to lay down a formal method for the training of the horse was probably **Xenophon** (500BC), and several Greek and Roman scholars followed his example, but the first recognised manual of instruction was produced by an Italian, **Frederico Grisone**, whose *Gli Ordini di Cavalcare* (*Rules of Riding*) appeared in 1550. The Frenchman **Antoine de Pluvinel** brought out his *L'Art de Monter à Cheval* (*The Art of Riding*) in 1623, and **William Cavendish, Duke of Newcastle**, produced his *General System of Horsemanship* in 1657. In the eighteenth century another Frenchman, **François de la Guerinière** laid the basis for the modern system of training the horse, and his *Ecole de Cavalerie* is as valid today as when it was written in 1733.

One of the first horsemen to base his training upon a study of the horse's psychology was **Federico Caprilli**, more generally remembered for the development of the forward seat for jumping and riding across country. An instructor at the Italian Cavalry School at Pinerolo, he died in 1907 aged only thirty-nine, but his influence on the development of modern riding has been considerable. **James Fillis** was an Englishman who studied in Paris, took French nationality, and published his *Principes de Dressage et d'Equitation* in 1890. In 1898 he was appointed instructor at the Imperial Russian Cavalry School in St Petersburg, a post which he held until his retirement in 1910 at the age of seventy-six. He died three years later, and is said to have attributed his long and active life to having ridden 'ten horses a day on weekdays and three or four on Sundays and holidays'!

The early centres of equitation were based on the royal courts of Europe, and what the Kings practised their courtiers copied, and so did the calvalry élite of the royal armies. Eventually it was the cavalry schools that became not only the repositories of knowledge but also centres for the development of dressage; Germany with Hanover and Potsdam, France with Saumur, and Sweden with Strömsholm, and to a lesser extent Italy with Pinerolo.

Although there were jumping events at the Paris Olympic Games of 1900, it was not until 1912 in Stockholm that the three equestrian disciplines of dressage, jumping and the three day event became established Olympic sports. And it was Sweden, in whose capital the Games were held, that dominated the dressage scene until the Equestrian Games returned to Stockholm in 1956 when quarantine regulations precluded their being held in Melbourne, Australia.

In Stockholm (1912), Antwerp (1920) and Paris (1924) Swedish officers took eight of the nine individual medals (teams were not introduced until 1928) and **Gustav Boltenstern's** successful career included medals thirty-six years apart, for he was silver medallist in 1912 and took the bronze in London in 1948. One of the great post-war dressage riders was **Henri St Cyr**, Olympic Champion of 1952 in Helsinki and of 1956 in Stockholm. And between 1928 and 1956 Sweden took home team medals from every Games.

St Cyr's unique double was coupled with another, for the silver medallist on both occasions was Denmark's **Liz Hartel**. What makes this all the more remarkable, however, is the fact that this elegant rider, who did much to popularise dressage in England with her brilliant displays on Jubilee at London's Horse of the Year Show, could only walk with difficulty and had taken to dressage as a form of therapy.

A strong hint that competitive dressage was one day going to be dominated by Germany was given in 1928 in Amsterdam, when **Carl Friedrich von Langen** led his team to victory and took the individual title himself. But France was to have her turn in Los Angeles (1932) when **Xavier Lesage** did the same, with **Pierre Marion** as the silver medallist, and again in London (1948) where **André Jousseaume** took the silver medal and the team the gold. Jousseaume also took the bronze medal behind St Cyr and Liz Hartel in Helsinki.

The first German rider to gain international recognition after World War II was **Colonel Felix Bürkner**, who won the dressage at London's White City, only to have the prize removed because his country had not yet been readmitted to the FEI. But a measure of Germany's domination is the fact that between 1964 and 1988 there were twenty-six team competitions at the Olympic Games and World and European Championships, and the German team took twenty-four gold medals and two silver. Germany's first post-war Olympic Medallist was **Liselott Linsenhoff**, who took the bronze medal with Adular, again behind St Cyr and Hartel, in Stockholm. Then with Piaff she won the Aachen Grand Prix, the most competitive event outside the championships, in 1955, 1956 and 1959, took the silver medals at two World Championships, was European Champion in 1969 and 1971, and Olympic Champion in 1972. Later she coached successful German teams, and her daughter, **Ann-Kathrin**, was a European Young Rider bronze medallist and has already won European individual silver and bronze and team gold medals as well as a team gold medal in the Seoul Olympics.

Josef Neckermann took the bronze medal in Rome (1960), a team gold medal in Tokyo (1964), individual silver and team gold in Mexico (1968) and individual bronze and team silver in 1972 in Munich. He won the FEI Championship that preceded the World and European Championships in 1961, was World Champion in 1966 and took the European bronze medal in 1969 and the silver in 1971. He also monopolised the Aachen Grand Prix from 1961 to 1965 and won the Grand Prix Special in 1971.

Harry Boldt was one of Germany's most consistent riders who, though the individual gold medals somehow eluded him, won a team gold medal at the Tokyo Olympics, and individual silver medals there and in Montreal, as well as at the 1966 World Championships and at two European Championships. He was German Champion three times, won two Hamburg Derbys, and with his great horse Woyceck won the Aachen Grand Prix and Grand Prix Special in 1978. Then when **Willi Schultheis** (see p119) retired as German team trainer he took over and produced the very successful teams of recent years.

Germany has produced so many outstanding dressage riders, but few can match the

ABOVE: *Gabriela Grillo (Germany) with Ultimo at the Olympic Games, Montreal 1976* (Leslie Lane)
LEFT: *Nicole Uphoff (Germany), Olympic Champion 1988, with Rembrandt at the European Championships 1989* (Bob Langrish)

record of **Reiner Klimke** (see p122). Among the country's great trainers were **Otto Lörke**, private trainer to the last Kaiser and still, well into his seventies, winning the Aachen Grand Prix in 1950 and 1951; and **Walter 'Bubi' Günther**, who spanned both the jumping and dressage disciplines. Of the ladies, **Rosemary Springer** dominated the early sixties, while **Liselott Linsenhoff's** career covered the twenty years from the mid-fifties to the mid-seventies. **Gabriella Grillo** was prominent in the late seventies and early eighties, while in **Nicole Uphoff**, individual and team gold medallist in Seoul at the age of only twenty-one, and European Champion of 1989, Germany has a Champion who is likely to be around for some time to come; and with fellow team gold medallists **Monica Theodorescu** and **Ann-Kathrin Linsenhoff** (European bronze medallist in 1989) to back her up, the team medals are likely to stay in Germany too.

At the Olympic Games and at World and European Championships only two nations other than Sweden have mounted a serious challenge to Germany as far as team medals have been concerned – Switzerland and USSR – and it was **Hans Moser** of Switzerland who won the Olympic gold medal in London in 1948. **Gustav Fischer** came near to repeating this success when taking the silver in Rome, but it was **Henri Chammartin**, Olympic Champion in Tokyo, who really served notice that the Germans could not have everything their own way. He was European Champion in 1963 and 1965, took four

Ann-Kathrin Linsenhoff (Germany) with Courage, European Championships 1989 (Bob Langrish)

other medals and was fourth in 1967. Since then team silver and bronze medals have continued to accumulate, but it was **Christine Stückelberger** (see p128) who came closest to breaking the German domination.

The Russian team is the only one to have wrested any team gold medals at all from the Germans, and surprisingly enough both of these were on German soil, at the Aachen World Championships of 1970 and the Munich Olympics of 1972. (They also, not unnaturally, won in Moscow in 1980.) The way was led by **Serge Filatov**, Olympic Champion in Rome and bronze medallist in Tokyo, and three times European silver medallist. **Ivan Kizimov** took the individual gold in Mexico and four other championship medals, and **Elena Petushkova** not only took home the silver medal (and team gold) from Munich, but was European Champion in 1970, and in the same year became one of the few foreigners (and the only Russian) to win the Aachen Grand Prix.

Although United States teams have proved the equal of any in the world in jumping and the three day event, in dressage they have made little impact at world level since **Hiram Tuttle** won a bronze medal on his home ground in Los Angeles in 1932, though their team did win medals there and in London (1948) and Montreal (1976). But **Patricia Galvin** won the Aachen Grand Prix in 1960, and their 1988 National Champion **Robert Dover** has shown good form in the World Cup, and actually headed the European League in 1987/88 missing a medal by one place in the 1988 Final.

The World Cup was inaugurated in 1985 with aims similar to those of its jumping counterpart, but also to try to bring the sport of dressage before a wider public. In a European and a North American League there are qualifying competitions during the winter for a final held in the spring, and the basis of all the events is a Grand Prix which qualifies for a 'Kur', a freestyle test to music of the rider's choosing, which must incorporate certain laid down movements. This 'Kur' is the crux of the competition, and has proved extremely popular with the public.

Another nation primarily noted for success in the other two disciplines is Great Britain, for whom the Channel has proved almost as much of a barrier as the Atlantic has for the Americans. The British team has not managed to win a medal at the Olympics, nor at World or European Championships, though the records show that in 1963 Great Britain won the unofficial team competition at the European Championships in Copenhagen; but as the only other team was from Romania, and the total British team score was not greatly in excess of the individual scores of the individual medallists, Chammartin, Boldt and Klimke, not too much importance should be attached to that!

But the fact that Great Britain is today able to produce riders capable of competing honourably at the highest level is mainly due to four redoubtable ladies who set an example back in the fifties and sixties. **Joan Gold** showed that British riders could take on the best when winning the Aachen Grand Prix in 1958. Three years later **Brenda Williams** took the bronze medal at the Aachen European Championships. **Joanna (Jook) Hall**, who became a much respected FEI dressage judge, won the Rotterdam Grand Prix, one of the major European competitions, in 1960, 1963 and 1968, as well as the Hamburg Derby (for ladies) in 1965 and 1967. And **Lorna Johnstone**, thirteen times National Champion between 1956 and 1974, achieved twelfth place at the Munich Olympics of 1972 at the age of seventy!

But the most successful British dressage competitor to date is **Jennie Loriston-Clarke**. As Jennie Bullen – her brother Michael rode for Britain in the Olympic three day event in Rome and Tokyo, while her younger sister Jane brought home a team gold medal from the three day event in Mexico – she enjoyed early success on show ponies and hacks. In dressage she has been National Champion seven times and has competed in five Olympic Games, and with her horses Kadett, Dutch Courage, and Dutch Gold has set a standard of elegance that many have envied but few have been able to imitate.

In the World Championships of 1978 she took the bronze medal with Dutch Courage, on whom she was also placed a most creditable sixth at the 1980 International Festival in Rotterdam, the European Championships of 1981 and the World Championships of 1982. She has won Grands Prix in Goodwood and Brussels, but perhaps her greatest impact has been in the World Cup, where in 1988/89 she won three qualifying competitions, headed the European league, and finished in fourth place in the Final, all with Dutch Gold.

Christopher Bartle is one of those true all-round horsemen who have shone in more than one discipline. An accomplished three day event rider, he was equal sixth in the dressage at the Los Angeles Olympics with Wily Trout, was fourth in the 1985 European Championships, won the Rotterdam World Cup qualifier in 1985 and was second in the 1986 final. Meanwhile his sister **Jane Bartle-Wilson** won the World Cup qualifier at Goodwood in 1986 and has twice been National Champion. **David Hunt**,

Jennie Loriston-Clarke, MBE (GB) and Dutch Gold performing the freestyle 'Kur' to music (Bob Langrish)

RIGHT: *Margit Otto-Crépin (France) – Corlandus – Goodwood 1988* (Bob Langrish)

LEFT: *Dominique d'Esmé (France) – Fresh Wind – Goodwood 1987* (Bob Langrish)

Willi Schultheis (Germany) – Pernod XX – Hamburg Dressage Derby 1950

and in 1974 he was appointed official trainer to the German team until his retirement at the age of sixty in 1982, though he carried on unofficially for another year until the appointment of Harry Boldt as his successor. He then returned to Canada to train the team that took all the dressage medals at the 1987 Pan American Games in Indianapolis. In all he has trained twenty-two Olympic horses, and has himself been German Champion thirteen times.

Perhaps because of his early years in a racing stable, Willi has usually preferred to train the Thoroughbred, or something very near it, in preference to the heavier Hanoverian or Holsteiner, and he showed a remarkable ability to take a horse off the racecourse, establish a relationship with him, and develop his natural brilliance, so that he produced a performance that was a joy to watch. The Thoroughbred Pernod, winner of sixty major competitions including the Hamburg Dressage Derby, he regards as the most brilliant horse he rode, while Doublette was, in terms of competitions won, the most successful.

'I prefer to train Thoroughbreds,' he says, 'but good ones that have not been ruined are hard to find and difficult to buy. If I have to train a warmblood, then he must have plenty of Thoroughbred in him.'

He made several visits to London's Horse of the Year Show, both at Harringay and Wembley, and he well remembers a pas de deux that he rode at Wembley with Rosemary Springer. Rosemary's horse missed the transition into the piaffe, and cantered, and Willi was considerably amused when told afterwards that the television commentator had said, 'Oh, what a pity, Schultheis has missed his canter and is trotting instead.' On another occasion at Wembley he was riding a pas seul on a brilliant ex-racehorse, and he sensed that the audience, while appreciating the technical merit of his performance, were not as enthusiastic as usual. Then, towards the end the horse gave a buck and a kick, and the applause was terrific. 'They told me afterwards,' he said, 'that they thought it was cruel to make a racehorse do all that dressage, but when they saw that he hadn't lost his spirit, they all cheered!'

Willi has many memories and has met many great horsemen throughout the world, but he will never forget the comment made by Colonel (now Sir Michael) Ansell after one of his performances at Wembley. Although blind, Colonel Mike had an uncanny ability to perceive what was going on in the arena, but on this occasion he said to Schultheis, 'That was wonderful; but if only I had been able to see it.'

Today Willi lives just outside Warendorf, where his wife trains over thirty racehorses, four of them imports from Newmarket. With a career that has spanned half a century, he has amassed a formidable collection of silver prizes, and has solved the problem of displaying them in a novel way. Those of which he is especially proud are still around him; the remainder he had chopped into small pieces and melted down to remove the impurities and finally he had the pure silver made into a low coffee table. In the centre are engraved the names of his favourite horses – Doublette, Pernod, Perkunos and Thyra, and round the outside are the names of all the others whose prizes form part of the table.

He is still schooling horses himself, and training a steady stream of dressage aspirants who come to him not only from within his own country but from as far away as Australia as well.

I wondered if today's pupils were as dedicated as those of the past.

Yes, they are, but with dressage more than with any other sport, the problem is not only to school the horse, but also to train the rider. Today's riders are too careful, they're too much afraid of making mistakes. The result is that they ride better in the practice area than they do in the actual test. When they get into the main arena they are more concerned with avoiding errors than with letting the horse show himself off to the best advantage.

There has probably never been a rider who has allowed horses to show themselves off better. Few instructors or trainers can have been responsible for the production of so many top class horses and riders. Certainly few riders have done as much to demonstrate that the serious business of dressage can also be fun to ride and a joy to watch.

Germany

REINER KLIMKE

For most of this century international equestrian sport has been bedevilled by distinctions between two types of sportsmen – amateurs and professionals. However, these distinctions have at last been virtually eliminated, and all are now categorised as competitors. But it is strange to find that the rider who has amassed no fewer than thirty-two medals at the Olympic Games and at World and European Championships can justifiably claim to be one of the very last true amateurs. For Reiner Klimke, with eight Olympic, seven World Championship and seventeen European Championship medals to his credit over a period of thirty-three years is a practising lawyer who has had to fit in the training of his horses (and he has trained them all himself), and his competitions, with the demands of a very exacting profession.

There are few people today sufficiently well placed to do this, but he is fortunate enough to live in the relatively small but important university city of Münster, in Westphalia, only five minutes from his office, with one of the great riding centres of Germany also a five-minute drive away. But there are not many young riders of today who would be prepared to put themselves through the punishing schedule that has enabled Dr Klimke to reach the top of his sport.

His love, and that of his family, for horses has enabled them to give preference to sport over holidays. He has trained his horses before breakfast, during the lunch hour, in the evenings and at weekends, and, apart from major events such as the Olympic Games, has taken his annual holiday in the form of days spent at competitions. And this dedication has carried him to the highest pinnacles of his sport – six Olympic, six World and thirteen European Championship gold medals for Germany, and an Olympic, two World and four European golds for himself. All these for dressage, but before these he had already won team gold and silver European Championship medals for the three day event (the first of these at Harewood in 1959), and had jumped clear round the notoriously difficult cross-country course at the Rome Olympics. It is also worth recalling that he was German Dressage Champion eight times, won four Grands Prix and two Grands Prix Specials in Aachen, and no fewer than fourteen Hamburg Dressage Derbies.

All this began in the shadow of the ruins of Münster immediately after the end of World War II. Reiner was born in 1936 in Münster, where his father was Professor of Medicine at the university. His father was sent to the Russian front, and Reiner was sent out to a farm where the only means of getting to school, six miles away, was by horse and cart. Thus began his association with horses. In 1946 the family was reunited in Münster, 98 per cent of which lay in ruins, but when his father returned the young Reiner was so afraid of this strange looking soldier that he ran away from him.

Fortunately the Westphalian Riding School, headed by Herr Stecken, whose sons Paul and Albert were to become respected dressage judges, was at this time restarting, and Reiner was able to take a few lessons there. And not far away at Westbevern were the Lutke-Westhues family whose sons Alfons and August were eventually to become mainstays of the German jumping and three day event teams. Reiner took part in his first show at Brakel, between Paderborn and Höxter, in 1951, and two years later he came to the notice of the man who did so much to revive German equestrian fortunes after the war. Dr Gustav Rau invited him to train at Warendorf, where for three years he shared a room with another trainee for the three day event team, Alwin Schockemöhle.

Until 1955 he was at school, and from 1955 to 1960 he studied law, and after taking his doctorate he emerged as a fully qualified lawyer in 1964. But by then he had already brought home four European Championship medals. In the run-up to the Stockholm Olympics of 1956 Reiner had been in training for the dressage, and Alwin for the three day event, but both were selected as reserves, and since officially there were none, they hitchhiked to the Games. Once there, Alwin decided that his future lay in jumping, and on returning home he gave the ride on his horse Lausbub to Reiner. So in 1957 he was a member of the three day event team that came second to Great Britain in Copenhagen, and two years later they took the gold medal in Harewood.

But Reiner had also taken the silver medal in the European Dressage Championships of 1955 on Scipio and the gold in 1962 on Arcadius, and it now became clear that he must make a choice between his career and his sport. But perhaps, given the proximity of home, office and stable, he could manage to combine the two. Perhaps not, however, in the three day event, that most demanding of equestrian disciplines. And so he made the decision to concentrate on dressage. He had, however, one last appearance for the three day event team, in the Rome Olympics, and to this day one of his most cherished memories is of completing that difficult cross-country course without jumping penalties.

Reiner considers he was particularly lucky in having been able to draw on the experience of teachers from the pre-war and post-war periods, so that he was able to combine the best of both. As a boy he used to watch the great Otto Lörke, who had been trainer to the Kaiser in Potsdam. The Kaiser had a stiff arm, and it was Lörke's task to train his horses so that they nevertheless remained under his control. One of his earliest mentors was Frau Kathe Franke, a formidable lady who had won jumping competitions at Grand Prix level in the days when such events were largely confined to cavalry officers, rode in international three day events, and who was for several years champion of Germany in dressage. Then there were Paul and Albert Stecken, and Frau Hertha Rau, wife of Dr Gustav, who developed a good and severely critical eye. 'If she said "Yes",' said Reiner, 'your performance was very good, but she very seldom said "Yes".'

Whilst he recognised the classical principles of the old German school, he felt that correctness and obedience were achieved at the expense of the horse's personality, and he has developed a style that enables the horse to express himself through a more elegant performance. Having been a successful three day event rider he appreciated the importance of free forward movement, and it was not long before he impressed the international judges in his new sport.

The story of his success is woven round the careers of three great horses. He won the first of six Olympic team gold medals in Tokyo in 1964 with Dux, who brought him his second team gold and an individual bronze four years later in Mexico. His tally included team gold and individual bronze at the World Championships of 1966, both the golds in the European Championships of 1967, and team gold in 1969.

The great Mehmed, originally a three day event horse but a moderate jumper whom Reiner bought as a six-year-old, entered the scene with the gold medal team at the European Championships of 1971, and added both team and individual titles in 1973, both the World titles in 1974, and team gold and individual bronze in the Montreal Olympics of 1976. (Though Mehmed was available for selection for Munich in 1972 he was passed over – and those were the only Games between 1964 and 1988 in which Germany failed to win the team event, and the only Games in which Reiner did not compete.)

The International Festival of Dressage at Goodwood in 1980, the substitute Olympic contest for the nations that boycotted the Moscow Olympics, saw the emergence of the greatest of Reiner's three great horses, though Ahlerich's performance there gave little indication of the brilliance that he was to display four years later in Los Angeles. Ahlerich's story is worth telling in more detail if only because it illustrates not only the technical ability, patience and sympathy of his rider and trainer, but also the pitfalls that lie in wait for anyone who aspires to the highest levels of dressage.

At the Westphalian auction in the spring of 1975 the four-year-old Ahlerich had made top price, largely because of the potential that he displayed when loose jumping, and indeed on his first competitive appearance in public it was his jumping ability that impressed the judges more than anything else. Over the next year the combined efforts of Reiner and his wife Ruth led Ahlerich towards his first dressage competition in the summer of 1976, where Ruth won on him in Class 'L' (Elementary), and on the following day Reiner rode him into third place in Class 'M' (Medium).

In January 1977 the six-year-old was placed third in his first Class 'S' (Advanced) and particularly impressed the judges with the correctness of his paces and the brilliance of his extensions. His training at home continued with flying changes until he could perform the fifteen in succession later to be required in the Grand Prix. For although Reiner relates the age at which he starts teaching a horse the various Grand Prix movements to that particular horse's ability, muscular development and temperament, he likes to introduce the movements as early as possible. 'I would have no intention of competing with him at Grand Prix level until much later, but unless he can perform the movements at home well before that time, he will never perform them with the brilliance and polish necessary to be a champion later.'

After Ahlerich's first win in Class 'S' in July 1977, Reiner began to introduce him to the two most difficult movements, the piaffe and the passage. In the autumn of 1977 he became Westphalian Dressage Champion, and then had his first taste of international success with three second places in Paris. In Bremen in February 1978 he entered and won his very first Grand Prix, and after winning the Grand Prix and Grand Prix Special for young horses in Aachen in June, he won the German Championship at Munich in July, a little over three years after the start of his training.

It might now have seemed that all Reiner needed to do in order to bring his brilliant young horse up to Olympic standard was to polish the rough edges and perfect his

Reiner Klimke (Germany) – European Champion 1962, 1967, 1973, 1985; World Champion 1974, 1982; Olympic Champion 1984

performance. But the really brilliant horse is no mere automaton, he has a mind of his own, and Ahlerich was no exception. In Dortmund in March 1979 he exploded in a transition from passage to piaffe, and so he was taken out of training for Ruth to exercise for a couple of months.

The bronze medal in the German Championships in Berlin in July restored confidence, and was followed by another Westphalian Championship in August, success at the Tournament of Winners in Münster in September, and a final Grand Prix victory in Zuidlaren (Holland) in December. All seemed set for Olympic year, and indeed after victory in the Grand Prix Special at the pre-Olympic show at Balve in 1980 the press reported that 'Dr Klimke presented Ahlerich in Olympic condition'.

Alas, at Goodwood's International Festival of Dressage (for the nations that had boycotted the Moscow games), Ahlerich once more showed that he was no mere machine. The exciting diversion of a television gantry poised aloft involved his rider in exceptional efforts to prevent him from jumping out of the arena altogether. Nevertheless they helped Germany to win the team event and received the bronze medal from Prime Minister Margaret Thatcher.

The 1981 European Championships in Laxenburg, near Vienna, are remembered for weather that reduced the arena to something akin to a ploughed field, and for the half-hour hack necessary to get there from the stables – Reiner likened it to the three day event, though there the roads and tracks normally come after the dressage! Reiner was happy to return home with another team gold medal.

And so to another World Championship year. The Swiss were hosts to seventeen nations in Lausanne, and their great hope was that their Olympic and World Champion Granat would provide Christine Stückelberger with a final victory on his home territory, and retire in a blaze of glory. Now at these Championships there were three horses, Granat, Ahlerich and another German contender Madras, whose previous successes made them ineligible to compete in the preliminary competition, Intermediaire II, something that did not bother the Germans at all. But Granat, now seventeen years old, lacked recent international experience.

But the rules were then changed so as to allow such horses to perform the Intermediaire 'hors concours' at the end of the competition in front of the judges but without being scored. Reiner was now in a slight quandary; should he allow the judges to compare his relatively young horse with the reigning World and Olympic Champion before the Grand Prix? When Granat drew the first start Reiner made up his mind.

Ahlerich's best hope of beating Granat lay in his more youthful and perhaps more brilliant trot. After Granat had performed his test, Reiner entered the arena, demanded and obtained a trot of the utmost brilliance from Ahlerich, and at the end of the trot movement, saluted and retired. If the change of rules had been to Granat's advantage, at the same time no rule stipulated that in these circumstances the whole test must be completed 'hors concours'. And at least now the judges would have no preconceived ideas as to the relative merits of Granat and Ahlerich, and all would depend upon their respective performances in the competition.

In the Grand Prix, which decided the team competition and constituted the first leg of the individual, Ahlerich made a couple of small mistakes and finished in second place, close behind Granat, leading the German team to a gold medal. But Granat had made no errors, so Reiner knew that an error-free test from Ahlerich in the Grand Prix Special could give him the title. Granat put in a winning performance, but Ruth Klimke reported that it had included a couple of mistakes in the canter changes, and Reiner felt that victory was possible. But he would have to risk everything in order to achieve it.

He asked for, and received, the utmost brilliance of which Ahlerich was capable, and the test was only marred by two very small mistakes, a tenseness in one of the canter pirouettes and a somewhat hurried final piaffe. The wait while the marks were added up seemed interminable. But minutes later Ahlerich was World Champion, and Reiner had won the title for the second time on a horse that he had trained himself.

In 1983 Ahlerich was allowed to rest on his laurels, though he did help Germany to another gold medal in the European Championships in Aachen, while Reiner made up for lost time in his office and also concentrated on his young horses. But the emergence of Denmark's Anne-Grethe Jensen and Marzog as European Champions, a combination that seemed to put the emphasis back onto fluency and elegance instead of mere technical correctness, spurred Reiner on towards the Olympic Games of 1984.

A big worry in Los Angeles was the heat and humidity, so Reiner began a slow process of acclimatisation that would enable Ahlerich to perform at his best in the 40°C (104°F) temperatures that could be expected on the afternoon of the test itself. Victory for Germany in the team competition was followed by the ultimate accolade for Ahlerich and his rider – individual Olympic gold.

Ahlerich was still only thirteen – Granat was seventeen when he retired – and in 1985 he added the Individual European title to his World and Olympic ones. Then a mysterious lameness kept him out of competition for over a year, though he recovered sufficiently to take the German Championship for the seventh time in 1988 – by a margin of over 100 points. His final appearance helped Germany to a clean sweep of all three equestrian team gold medals at the Seoul Olympics, and he then retired to a life of luxury as Ruth Klimke's hack.

Reiner, too, might now have been expected to rest on his laurels, but even when he does so the name of Klimke is unlikely to disappear from the scene. His son Michael has already won European medals for dressage, taking team gold and individual bronze at the 1989 Young Riders Championships, and has already won senior Grands Prix. His daughter Ingrid has been successful in German Young Rider three day event competitions.

He is happy that his children can learn from himself and from Ruth, but he doubts whether many of the present young generation would make the sacrifices that he did for his sport. 'I used to bicycle 30 kilometres each way from Münster to Warendorf in all weathers in order to ride. But then there was no television, no discos, I just had my studies and my riding.'

Apart from the difficulty of finding dedicated youngsters, Reiner sees difficulties ahead for the sport.

Our horses are now much better than before, the performance of dressage is more elegant and pleasing to watch, and interest in dressage has grown, partly due to the World Cup. But the standard of riding hasn't kept up with the improvement in horses. The standard at the 1989 European Championships in Mondorf, for example, was not very high. The problem is going to be that we no longer produce trainers. Our former trainers were the products of the Cavalry Schools or were trained by them. Today's good riders don't want to become trainers, they want to compete, and now that Boris Becker and Steffi Graff can compete in the Olympics it is possible for them to do so too. So as the old trainers retire, who will replace them? And our elegant and successful young lady riders of today rely very much on their trainers.

Reiner is not sure whether his best moment was Mehmed's World Championship of 1974, his regaining of the title with Ahlerich in 1982 or his Olympic gold medal in Los Angeles. In fact, true horseman that he is, he is not sure that the moment that gave him the greatest satisfaction wasn't that clear cross country round on Winzerin during the Olympic three day event in Rome.

Switzerland

CHRISTINE STÜCKELBERGER

At the dressage training area in Bromont, site of the equestrian events of the Montreal Olympics of 1976, a sizeable throng of spectators, mainly other riders of various teams, used to gather to watch the slim, elegant girl on the large and apparently unruly horse as they worked their way towards the dressage competitions of the Games. Sometimes the horse appeared totally to disregard the rider on his back, and sometimes it seemed nothing short of miraculous that she managed to stay there; at others he performed the movements of the Olympic test almost perfectly. In the individual Olympic competition Christine Stückelberger and Granat produced a display of dressage that for sheer technical merit has seldom been bettered, and which brought them the gold medal, fifty-one points ahead of Harry Boldt and Woyceck, and ninety-one ahead of the bronze medallist, Reiner Klimke and Mehmed.

With Granat and his successor Gauguin de Lully, Christine won six Olympic medals, including two individual golds and a bronze, seven medals at the World Championships, including an individual gold and two silvers, and at the European Championships she was Champion twice, silver medallist twice, and took home a total of ten medals. In the World Cup she has won eleven preliminary competitions, headed the European League in 1986/87 and was runner-up the following year, and in the four finals that have been held so far she was third in 1986, the winner in 1987 and 1988, and second in 1989. She was National Champion of Switzerland from 1970 to 1979 and again in 1986, and has won over thirty of the world's most important Grands Prix and Grands Prix Specials.

The story starts back in 1947, when Christine was born in the village of Wallisellen, a few kilometres north of Zürich. Her father was a doctor, who had ridden occasionally during his army service, and her mother, daughter of the President of Switzerland, loved animals, especially dogs and horses, and had taken riding lessons before her marriage. Christine evidently displayed this love of animals from an early age, for she first sat on a horse in a stable when a mere two years old!

Her formal training began at the age of eleven, when she started taking lessons from Georg Wahl of the Berne Riding School, and it is he who has guided her through her career ever since. Her first major successes came on an Irish Thoroughbred gelding

OPPOSITE
Christine Stückelberger (Switzerland), Olympic, World and European Champion, winner of the International Dressage Festival, Goodwood 1980 (Findlay Davidson)

called Merry Boy, who went on to take Christine to the European Championships of 1969, 1971 and 1973, and to the World Championships of 1972. 'Every year,' she says, 'I won two competitions on him in Aachen, and I thought I would never have a better horse. I certainly never imagined that I would one day have a horse called Granat who would be much better.'

'Much better' was something of an understatement, for Granat was eventually to take her to the top of the world. His early history, however, did not appear to be all that promising. A Holstein gelding by the stallion Consul out of the very successful mare Salmai, he showed very good movement, especially at the trot, which had excellent natural cadence. But as a young horse he was far from handsome, even perhaps rather ugly, for he had a poor neck and was a little too long in the back. But something about him appealed to Christine, who bought him as a four-year-old from Fürst (Prince) Magalow in Bavaria in southern Germany in 1969, and as his training progressed and he developed more muscle he became, in the words of his new owner, 'beautiful and very athletic'.

But before serious training could begin it was discovered that Granat was blind in one eye! This was three months after Christine had bought him, and his story might well have ended there and then. But when she told his former owner, he was so horrified that he generously refunded the entire purchase price, and so the horse that was to become one of the greatest that the sport has ever seen was really a gift.

Granat's blindness in one eye explains his often unruly behaviour, for if he heard something that he was unable to see he became 'a little bit crazy', and this not unnaturally made him difficult to train. But fortunately he was blessed with a wonderful temperament. 'He became very attached to Georg Wahl and to me; we could speak to him and he understood everything.' Sometimes extraordinary measures had to be taken in order to overcome his disability, and Christine describes how they overcame one particular difficulty.

> When Granat was five years old I rode him in Vienna in a test for young horses which included a half pirouette on the forehand. Because he was blind in his right eye he refused to turn on the forehand. So when we exercised the test Georg Wahl stood at 'B', spoke to Granat, and gave him a lump of sugar. Each time we wanted to exercise this movement we went to another indoor school in the same village, and whenever Granat heard Georg, he turned, and then received his sugar. In this way we taught him to turn on the forehand.

Fifteenth place at the Munich Olympics of 1972 at the age of only seven, fifth place in the World Championships in Copenhagen two years later, and the Olympic gold medal in Montreal at the age of eleven, are evidence of Granat's brilliance and intelligence and of the patience of his trainer and rider, and when he died in 1989 at the age of twenty-four Christine felt that she had lost a real friend.

But the year before Granat won his Olympic gold medal in Montreal, a horse called Gauguin de Lully was born in Switzerland by the Swedish stallion Shagall out of a Swedish mare – but because he was born in Switzerland he was entitled to Swiss nationality. At the age of eleven Gauguin de Lully took the silver medal in the 1986 World Championships in Cedar Valley, near Toronto, and in the next two years won the Nashua World Cup Finals in 's-Hertogenbosch (Holland) and Essen (Germany), and took the individual silver and team bronze medals at the Olympic Games in Seoul. After the 1987 European Championships in Goodwood (England), in which he had won the bronze medal, Gaugin was disqualified for failing a routine drug test, when a forbidden substance was traced to a proprietary brand of horse feed. But many competitors were having similar problems at this time, and the fourth-placed horse, to whom the medal was awarded, was himself then disqualified for the same reason! Christine also has the eleven-year-old Opal, a chestnut gelding bred in Holland, whom she bought in England, and who has recently started his career at Grand Prix level.

Christine acknowledges that she owes much to her good fortune in coming under the influence of a trainer as sympathetic and as dedicated as Georg Wahl. But there are other reasons, too, for her success.

I think that one of the reasons for my success is that I love my horses very much and accept them as real personalities. I have a very close contact with my horses. To a young rider today I would say that he must love his horses and must have the patience to spend a lot of time on them. When he is starting it is very important that he goes to a good teacher, and he must spend plenty of time on the lunge in order to achieve a good seat right from the beginning.

Christine has seen the sport develop considerably during her riding career, and has indeed contributed considerably to its development.

The level of performance in dressage is much higher now than when I started in competitions. For example, a lot of horses are now showing excellent piaffe and passage. The breeding of horses has also improved, and young horses are now much better movers. But one improvement that I would like to see introduced concerns the judging; any irregularity in a horse's movement should be much more strictly marked because it shows that the horse was worked too hard or too early, or was wrongly worked.

Christine looks back on her triumph in Montreal as the highlight of her career so far. But those who consider that pursuit of excellence in dressage entails no physical risk would do well to take note of what happened in the spring of 1989. Christine was schooling a young stallion in her indoor school and allowed him a moment of relaxation. Suddenly, as young horses will, he bucked, and having the freedom to do so, continued bucking. With the reins loose, Christine was thrown against the wall of the school, breaking her back in two places. Two operations and a long period of convalescence followed, and this incident has inevitably affected her plans for the future.

As a result of my accident I was nearly paralysed because I broke my back, and now my biggest wish is to be healthy again. For the moment equestrian sport has to take second place. But in 1990, if I am healthy, I would like very much to take part with the Swiss team in the World Equestrian Games in Stockholm, either with Gauguin de Lully or with Opal. But if I have to do less riding for a while, then I have other interests – I am very fond of music, both modern and classical, and also dancing, tennis, travelling and the study of ancient history.

We can but hope that someone who loves her animals as much as Christine does will soon be restored to full health so that the thrill that she has given in the past to spectators both in championships and in the World Cup may once again grace the world of dressage.

Part IV

SHOW JUMPING

TOGETHER WITH FLAT RACING, show jumping is one of the most universal of equestrian sports. But there are many more jumping riders than jockeys, and their careers generally span a longer period than in other equestrian sports, except perhaps dressage. Statistics alone, in terms of success in the Olympic Games, World and Continental Championships and major Grands Prix, are not sufficient to establish relative merit, since the accident of geography would exclude consideration of many Americans. But if the United States riders, for example, do not often have the opportunity to compete in Europe, their performances in the World Cup Finals alone have shattered any European complacency.

Up to 1989, ten of these finals have been won by North Americans – seven by the USA and three by Canada – and apart from the single European victory, only twelve of the possible thirty-three medals have been retained in Europe, although that is where every final except two has been held.

If anyone merits the title of 'the Father of Modern Jumping' it must surely be **Federico Caprilli**, the Italian officer who introduced the forward seat, and though he died in 1907 at the age of only thirty-nine, his influence was evident in the Italian teams of the inter-war years – in 1923, for example, Italy won all four Nations Cups contested (Nice, Rome, Brussels and London.) Ireland, too, was a force to be reckoned with, and **Dan Corry**, **Jed O'Dwyer** and **Fred Ahearn** formed the basis of the team which scored a notable victory in Lucerne in 1935 with a zero score, twenty-four ahead of Switzerland, who were second. **Paul Rodzianko** of Russia, later a great trainer of British and Irish riders, and **Jack Talbot-Ponsonby**, triple winner of London's King George V Gold Cup, were other consistent winners, but the greatest team of the immediate pre-war period came from Germany.

Kurt Hasse, **Harald Momm**, and **Marten von Barnekow** were joined in 1937 by **Hans-Heinrich Brinckmann**, and until the war put an end to international competition this young cavalry officer helped Germany to win ten Nations Cups, and himself won seven major Grands Prix, mainly with three stallions, Oberst II, Wotansbruder, and Baron IV. There can be little doubt that had his equestrian career not been cut short by hostilities, he would have joined the ranks of the greatest riders. As it was, he did much to resurrect the sport in Germany after the war, and then spent two years training the Egyptian team to such good effect that they came fourth out of fifteen teams behind Germany, the USA and Italy at the Rome Olympics in 1960.

Back in his home country Brinckmann not only trained the German team, but became

The Piazza di Siena, Rome, one of the most famous and picturesque arenas in the world (Findlay Davidson)

one of the most knowledgeable and respected course designers in the world, and the courses at Aachen, and especially those for the Munich Olympics of 1972 and for the Aachen World Championships of 1978, were regarded as classics. Though he may have been denied the highest honours because of historical events, Brinckmann's influence on the sport over half a century has been immense.

There have been other riders, too, who would surely have joined the ranks of the greatest but for the fact that World War II either terminated their careers prematurely, or delayed their entry to the sport until an age at which many are considering retirement. Perhaps the most intriguing of these was the Mexican **Humberto Mariles Cortés**.

His gold medal, together with that of the Mexican team, will never be forgotten by those who witnessed it in Wembley Stadium as the 1948 London Olympics drew to a close. With only three riders to a team – the fourth was not added until Munich in 1972 – the elimination of nearly half the starters resulted in the elimination of eleven teams out of fourteen. But Cortés had trained his team to perfection, and when he entered the arena as the last to go, he knew that he had six fences in hand for Mexico to win the gold medal, but that he could only afford one mistake to take the individual gold as well. The faults of previous competitors had been spread round the course, but the last two fences posed a particular problem, and no rider so far had managed to clear the water and then collect his horse in time to negotiate the final wall.

Cortés took the one-eyed Arete round slowly and clear as far as the water, and there was silence in the stadium as he approached it without any increase in pace. To the amazement of all, Arete was allowed to pop into the water, and consequently was the only horse to arrive at the wall sufficiently balanced to clear it; 4 faults for jumping and $2\frac{1}{4}$ for time, and two gold medals were theirs. A superlative piece of intelligent riding by a great horseman! And over the next decade Cortés himself won nine of the North American Grands Prix, and his team took no fewer than thirteen of the North American Nations Cups as well as those of Rome and Madrid.

Cortés rose to the rank of general, but in 1964 the equestrian world was shocked to hear that he had been charged with shooting a man with whom he was involved in a traffic accident in Mexico City. He claimed self-defence, but left Mexico before the sentence of twenty years imprisonment was pronounced. Returning two years later, he served five years in prison, but a year after his release when supposedly working for the Mexican Tourist Board in Paris, he was picked up and charged in conjunction with others with transporting heroin. He denied any involvement, but was later found dead in his prison cell, and it was never clearly established whether the cause of death was natural or suicide. A tragic end to the life of a great rider!

Before 1939 British Army teams had usually managed to win the Nations Cup in London, but had only ever won five elsewhere. After the war, however, the vision of one man and the horsemanship of another brought about a change that was to result in an Olympic medal at every Games from 1948 to 1968, and eventually to thirteen wins out of twenty-three in the President's Cup and its successor the Gucci Trophy, the league table for Nations Cups. If the inspiration for this lay with **Colonel Mike** (now **Sir Michael**) **Ansell**, an outstanding horseman before the war but blinded in action in its early days, the victories in the field were brought home by **Harry** (now **Sir Harry**) **Llewellyn**.

After a successful pre-war career as an amateur steeplechaser, which had included a second and a fourth in the Grand National, and an equally successful military interlude as a staff officer in North Africa, Italy and North West Europe, Harry Llewellyn had then turned to jumping, and his appetite for international competition was whetted when he became the first civilian rider to win, with Kilgeddin, the Puissance in Rome in 1947. He then bought the seven-year-old horse with which he was to become one of the most successful riders in the world over the next six years.

Foxhunter's subsequent successes have tended to overshadow what was no mean feat by horse and rider at the Olympic Games in London only a year later. From forty-four riders from fifteen nations only twenty-three riders and three teams managed to complete the course, and for a horse of Foxhunter's experience to do this with only four fences down was a tribute to his rider. And never before or since has one rider owned a

OPPOSITE
Christine Stückelberger (Switzerland) – Olympic Champion 1976, 1980, World Champion 1978, European Champion 1975, 1977 – Gauguin de Lully, Seoul 1988 (Bob Langrish)

TOP LEFT: *Paul Schockemöhle (Germany) – European Champion 1981, 1983, 1985 – Deister* (Bob Langrish)

TOP RIGHT: *Pierre Durand (France) – European Champion 1987, Olympic Champion 1988 – Jappeloup de Luze, Hickstead 1989* (Bob Langrish)

LEFT: *Nelson Pessoa (Brazil), – European Champion 1966 – Miss Moet, Puissance Wall record holder* (Bob Langrish)

OPPOSITE

David Broome, OBE MFH (GB) – World and Triple European Champion – Countryman, Seoul 1988 Bob Langrish

Sir Harry Llewellyn (GB) on his Olympic team gold medallist Foxhunter in 1952 (Sport & General)

complete Olympic team, for Llewellyn also owned Kilgeddin, ridden by **Henry Nicoll**, and Monty ridden by **Arthur Carr**. (Arthur Carr's round was one of utter determination, for Monty, who subsequently became one of the most successful horses in Europe in speed competitions, refused the first fence, and to go on to complete the course in those circumstances was a considerable feat of horsemanship, which helped the team to take the bronze medal.)

At the next Olympics in Helsinki in 1952 a first round disaster was followed by a second round triumph. Anxious to preserve Foxhunter for the second round, Llewellyn admits that he did not work him enough before the first, in which they knocked up an uncharacteristic 16¾ faults, thus apparently destroying any chance of a team medal. But in the second round, thanks to the efforts of **Wilf White** and **Duggie Stewart**, a clear round or one fence down from Foxhunter would mean a gold medal for Great Britain.

OPPOSITE

TOP: *Joe Fargis (USA) – Olympic Champion 1984 – Mill Pearl, Hickstead 1989* (Bob Langrish)

BELOW LEFT: *Nick Skelton (GB) – Winner, Hickstead Derby 1987, 1988, 1989 – Burmah Apollo* (Bob Langrish). BELOW RIGHT: *John Whitaker (GB) and Milton – European Champions 1989, World Cup Champions 1990* (Bob Langrish)

Peter Robeson, OBE (GB), Olympic bronze medallist 1964. Seen here winning the Amateur Championship on Grebe at Cardiff 1980 (Bob Langrish)

This time Foxhunter jumped like the great horse that he had become, and the team took home not only the first British Olympic equestrian gold medal, but the only British gold of the Helsinki Games.

Between 1948 and his retirement in 1954, Foxhunter won two Olympic medals, seven major Grands Prix, including three King George V Gold Cups (the only horse ever to do this), and helped the British team to win a dozen Nations Cups. Harry Llewellyn himself was winning on other horses, too; Kilgeddin and Monty were two of them, and there is little doubt that had he not entered the world of international jumping relatively late in life he would have equalled the records of the world's outstanding riders.

Inspired by these successes, British riders went from strength to strength. One who was for long regarded as a model for his quiet but effective style of riding was **Peter Robeson**, Olympic bronze medallist in Stockholm (1956) and in Tokyo (1964), and still riding in the Olympics in 1976.

It was unfortunate that a decision by the British Equestrian Federation in 1972 to turn most of the leading riders into professionals deprived British teams of possible Olympic medals until the IOC reframed their rules, so as to permit the readmittance of former professionals. This was in response to a call by the President of the FEI, Prince Philip, for nations to set their houses in order in this respect, but no other nation followed the British lead.

One who was affected by this was **Harvey Smith**, who first came to prominence when he came third to **Graziano Mancinelli** and **Alwin Schockemöhle** (see p181) in the 1963 European Championship in Rome. In 1967 he took the silver medal in Rotterdam behind **David Broome** (see p175) and ahead of Schockemöhle, and in 1970 he was third to Broome and Mancinelli (with Schockemöhle behind him) in the World Championship in La Baule. The following year he was runner-up to Hartwig Steenken in the Aachen European Championship, and over a decade later helped Great Britain to victory in the European at Hickstead. Twenty-eight major Grands Prix wins in nine countries testify to his versatility, and he has carved something of a niche for himself as a Derby specialist, winning no fewer than eight, a record he shares with **Eddie Macken** (Ireland). Above all he has earned a reputation for being able to get the best out of some horses that others considered unridable, and his major successes have been achieved on

Harvey Smith (GB) – European Championships, bronze 1963, silver 1967, 1971; World Championships, bronze 1970 – here winning the Daily Mail Cup with Sanyo Shining Example (Bob Langrish)

Fritz Thiedemann (Germany) riding Meteor, whose record of medals at three consecutive Olympic Games is unique (Sport & General)

some fourteen different horses. An outspoken protagonist on behalf of competitors, he has also trained his two sons, Robert and Stephen up to international standard.

Another British rider who has missed the opportunity of Olympic medals through enforced professional status is **Malcolm Pyrah**, who has not been slow to pick up honours elsewhere. He will long be remembered in Britain for his unselfish devotion to the interests of the national team, first with Law Court, on whom he won team gold medals at the World Championship in Aachen in 1978 and at the European Championship at Rotterdam in 1979, and then with Anglezarke, on whom he won three World medals, including the individual silver in Dublin in 1982, three European, and a dozen major Grands Prix.

Three young British riders who burst upon the scene in the late seventies were **Nick Skelton** (see p199) and **John Whitaker** (see p201) and his brother **Michael** (see p204).

In the early fifties the West German team re-emerged as a power on the world scene, and in 1952 **Fritz Thiedemann** took the bronze medal in Helsinki. Of slight build himself, his greatest successes were achieved on the gigantic Meteor, and to those who had watched him performing very adequate dressage as part of the warming up process for this enormous horse it came as no surprise when Fritz also earned a team bronze medal at the same Games for dressage. He was to win team gold medals in Stockholm and Rome, he was runner-up in the first World Championship in Paris in 1953 and he was European Champion in 1958, but he will probably best be remembered for his achievements in the greatest of all Derbys, Hamburg. Fritz won this five times between 1950 and 1959, and on five different horses. Among his many Grand Prix victories were those in Aachen, New York and the King George V Gold Cup at the White City, London.

With the example of **Hans Günter Winkler** (see p154) to follow, there was no shortage of top-class German riders from then on, and for three successive Olympic Games the German team took the gold medals – at Stockholm, Rome and Tokyo, where **Hermann Schridde** also took the silver medal, with team bronze to follow in Mexico. In 1965 Schridde was European Champion, and he was later appointed trainer to the German team. (He died tragically in a flying accident while still holding this post.) **Hartwig Steenken** and **Gert Wiltfang** were two who rode for Germany in the seventies, and both helped their team to a gold medal in Munich in 1972. Steenken became European Champion in 1971 in Aachen, World Champion in 1974 at Hickstead, and runner-up to the European Champion in 1975, where Germany made a clean sweep of the medals. Mainly associated with the great Simona, Steenken's career was also tragically cut short when in 1978 he died as a result of a motor accident.

With Roman, **Gert Wiltfang** became World Champion in Aachen in 1978, and European Champion in Rotterdam the following year, when he also won the Hamburg Derby. Germany has also produced one of two great pairs of show jumping brothers, **Alwin Schockemöhle** (see p181) and his younger brother **Paul** (see p186), who took over as Alwin was retiring.

Germany has also both exported and imported talent. In 1971 **Hugo Simon** helped Germany to win the Rotterdam Nations Cup. He had however been born in 1942 in that corner of Europe where the borders of Germany, Austria and Czechoslovakia meet, and because of post-war 'tidying up' of the boundaries he found himself eligible to ride for Austria. Sensing a more assured future if he did that, he changed his nationality, and in 1972 he was fourth in the Munich Olympics riding Lavendel. His record in Championships is impressive, for in World Championships he has finished third and sixth, while in the European he has been five times in the top five. But his record in World Cups is even better. In 1979 he won the first running of the World Cup Final in Gothenburg, being the only European rider to have beaten the North Americans in this contest. He has ridden in every World Cup Final except one, and has finished eight times in the top ten. In 1980 he won the substitute Olympics in Rotterdam, and he has won three Hamburg Derbys, most of this with Gladstone, whom he acquired on the death of his former rider Hartwig Steenken, and latterly with The Freak and Winzer.

Franke Sloothaak was born in Holland in 1958, and at his first show at the age of ten he was second in dressage and jumping. He had won over forty jumping classes by the time he was twelve, which meant that he had accumulated too many points to remain in juniors, while his horse, just one centimetre over the height for ponies, was too small to jump in the senior classes. In 1972, aged fourteen, he won a team silver medal for the Netherlands in the Junior European Championships in Cork, repeated the performance in Lucerne two years later, and shared the individual silver medal in Brussels in 1976. In 1977 he went to work with Alwin Schockemöhle in Germany.

Since he seemed unable to secure a place in the Dutch team, Franke took out German nationality, and in 1980 he won the Dortmund World Cup qualifier with Rex the Robber. In 1981 he became German Champion, and between 1980 and 1988 he won twelve major Grands Prix on twelve different horses. When Alwin reduced his jumping stable to concentrate on trotting, Franke moved across to join Paul Schockemöhle, and in 1984 he went with the German team to the Los Angeles Olympics where they took the bronze medal, with Franke and Farmer in eleventh place. Another European bronze medal with the German team followed in 1985, and in the Seoul Olympics of 1988 came the clean sweep of all the equestrian team gold medals – dressage, jumping and the three day event. With the giant Walzerkönig, Franke finished in seventh place, and in 1989 he won with him the important Grands Prix in Aachen, Zürich and Stockholm.

It is interesting to note that the rider who was overlooked by his native country, Holland, is now sponsored by the Dutch firm of Optiebeurs.

Since World War II, the fortunes of Italy have rested squarely on the shoulders of another remarkable pair of brothers, **Piero** and **Raimondo d'Inzeo** (see pp166–74), backed up for much of their long careers by **Graciano Mancinelli**. One unfortunate result of their domination has been the dearth of Italian success since their retirement in 1977; indeed Italy failed to win a Nations Cup from 1978 until 1985, whereas between 1950 and 1977 there were only eight seasons in which a d'Inzeo did not help Italy to win a Nations Cup.

Mancinelli's career started back in 1952 in the Junior European Championships, and he appeared on his first Nations Cup winning team in 1960. He was European Champion in 1963 and formed part of the bronze medal team of the Tokyo Olympics in 1964. In 1970 he was runner-up in the World Championships at La Baule, and the highlight of his long career was winning the individual gold medal with Ambassador at the Munich Olympics of 1972. He helped Italy to win thirty Nations Cups, the last being in 1985.

France was particularly strong immediately after World War II, and again from the middle seventies. One of her most charismatic riders, and the first civilian to challenge the supremacy of the military, was **Jean d'Orgeix**, something of a genius and a star at whatever he turned his hand to – film star, aerobatic ace, racing driver, and a brilliant horseman. In 1947 he helped the French team to win the Prince of Wales Cup (the Nations Cup) in London, and the following year he took the bronze medal in London, being the first civilian to win an Olympic medal. With Sucre de Pomme, Marquis III and Arlequin D he exhibited dash and style which thrilled those who saw him – and he never wore spurs.

One of his contemporaries was a quiet and unassuming farmer from the foothills of the Pyrennees, who was to dominate the French scene for a quarter of a century, **Pierre Jonquères d'Oriola** (see p150). There was a period when the French did not win many Nations Cups, but the challenge of the Olympics usually brought out the best in

Franke Sloothaak (Germany) with Walzerkönig, Olympic Games, Seoul 1988 (Bob Langrish)

them, and with riders such as **Guy Lefrant** and **Marcel Rozier** their team took silver medals in Tokyo and Mexico. But in Munich they failed to qualify for the second round, and d'Orgeix was brought back to train the team for Montreal in 1976, where they duly took the gold medal. The eighties, however, saw the real renaissance of the French team, with **Michael Robert**, **Frederic Cottier**, **Gilles Bertran de Balanda** and **Pierre Durand** (see p195).

Spain won the team gold medal in Amsterdam in 1928, and the silver in London in 1948, but since then their most successful rider has been **Francisco Goyoaga**. With Quorum, he won the first World Championship in Paris in 1953, was third in 1954 in Madrid, second in Aachen in 1956, and he won sixteen major Grands Prix, mainly with Fahnenkönig.

It seems strange that Ireland has never won an Olympic medal of any sort, and in fact has only managed to be represented on five occasions. Since 1948 she has produced three very successful riders in **Seamus Hayes**, winner of two Hickstead Derbys, **Tommy Wade**, twice winner of the Dublin Grand Prix with the diminutive Dundrum, and **William Ringrose**, winner of Grands Prix in New York, Harrisburg, Rome and

Nice. But in the World Championships of 1974 at Hickstead there was some surprise when Hartwig Steenken (Germany), Hugo Simon (Austria) and Frank Chapot (USA) were joined in the final by **Eddie Macken**, and even more when he forced Steenken to a jump-off and took the silver medal with Pele. But to show that this was no fluke, he was runner-up in the European Championships of 1977 in Vienna. He then took the World silver medal again in Aachen in 1978, and but for a quarter of a fault Ireland might have had a World Champion.

This time Eddie was riding Boomerang, and with him he won Grands Prix all over Europe and North America, as well as two Hamburg and four successive Hickstead Derbys. To win even one Derby at Hamburg or Hickstead is difficult enough; to win six of these in the space of four years implies an exceptionally high standard of horsemanship. In all Eddie won eight Derbys, a record he shares with Harvey Smith.

Of the other European nations, **Johan Heins** of Holland was European Champion in Vienna in 1977, while the Swiss took the team Championship in 1983 at Hickstead, and their leading rider **Paul Weier** won four Lisbon Grands Prix in succession with Wulf. But one of the most consistently successful riders in Europe has been the Brazilian **Nelson Pessoa** (see p188).

Of all the nations, the one that is universally admired for the style and skill of her riders is the United States, and apart from their outstanding success in the World Cup, when they have sent teams to Europe they have proved very hard indeed to beat. Their first Olympic medal came in Los Angeles in 1932. The Nations Cup was something of a farce, for only three teams competed and none succeeded in getting their three riders round the course, but **Harry Chamberlin** took the silver medal behind **Baron Takeichi Nishi** of Japan. But the fifties saw the emergence of four great riders: **Hugh Wiley**, **William Steinkraus** (see p160), **Frank Chapot** and **George Morris**.

This was the team that won the Pan American Games of 1959 in Chicago, and Frank Chapot rode in six Olympic Games (a record only equalled by Hans Günter Winkler and bettered by the brothers d'Inzeo), winning two team silver medals, and he shared the bronze medal with Hugo Simon in Hickstead's World Championship of 1974 and (strangely enough) was runner-up in the European Championship of 1966 in Lucerne.

When Hungarian **Bertalan de Nemethy** was appointed team trainer he produced a new generation of young riders in the same mould: **Michael Matz**, third in the World Championships of 1978 in Aachen, and winner of the 1981 World Cup Final in Birmingham, Pan American champion of 1979 and the only rider to win six Pan American medals; **Buddy Brown**, Pan American runner-up in 1975; **Joe Fargis** (see p191) whom he regards as one of the best in the world today; **Conrad Homfeld**, Olympic silver medallist in Los Angeles, World silver medallist in 1986, and World Cup Champion of 1980 and 1985 (and he was third in 1986 and fourth in 1983).

Canada has only taken part in four Olympic Games, but surprised the world by taking the team gold medal in Mexico in 1968, where **Jim Elder** took sixth place in the individual competition after jumping off for the bronze medal with David Broome, Hans Günter Winkler and Frank Chapot. They then showed that this was no fluke by repeating this victory in Rotterdam in 1980. Meanwhile **Jim Day** had been fourth best individual in Munich, and **Michel Vaillancourt** had taken the silver medal in Montreal. But their most successful rider of recent years has been **Ian Millar**. Runner-up in the

World Cup Final of 1986, and fifth in 1987, he won it in 1988 and again in 1989, each time with Big Ben.

So far we have not mentioned the ladies. Until 1956 they were not allowed to compete in the Olympic Games, and were only admitted to the World Championships on equal terms with the men in 1978 after having had three Championships of their own. They had their own European Championships from 1957 to 1973, and joined the men in 1975. The first lady to ride in the Olympics was perhaps the best there has ever been: with Flanagan, **Pat Smythe** also became the first lady to win an Olympic medal, taking bronze with the British team in Stockholm. She won the first Ladies European Championship in 1957, and won it three times in succession from 1961 to 1963. She won the British Ladies Championship eight times, and won the second running of the Hickstead Derby in 1962.

The most successful lady Olympians were the British girls **Marion Coakes**, silver medallist in Mexico in 1968 with the tiny Stroller, and the silver medallist of 1972 in

Frank Chapot (USA) – bronze medal, World Championships 1974; silver medal, European Championships 1966; team silver medals, Olympic Games 1960, 1972– with Tally Ho at the White City, London 1959 (Leslie Lane)

Conrad Homfeld (USA), silver medallist, Olympic Games 1984, World Championships 1986, and World Cup Champion 1980 and 1985 (Bob Langrish)

Munich, where **Anne Moore** and the equally diminutive Psalm pushed Graciano Mancinelli and **Neal Sharpiro** (USA) into a jump-off. Stroller also won the 1965 Ladies World Championship, and both the Hamburg and Hickstead Derbys, while Psalm won the ladies European Championship in 1971 and 1973. **Heidi Robbiani** (Switzerland) won the bronze medal in Los Angeles, and then took the silver medal in the Open European Championship of 1985 against the men.

In 1976 **Debbie Johnsey** (GB) came fourth in the individual competition in Montreal, and **Janou Lefèbvre** (FRA) earned team silver medals in Tokyo and Mexico, also taking the World Ladies title in 1970 and 1974, and the European in 1966. The youngest winner of the European Championship was Britain's **Ann Townsend** (at nineteen), and the most versatile was **Anneli Drummond-Hay** (GB), who, having won the Burghley and Badminton three day events with Merely a Monarch, took the European title with him in 1968, and also won the Hickstead Derby with Xanthos. The late **Caroline Bradley** (GB) won team gold medals at the 1978 World and the 1979 European Championships, and won the Hamburg Derby in 1975 and the Queen Elizabeth II Cup in 1978 and 1980. **Liz Edgar**, wife of Ted and sister of David Broome, has won five Queen Elizabeth II Cups and the Aachen and New York Grands Prix.

From Canada **Gail Greenhough** came to Aachen in 1986 to trounce the men in the World Championship by being the only rider to jump clear on all four horses in the final. The ladies of the United States seem to have made the World Cup Final a speciality of theirs; **Melanie Smith** was second in 1980, won in 1982 and was third in 1983; and they produced the runner-up in 1979, **Katie Monahan**, the winners in 1986 and 1987, **Leslie Burr-Lenehan** and **Katherine Burdsall**, and the third in 1987, **Lisa Jacquin**. But perhaps the most stylish of the American ladies was **Mary Mairs**, who with Tomboy rode for the successful United States team of 1962, 1963 and 1964, and, after marrying Frank Chapot, 1965 and 1966, also winning the Pan American Games of 1963.

Finally, mention must be made of two riders from Australia. **Jeff McVean** came to England in the seventies, bringing with him an acrobatic style that amazed all who saw it, but which he soon realised was unsuited to the demanding European courses, and in 1978 he won the King George V Gold Cup in London. The other is **Kevin Bacon**, in 1989 surely the senior rider (in age) on the European circuit, but still capable of winning the Biarritz Grand Prix in the autumn of that year.

Pat Koechlin-Smythe (GB) – Ladies European Championship 1957, 1961, 1962 and 1963 – Flanagan (Leslie Lane)

France

PIERRE JONQUÈRES D'ORIOLA

Only three riders have ever won two individual Olympic gold medals: a Dutchman, Charles Pahud de Mortanges for the three day event in 1928 and 1932; a New Zealander, Mark Todd for the same sport in 1984 and 1988; and a Frenchman, Pierre Jonquères d'Oriola for jumping in 1952 and twelve years later in 1964. During an international career that started in 1947 (and but for World War II would have started earlier) and continued through to the seventies, he also won the World Championship and silver and bronze medals, was runner-up in the European Championship, won two Olympic team silver medals, was four times champion of France, rode in over a hundred Nations Cups, winning twenty of them, and recorded a host of major Grands Prix wins, including the King George V Gold Cup in London and those in Aachen, Brussels, Lucerne, Paris, Rome and Madrid.

How great a part heredity plays in the emergence of a great horseman will for ever remain a subject for discussion, but certainly d'Oriola's ancestry gave him every advantage that might be available in this respect. His grandfather was Ecuyer (Instructor) to the Cadre Noir at Saumur, and his father was a distinguished jumping rider who gave Pierre his first lessons on a pony when he was only four years old. 'My greatest pleasure,' he recalls, 'was to gallop and jump across the country near our home.'

Pierre learned also from Colonel St André, and from two well respected figures on the international scene in post war years, Colonels Cavaillé and Clavé, the first as Chef d'Equipe to the French team and the second as an International Judge. And it was with the French team in 1947 that Pierre first made his mark on the international circuit. In those days in Nations Cups there was a prize for the best individual performance, and at Nice in 1947 the French won the cup and Pierre took the individual prize. All in all his debut was an impressive one, for with the brilliant little Anglo-Arab gelding Marquis III he also helped France to win the Nations Cups in Lucerne, London and Ostend, and won the King George V Gold Cup at the White City and the Ostend Grand Prix.

Competition for inclusion in the Olympic team for London in 1948 was intense, with only three riders permitted, and with Jean d'Orgeix, the bronze medallist, Max Fresson (equal seventh) and Pierre Maupeou selected, D'Oriola had to wait until 1952 in Helsinki for his chance. Riding the Anglo-Arab gelding Ali-Baba in the two round competition for both team and individual medals, in the first round, in which Fritz Thiedemann achieved the only clear round for Germany on Meteor, Pierre lowered two fences which left him in twelfth place.

But in the second round Meteor lowered two while Ali-Baba jumped the only clear

Pierre Jonquères d'Oriola (France), double Olympic Champion, riding Voulette at the White City, London 1958 (Sport & General)

round, and a jump-off for the medals between the five riders on a total of eight penalties ensued. Wilf White (Great Britain), who but for an unlucky foot in the water would have won the individual gold medal outright with four penalties, lowered three, Meteor and Bigua (for Brazil) lowered two each, Oscar Cristi and Bambi secured the silver medal for Chile, and only Ali-Baba jumped clear to give Pierre the gold.

The following year saw the first running of the World Championships, in Paris, and at the end of the three qualifying competitions Pierre, again with Ali-Baba, had achieved easily the best performance with placings of second, equal first and first. But in the change-horse final the joker in the pack was Piero d'Inzeo's Uruguay, who amassed a total of thirty-two penalties, four each for Francisco Goyoaga (Spain) and Fritz Thiedemann, and twelve each for Pierre and, surprisingly enough for Piero. In the end Pierre's clear rounds on Ali-Baba and on Goyoaga's Quorum, and one fence down on Thiedemann's Diamant were good enough to give him the bronze medal behind the Spaniard and the German in that order.

In 1954's World Championship – they were held annually until 1956 and thereafter every four years – the holder of the title entered the final on a wild card in addition to the four qualifiers, and again Pierre, this time on Arlequin D, showed much the best form in the qualifying competitions. But he had to be content with the silver medal in the final behind Hans Günter Winkler for Germany.

The 1955 formula was even less comprehensible, for the four riders qualified for the final could ride different horses from those on which they had qualified, and when a jump-off was also found to be necessary between Winkler and Raimondo d'Inzeo, neither of them rode the horses that they had ridden in the final! For the final Winkler nominated Orient in place of the perhaps easier Halla, and Ronnie Dallas (Great Britain) replaced Marmion with Bones, with whom Pierre could establish no rapport and had to be content with fourth place.

But eleven years later in Buenos Aires (1966) Pierre, now forty-six years of age and riding the mare Pomone B, took the Championship in a final in which the sixteen rounds produced no fewer than 100.25 penalties. (And on this occasion the faults of a rider on his own horse were augmented by 25 per cent and the silver medallist, José Alvarez de Bohorques (Spain) equalled Pierre's score but faulted three times on his own horse!)

But the crowning achievement of Pierre's long career came in 1964 at the Tokyo Olympics. Again one competition decided the team and individual medals, and in the first round no one had jumped clear, Pierre's nine penalties on Lutteur B leaving him in fourth place behind Peter Robeson (Great Britain), John Fahey of Australia and Joaquim Duarte Silva of Portugal. As Pierre entered the arena for the second round only Hermann Schridde and Dozent for Germany had jumped clear but with 1.25 time penalties. Pierre's round was a truly classic performance, clear and within the time. Once again he was Olympic Champion, and team silver medallist as well.

Meanwhile the formula for the European Championships had also been subject to experiment and change, and in 1959 in Paris the change-horse final was used. With participation still allowed from outside Europe, the competition was as hot as it has ever been; with Hugh Wiley and William Steinkraus of the USA in fifth and sixth places, the final was contested by four superstars in the shape of Hans Günter Winkler, Piero d'Inzeo, Fritz Thiedemann and Pierre d'Oriola, who ended up with the silver medal behind Piero d'Inzeo. (For some reason his brother Raimondo was not entered on the somewhat odd grounds that the reigning World Champion should not compete at this lower level.)

Whilst continuing to win his share of the major Grands Prix, Pierre continued also to make his presence felt at the European Championships, finishing eighth in 1967 in Rotterdam and fourth in 1969 at Hickstead, and fourth again in Aachen with Tournebride in 1971, the year in which he won his final major Grand Prix, the Aachen Championship, with Moët et Chandon.

Now retiring from major international competition, Pierre began to spend more time on his farm and his vineyards near Perpignan, on the Mediterranean coast just North of the Spanish border. But even in his seventieth year he still rides. 'Yes, certainly,' he says, 'and even in certain competitions confined to veteran riders!', and he is a welcome and familiar sight at the many shows to which he is invited, and especially at the World Cup show in Bordeaux. But thinking back to the days when he was in his prime he has certain misgivings about the sport today.

I think that it has become too artificial. We must not let the spectacular side take precedence over the natural and truly sporting side of equestrian sport. I think that each show ought to keep its own particular character and tradition, and I also would like to see more variation in the types of obstacle, and in some cases more solid fences.

He finds advice to the young rider of today not easy to give, 'Because I was an instinctive rider, and I never worked very hard at it. But above all I would say that a young rider must have two qualities – patience and the will to win.'

But though Pierre may not admit to having worked hard at his riding, he certainly set an example which any young rider would be wise to follow. His style combined the natural flair that has always been the hallmark of the best French riders with a calmness that brought the best out of the many horses that he took to the top – Ali-Baba, Arlequin, Aiglonne, Charleston, Lutteur, L'Historiette, Marquis III, Virtuoso, Voulette, to name just a few. And if the mark of the truly great horseman is to achieve a considerable number of victories against the highest opposition on a number of different horses over a considerable period of time, then none deserves this accolade more than Pierre Jonquères d'Oriola.

Germany

HANS GÜNTER WINKLER

There are many who would say that in Hans Günter Winkler Germany has produced the greatest jumping rider of all time, and certainly his record of seven Olympic medals, five of them gold, two World Championships and a European Championship, forty-two winning appearances for Germany in Nations Cups, and victories in virtually all the World's major Grands Prix is unlikely ever to be bettered.

For many great riders, World War II either brought their careers to an abrupt end, or it delayed their start so that they were nearing the normal age for retirement as soon as they neared the top. For Winkler, though the situation in Germany at the end of the war was far from promising for anyone contemplating a sporting career, it nevertheless provided the spur to his ambition, which had always been to become a great rider in the model of the German Cavalry officers who had been so successful in the immediate pre-war years.

His family, originally from Frankfurt on Oder, on what is now East Germany's border with Poland, moved to Wuppertal in the West, where Hans Günter was born in 1926. His first pony arrived when he was six.

'He wasn't like the English ponies, he was very naughty and bad tempered, a real monster, and my first success was to dominate and school this mean animal.'

He had dreamed of becoming a cavalry officer, but the year 1942 saw him, at the age of sixteen, in the Light Artillery. During the very last weeks of the war his father was killed, and his mother was living alone in bombed out Frankfurt (on Maine). It was, as he says, a time for survival, for trying to obtain enough food. But a friend of his father's, Herr Eckhardt, had run the stables of the Landgräfin of Hessen in Kronberg, and though most horses had been requisitioned for the German Army, some of the best had been allowed to remain with their owners. Here Hans Günter worked the horses and learned the rudiments of dressage.

At this stage this young man's ambition and dedication might well have been exploited by USET (the United States Equestrian Team) instead of the DOKR (Deutsche Olympiade Kommittee fur Reiterei). The US Army had taken over Schloss Kronberg, and most mornings young Winkler was sent out riding as escort to General Eisenhower, who later as President of the United States was to receive the World Champion at the White House. A member of the General's staff offered him the chance of emigrating to the States and of becoming an American citizen. But, though such a proposition must have seemed unbelievably attractive to a young man in Germany then, this would have meant abandoning his mother, and he declined the offer.

But his first taste of success did come in American uniform! There were various local military teams that used to compete at shows run by the Army, and the Kronberg team were determined to win. 'So they put me in an American lieutenant's uniform, and we won.'

Then Hans Günter rode racehorses for a while, and gained useful experience until the trainer legged him up one morning and realised he was on the heavy side for a jockey, whereupon he only gave him the less fancied rides. In 1948 came the opportunity to ride jumpers, and he managed to buy his first horse for 600 marks. Eventually after several successes he was noticed by Dr Gustav Rau, who was endeavouring to revive the sport of jumping in Germany at that time. In 1949 the first German team to compete since the war took part in the British Rhine Army Show at Bad Lippspringe; it consisted of Fritz Thiedemann, Georg Eppelsheimer, Hans Günter Winkler, and Freiherr von Nagel, cousin of Clemens von Nagel, who bred so many good jumping horses at Vornholz. In 1950 Hans Günter was invited to train at Warendorf, and in 1952 he rode in his first Nations Cup in Bilbao, Spain, but this trip was not the greatest success.

It was a disaster. I spent more time in the fences than over them! Although my early idol had been Micky Brinckmann, I was now riding with Fritz Thiedemann, but his style, on his heavy Holstein horses, didn't suit my horses, and when I saw French riders like d'Oriola, Lefrant and du Breuil, I realised that a more forward style, 'galloping with control', was what was needed for horses like Rebell and Halla.

Halla was foaled in 1945 out of a French mare by a trotting stallion, and started life on the racecourse, winning a steeplechase in Frankfurt. Dr Rau persuaded her owner Gustav Vierling to let her train as a three day event horse for the 1952 Olympics in Helsinki, for which she proved temperamentally unsuited. But apart from that, one of the other riders in training, no doubt hoping to enhance his own prospects, objected to Winkler on the grounds that he was, technically at any rate, a professional. Hans Günter was precluded from further consideration for the Games, but was able to disprove the allegation, and meanwhile he had been offered Halla as a jumper.

Halla was really a freak. She could jump unbelievably wide, up to seven metres, and had unlimited scope, but was almost impossible to ride. No other horse has ever sent so many poles flying. It took me two years to train her. Gradually she came to understand that she must jump high, and then we started winning, and after that she jumped the Puissance as if she was jumping cavaletti.

In 1952 Hans Günter was German Champion for the first time, in 1953 he won the King of Cambodia's Trophy for the most successful rider in the world in international shows, and in 1954 he won the World Championship in Madrid with Halla and Alpenjager. The following year he successfully defended his World title in Aachen in a jump-off with Raimondo d'Inzeo, and in 1956 he joined Fritz Thiedemann and Alfons Lütke-Westhues for the Olympic Games in Stockholm. The story of the German team's success and of Winkler's own gold medal is legendary.

As we approached the penultimate fence, a vertical at 1.6m (5ft 3in), we were clear so far, and no other rider in the first round had achieved less than eight faults. Because Halla didn't have the best of front legs I had to bring her close to her fences, and because of her temperament I had always to sit lightly and ride her with a long rein. But now she took off early, and because I had pulled a muscle five weeks before, she threw me into the air, and I ruptured the stomach muscles. Five strides away was the final gate, and because I could do nothing, she had it down. But fortunately the finish was directly beyond the gate, and at the end of the round we were in the lead with four faults.

In those days there were no medical facilities like we have today, and with only three riders in the team, which was also in the lead, I had to ride again. I knew that if I allowed myself to be taken to hospital I wouldn't come out. I also knew that if I let the team down people would never forgive me; if I had broken something people would have understood, but because there was nothing to see it was different. They gave me some tranquillisers, and as long as I was sitting down it was OK. But then, after two hours, I had to remount and it was a disaster.

Dr Büsing, our vet, gave me some pills, but the trouble was that the medicines in those days were not very sophisticated, and anything strong enough to kill the pain also dulled the brain! Then they gave me more pills, and finally some morphia, and I managed one or two practice jumps. But then I began to feel dizzy and to have double vision, so I was given some strong black coffee. And so I entered the Olympic arena.

Then came the miracle. Halla was just like a dog, she realised that I was ill and felt that I couldn't help her. All I could do was to guide her to the fences, and when she took off I could only sit back, falling onto her as she landed, and I couldn't help crying out with pain. Partly because of this and partly because of my light way of riding her on a long rein, she didn't run away as she would have done before, and she just helped herself. It was a very big, stiff course with a lot of distance problems, but she jumped clear.

So Hans Günter won the individual gold medal ahead of the two d'Inzeo brothers, and Germany took the team title. In subsequent Olympics, Halla was fifth in Rome in 1960, and second best individual in the team competition which brought Hans Günter his third gold medal; Fidelitas and Torphy brought home team gold medals from Tokyo and Munich, and Enigk (fifth individual) and Torphy won team bronze and silver in Mexico and Montreal respectively.

As well as winning two World Championships, Halla won the European Championships in 1957 (together with Sonnenglanz), and was third in 1958 in Aachen and fourth in 1959 in Paris. Hans Günter was third in 1961 in Aachen and shared the silver medal with Piero d'Inzeo in London in 1962 (with Romanus and Feuerdorn), and was third again at Hickstead in 1969. He has won almost all the major Grands Prix in the world, including three in Aachen and two King George V Gold Cups in London. For Germany he has ridden in 107 Nations Cups, in which the team won forty-two times and were only outside the first three on fifteen occasions.

What enabled him to be so successful?

OPPOSITE
Hans Günter Winkler (Germany) with Halla at the Olympic Games, Stockholm 1956 (F. Peyer)

I think a strong will was a big help. After the war in Germany I was determined to be a success. Then I think that to succeed as a rider you must become a complete horseman. It's like motor racing, it's not just a question of driving, you must know your engine and know about tyres. It's the same with horses, it's not only riding and jumping. I was schooled in dressage, I rode in races and three day events – I was second and third in Bad Harzburg and in Bad Hersfeld – and I schooled horses to Class 'S' in dressage – one of those I trained took part in the Helsinki Olympics.

You need luck, but you can make your own luck to a certain extent, and attention to small details can just make the difference between winning and losing. A good rider will win, but when he loses he analyses the reasons, like Lester Piggott.

So what would be his advice to a young rider?

I am now very much involved with the training of young international riders, and it's much more difficult than it used to be. In the old days we jumped farm horses; now we breed jumpers. But the quality of riding hasn't kept pace. When I started we had very little; riders were tougher, they had to think more, and give more of themselves. To succeed you have to go beyond your own limitations. Today's riders have it too easy, they don't understand the effort needed, and they think they can buy their way to the top.

But you can't succeed without a proper base, so my advice would be to become a complete horseman through sound basic training. Why are the Americans so successful? They can field three Nations Cup teams at any time. Because they have a proper system of basic training for their riders, who are taught how to sit on a horse properly, and from this base comes success in dressage, jumping or three day events.

Hans Günter has mixed views on the state of the sport today.

Having just come back from Aachen, with 45,000 spectators for the Grand Prix, wonderful jumping and good sport, I'm tempted to say that all is well. Certainly we are one of the better sports. But where there's a lot of sun, there's a lot of shadow too. There has been an explosive increase in riding, but the base for it hasn't grown. In the old days the base came from the Cavalry; grooms had been orderlies, instructors·in the country riding clubs had been sergeant-majors, the officers filled the higher positions and the general was in charge of the whole thing. They were all horsemen, and they all loved horses.

Now they think you can make a horseman in three years. For example, if you want an English groom you don't take one of those who has been officially trained and who has initials after his name, you take someone with plenty of experience from one of the big competition stables. Also, an Army career gave people security. People like Colonel Mike [Sir Michael Ansell] weren't afraid to make unpopular decisions, and they knew how to deal with the 'difficult' riders. The new functionaries want above all to keep their own positions, so they are making compromises.

So what improvements would he like to see on the international scene?

I wouldn't change much, but I'd like to see the Rule Book used firmly for the good of the sport. If the FEI isn't prepared to act, then the riders must do something. I think we have fewer black sheep than other sports, but we must control them and clean up the sport. People talk about the use of drugs and the rapping or polling and the blistering of horses' legs that goes on at shows, but no one is prepared to be specific about who is doing these things. In racing they are much tougher in these matters.

We have the rules and they must be applied. People think that democracy means complete freedom to do what you want, but it really means self-discipline for each person, and democracy only works where you have strong leaders. The successful riders are all self-disciplined.

We must also think of our horses. Today with the World Cup there is no rest, and all these big shows want the top riders with their best horses. In racing if you have a Classic horse you don't run him very often, but in jumping I think we have to make rules to protect the horse. Also, the top riders no longer have the time to bring on their young horses, whereas we used the winter for schooling. Now if they lose a top horse they have to buy another one.

Certainly Hans Günter in his time schooled and produced a host of young horses. Everyone associates him with Halla, but they tend to forget all the other Grand Prix and Nations Cup winners – Orient, Fidelitas, Enigk, Alpenjäger, Sonnenglanz, Romanus, Feuerdorn, Fortun, Cornelia and Torphy. But after Halla he considers the unfortunate Terminus to have had the greatest potential. A big thoroughbred, he joined Hans Günter only a month before leaving for the North American circuit in 1970, and after winning a class in Harrisburg he went on to win a speed class, the Puissance and the Grand Prix in New York. Then the next season in Dublin, when jumping off he slipped on a bad patch of ground on the approach to a huge silver birch oxer, tried to jump the fence, and turned a somersault. Though it was a spectacular fall, both horse and rider seemed unhurt. But one of the heavy birch poles 'whipped', fell on Terminus and broke his fore leg.

Now Hans Günter lives on the outskirts of Warendorf in the lovely house that he built in the woods and has since several times extended, surrounded by countless silver trophies and mementoes of a career that spanned four decades. In his stable, amongst a myriad of rosettes, is a selection of young horses, looked after by a Scottish lad and ridden by a young rider whom he is training. Responsible for the training of young riders for the German team, he also acts as public relations consultant for one of the largest German companies, and in his spare time – when there is any – enjoys game shooting, tennis, swimming and skiing.

In spite of all the advantages that are available to the top riders of today, it is unlikely that anyone will ever equal Hans Günter Winkler's tally of Olympic, World and Continental Championship medals, nor his record of success in Nations Cups and in the major Grands Prix of the World. He is what he advises young riders to try to become – the complete horseman.

WILLIAM STEINKRAUS

The FEI is fortunate to have as a Bureau member and as President of the World Cup Committee someone who is not only one of the world's most accomplished and stylish horsemen, and an Olympic Champion, but who also has the breadth of vision of someone whose career has been spent, when not in the saddle, in the world of business. Add the sensitivity of a practising musician, and his admission of a real love of horses, and you find someone who is deeply concerned about the best interests of the sport.

Bill Steinkraus was born in Ohio, though his earliest memories are of Connecticut where his family moved four years later. They had no equestrian background, but Bill discovered horses during his first visit to summer camp at the age of ten; by his second year they couldn't tear him away from the stables, and complained that he didn't seem too interested in other activities. From then on his riding developed as the opportunities presented themselves.

His first instructor was a lady riding teacher in Connecticut who kept a pack of foxhounds. He whipped-in to her, and she instilled in Bill a love of hunting which he has never lost. His next was Gordon Wright (who also taught George Morris, who was later to ride with Bill on United States teams), and the third was M. W. 'Cappy' Smith, a famous dealer, who gave him the opportunity to gain experience on a large number of high class jumpers. In 1941 came his first big success with victory in the United States Equitation Championships, both on the flat and for jumping.

Then in 1943 came the entry of the United States into World War II, and Bill found himself in the 124th Cavalry Regiment destined for India, where they were to meet up with horses from Australia, en route to relieve Merrill's Marauders against the Japanese in Burma. 'We took all our saddles and bridles and equipment, but ended up not with horses but with mules. Eventually we and a sister regiment went into Burma as an infantry brigade with all our artillery, mortars and heavy equipment carried by these animals. If it hadn't been for them we wouldn't have made it, as the only way to get up some of the slopes was to hang on to the mules' tails.'

In 1945 Bill returned home to complete his university education and to resume competition riding, and six years later he won a place on the United States Equestrian Team (USET). But in those days it was still possible to combine a sporting career with a professional one, and apart from horses another passion of Bill's had always been music. He had learned to play the violin, and had then progressed to the viola, since that instrument opened the door to playing with a symphony orchestra. And though this was primarily a hobby – and he still plays the viola in chamber music today – he was for a time involved professionally in concert management, and his career might well have developed in that field had not an opening presented itself in Wall Street, and through that another role in the world of books. It was in this field, as an editor and publisher, that his career finally developed.

Meanwhile he had ridden in his first Nations Cup in 1951, and the following year he rode the gelding Hollandia to eleventh place and a team bronze medal in the Helsinki Olympic Games. Four years later he became one of only two riders ever to be first and second (with First Boy and Night Owl) in the King George V Gold Cup at the White City, London, and rode Night Owl into fifteenth place at the Stockholm Olympics. The Grand Prix of Rotterdam in 1958 (Ksar d'Esprit) and the International Championship of Germany in Aachen in 1959 (Riviera Wonder) were followed by team silver medal and another fifteenth place in the Rome Olympics of 1960 and a second King George V victory in 1964, with Sinjon.

Mexico in 1968 provided the high point of Bill's equestrian career, when he won the individual gold medal with Snowbound. The Olympic Games always means more than any other sporting event, and ever since 1912 the United States had been trying to win a gold medal for jumping. 'So my lucky performance in Mexico – and it takes plenty of luck for everything to come just right on that one day out of four years – was the culmination of a lot of effort by many people over half a century.'

An interesting horse that Bill rode was the grey Bold Minstrel. After bringing home team silver medals from the three day events at the Pan American Games and the Tokyo Olympics, he was taken over by Bill and won a team silver medal for jumping at the 1967 Panam Games and then numerous international jumping competitions in North America and Europe, setting the Puissance record at Madison Square Garden at 7ft 3in (2.21m). 'In his prime,' says Bill, 'he could have made anybody's Olympic team in any of the three disciplines.'

In 1971 Bill returned to the White City to win the John Player Championship with Fleet Apple, on whom he scored his thirty-fifth and thirty-sixth Nations Cup wins at Aachen and Harrisburg. His final three wins were on Main Spring in 1972, to add to well over a hundred individual international victories. On his last Olympic appearance for USET at Munich, Snowbound was lame after the individual competition, but in the team competition on Main Spring he returned the best individual score of the day with just one fence down over the two rounds to give the USA the Silver Medal. Retirement from the saddle at the end of that year by no means ended his involvement with USET, for as President and later Chairman he presided over their many successes over the next two decades.

Looking back on his career, Bill reflects upon the reasons for his success, and on the advice he would give to a young rider today.

I think my success has been due to favourable preconditions, to many people who gave me the best they had, to a degree of natural talent, and especially to a lot of hard work. I don't think that anyone can succeed in sport or in life on talent alone. All those who have been successful have been hard workers; some were not even very talented to begin with, but they made up for that by application. I was also a monomaniac about horses, so for me it didn't seem like work. I adored horses and still feel like a king when I am in the saddle, and I am thankful that I never reached the point where riding was an obligation rather than a pleasure. It has always amazed me that this wonderful animal, one of God's finest creations, with all its remarkable physical

attributes, is prepared, and mostly with very good grace, to do the sometimes quite extraordinary things we ask it to do.

To the parent of a child I would say 'Be sure that you are not imposing your own ambition on your child'. Then if the child really wants to make a career with horses, I would say, 'Be sure that you really love it, because there will be a lot of cold wet days and a lot of drudgery, and if you don't really love horses, do something else'. I would then advise the young rider to get as sound a foundation as possible, and then to be prepared to accept opportunities as they occur. For example, there comes a time when a young rider must move on from one teacher to another. It may be difficult to make the move out of loyalty to the existing teacher, but unless opportunities are accepted as they present themselves, a rider will never progress.

Then there will come a time when a rider must get out on his own; he can't always rely on the advice of his teacher, eventually he will have to make his own decisions. An excellent example of this is Steve Cauthen; if he hadn't taken the decision to move to England when the opportunity presented itself, I don't think he would have been the rider that he is today.

In response to a question concerning the relationship between music and riding, Bill has some interesting observations on the interaction of the two.

There was recently a study carried out on the development of an athlete and a musician, and the conclusion was that to achieve success each must progress through the hands of several teachers; the first must be someone who can install the basic fundamentals and at the same time develop the enthusiasm and passion of the child; the second teacher must teach him to be technically proficient; and the third must be world class. And to succeed he must reach the third stage by the time he is sixteen. I was lucky enough to have, in effect, these three teachers, and some great coaching later on as well.

There are perhaps some superficial connections between music and riding, sensitive hands, a sense of rhythm and flow for example, but there are a couple of specific things that I learned as a musician which I found much more helpful. The first is the musician's way of isolating difficult technical problems, breaking them down and reducing them to the simplest terms, then practising them separately and putting them back together. With the violin, for example, if you have a difficult passage, you analyse the problems, break them down into passages for the left hand and for the bow arm, develop exercises to overcome the problems, and then put the whole passage back together, so that in the end you can play the passage which was so difficult before.

You can do the same thing with a difficult riding problem; you can isolate the things that make it difficult, develop exercises that enable the horse to overcome them, and then put it all back together. This makes it much easier for the horse than trying to work it all out at once. Let us see how this might apply to jumping, for example.

A course can be broken down into four basic ingredients: the line or track, the striding or distance between fences, the type and size of fences, and the speed at which the course must be ridden. In training each of these problems can be reduced to its simplest terms. The obstacles, for example, can be reduced to something well within the horse's capability, leaving only the problems of line, striding and speed to be solved; you can use gymnastic exercises to solve distance problems, again using obstacles that are well within the horse's capability; different types of obstacles and varying speeds can be treated in a similar way, and finally you can put the whole thing together in order to jump a course.

I have found this way of solving problems to be particularly helpful. I have also found that the way in which a musician memorises a composition can be adapted to memorising a course, so that I memorise not just the separate obstacles but firstly the basic structure or layout of the course and then the connection between each obstacle.

From his viewpoint in the FEI Bill is well qualified to air his views on the state of the sport today.

I think the quality at the top is not necessarily higher than in the past, but it is higher in the middle, and at the bottom it is immeasurably higher, both as regards riders and horses. The great riders and great horses of the past would still be great today, and they would have adapted to today's conditions. In fact conditions were sometimes more difficult in the past than they are today. Games courses, for example, were bigger, and distances tougher. In the Rome Olympics we had a distance of thirty feet, one and a half strides, from a triple bar to an oxer. Today the Chefs d'Equipe wouldn't allow that to happen.

I think our sport has benefited from increased public involvement, especially through television, and I think we have kept or even improved our position in the world of sporting entertainment. However, I fear that the business aspect of sport is beginning to take precedence over everything else, and this is very dangerous. This is even beginning to apply to the Olympic Games, which for me are something unique and not just another television special.

With his intense love of horses, Bill is acutely aware of the need to protect horses from ambitious riders, owners or sponsors.

If you have a top class racehorse you may only run him eight or ten times a year, even though there is a stakes race every week. I think jumping riders have to learn in the same way to pick and choose, to plan a campaign for their horses, because there's a very true saying, 'If you don't wait for your horse, he's surely going to make you wait for him'. The ultimate responsibility lies with riders; too many good horses arrive at the World Cup Final or World Championships without enough petrol left in the tank. The great riders plan for the great occasions: Hans Winkler was a wonderful rider who achieved a very high percentage of his victories in important competitions; Joe Fargis is the same, he hardly ever wastes his horses trying to win a small class.

In general I think we have to regulate the sport so as to protect the horse, for example, to improve the footing in jumping arenas, to eliminate some of the things that are practised in order to make a horse jump more cleanly, and to improve course building and judging. But on the whole I think the top administrators are able and dedicated people who have the best interests of the sport at heart.

On the question of championships, Bill feels that the present formula for the European and Continental Championships is about right (a speed class on the first day, a Nations Cup on the second, and a Grand Prix on the third).

If the first competition is run over a large enough course, then judging it on Table 'C' does ensure that the rider whose horse has one unlucky fence down is not completely without hope. If it were under Table 'A', if the course builder had made the course slightly too easy there might be a dozen clear rounds and no rider with a fence down would have a chance. As it is he may be able to climb back. [In Rotterdam in 1989, for example, the Olympic Champions Pierre Durand and Jappaloup were able to climb from nineteenth position after the first day to fourth after the second.] But the course for the first day must be big enough, and not just a 'scurry'.

I do have reservations, however, regarding the formula for the World Championship, where the four riders in the final ride each other's horses. I ask myself three questions. Is it reasonable to determine the World Champion in a final in which all four riders start from scratch? Should not their performances during their progress to the final count? And what most truly distinguishes the World Champion? Is it what he can do on a strange horse in a couple of minutes over a moderate course? And finally, is it reasonable to determine the World Champion by using a form of competition – 'catch' riding – that is otherwise hardly even a part of our sport? (Our last Champion, Gail Greenhough, had never ridden in such a competition in her life!) Of course, the public love the final (and so do some riders), but I think there is room for improvement here, and I hope that this will evolve.

Certainly the evolvement of international jumping will lie in safe hands so long as Bill Steinkraus' influence can be brought to bear, because for him the welfare of the horse is of prime importance.

William Steinkraus (USA) – Olympic Champion 1968 – Bold Minstrel (Olympic team silver medal, Three Day Event, Tokyo, and international show jumper)

Italy

PIERO D'INZEO

Findlay Davidson

Think or speak of Italian show jumping, and immediately it is the brothers d'Inzeo who come to mind. For thirty years, between 1947 and 1977, they completely dominated the sport in their own country, and between them won almost every major prize on the international circuit. So complete was their domination that since their retirement Italy has no longer been the force that she was. Since 1977, when Piero won the Barcelona Grand Prix on Easter Light and both brothers rode on the winning Nations Cup team, there have been very few Italian victories in Nations Cups or Grands Prix, and not a single Italian medal in the Olympic Games, World or European Championships or the World Cup. During the period of the d'Inzeos' involvement Italy headed the table for individual Olympic medals, came second to Germany in the world Championship individual rankings and were third behind Germany and Great Britain in the European ratings, and there was scarcely a Nations Cup in Europe in which the Italian team did not figure prominently.

Their father, Carlo Costante d'Inzeo, was a warrant officer instructor in the Italian cavalry, and it was he who started them on their paths to success. Piero was set on a military career from the start, and in 1942, at the age of nineteen, he entered the Military Academy at Modena. In 1946 he made his first appearance on the Italian team, and the following year scored his first Nations Cup victory at Rome's Piazza di Siena with Tulipano. In 1948 he made the first of eight Olympic appearances with Italy's show jumping team, but the experience was far from happy, since his own horse fell ill shortly before the Games, and he rode Briacone, who was eliminated for knocking down the flag on the first fence – for which today there is no penalty.

Later in the year Piero won the first of two successive Grands Prix in Paris with the massive Destino, and he then formed a partnership with the first of his great horses, the French-bred Uruguay, with whom he won the first of his four Aachen Grands Prix in 1952. But at the Helsinki Olympic games of that year, when he had justifiably high hopes of a medal, he was eliminated for missing his start time after a misunderstanding concerning the procedure for weighing out before jumping. He was, however, sixth in the three day event on Pagoro.

The year 1953 saw the inauguration of the World Championship in Paris, and after qualifying for the change horse final with Uruguay, Piero finished in fourth place. Meanwhile he and Uruguay had established themselves as the mainstays of the Italian team, winning Nations Cups in Aachen in 1952, and in Rome (1952, 1953 and 1955), and in Paris and Pinerolo (1955). Then came Piero's first moment of triumph at the

Stockholm Olympics of 1956. In the single competition for team and individual medals, Uruguay finished the first round in equal third position, and just one refusal in the second round gave them the bronze medal behind Hans Günter Winkler and his brother Raimondo, with Italy taking the team silver medal.

In 1957 Uruguay took the first of Piero's three King George V Gold Cups at the White City, London, and the following year saw the beginning of four notable appearances in the European Championships. Amongst the many great horses that he produced Piero is perhaps best remembered for his performance on the Irish gelding The Rock. A big strong grey, often fighting for his head but sympathetically and quietly ridden, he separated Meteor (Fritz Thiedemann) and Halla (Hans Günter Winkler) for the silver medal at the 1958 Championships in Aachen. In 1959 they won the Championship in Paris from Pierre Jonquères d'Oriola, two years later Piero was again runner-up in Aachen to David Broome, and in 1962 he shared the silver medal with Winkler at the Rome Olympics.

During this period The Rock won two successive King George V Gold Cups in London, two Grands Prix in Aachen, as well as those in Barcelona, Dortmund, Dublin, Lucerne and Rome, and at the 1960 Olympics at the Piazza di Siena they took the silver medal behind Raimondo as well as team bronze. But Piero had the ability to train and ride many different horses, and his seven victories in the Rome Grand Prix were all obtained on six different mounts: The Rock in 1958, Sunbeam (1962), Navarette (1967), Fidux (1968), Red Fox (1970), and Easter Light in 1973 and 1976.

When he retired from active participation in international competition, Piero had ridden in over forty winning Nations Cup teams, a record bettered only by Frank Chapot (USA). But his equestrian career had not been pursued entirely at the expense of the military; towards the end of his military service he commanded the Reconnaissance Squadron of the Montebello Lancers, stationed just outside Rome, and was finally Commandant of the Officers School at Caserta.

Looking back on his long competitive equestrian career, the moments he likes to remember best concern not his eight Olympic appearances nor his six Olympic medals, nor his European Championship, but his three victories in the King George V Gold Cup at the White City, London, with Uruguay in 1957 and with The Rock in 1961 and 1962. And after a career that spanned more than three decades he has forthright views on the state of the sport today and the direction in which it is heading.

The sport is quite different today from what it was when I was competing. Now there are no more sportsmen, only professionals. One of the reasons for this lies in the modern form of sponsorship. The sport would be in much better shape if sponsorship were confined to events and competitions rather than individual riders. Then riders would have to save their horses in order to win the major prizes, whereas, today, if a rider loses a good horse he expects his sponsor to buy him another.

And young riders today do not seem to be prepared to work hard enough at their sport. Patience, dedication, hard work and sacrifice form the basis for success, and a young rider must realise that before expecting success in competitions he must prepare himself by achieving a sound basis of general equitation.

Piero's outstanding success as a show jumping rider has overshadowed his other achievements. Apart from his sixth place in the three day event in the Helsinki Olympic Games of 1952 he has also ridden with distinction on the polo field, in steeplechases and in other cross-country events. Nor are his sporting interests confined entirely to horses; he is a keen yachtsman, and these days, though he still rides and trains young horses, he likes nothing better than to escape to the coast for a day's sailing.

The care which he exercised in the training and production of his young horses, and the length of their careers in top-class internatioonal competition, are evidence of his skills as a rider and of his love of the horse. His quiet but firm style of riding was typical of the best of Italian horsemanship, and he must be considered one of the best judges of stride that the world of show jumping has ever seen.

Piero d'Inzeo (Italy) – eight Olympic appearances and six medals. Seen RIGHT *riding his 1957 King George V Gold Cup winner Uruguay at the White City, London. He won his second and third King George V Gold Cups on The Rock,* BELOW, *in 1961 and 1962 (Leslie Lane)*

Italy

RAIMONDO D'INZEO

Findlay Davidson

The younger of the two d'Inzeo brothers was born in 1925 and like Piero started riding at the age of nine under the expert tuition of his father. He competed successfully in junior competitions, but for a while it seemed that he was more interested in a career in engineering than with horses, and he completed two years of a university engineering course before joining the Italian cavalry. In 1952 he transferred to the Carabiniere, a force of paramilitary police which to this day retains a mounted regiment in Rome. It would be a brave man who endeavoured to pronounce on the relative merits of the two brothers as horsemen, but though their style of riding was similar, thanks to their father, if Piero was in some ways the more stylish, then Raimondo was perhaps the more competitive. What is in no doubt is the debt that Italy and the world of jumping owes to these two brothers: between 1947 and 1977 there were very few Italian teams that did not include at least one, and usually two, d'Inzeos. Scarcely an important individual trophy does not bear the name of one or other or both of them as winners.

Raimondo's first appearance in the Nations Cup, riding Magnifico, was on the winning team in Geneva in 1947, and when he retired over thirty years later he had helped Italy to win thirty-two trophies, and had represented his country in over 150 Nations Cups. At the Olympic Games in London in 1948, where the entire Italian team (including his brother) was eliminated in the show jumping, Raimondo finished in thirtieth place in the three day event at Aldershot. Nations Cup wins followed in Rome in 1950, when he rode Uranio, in 1951 with Destino, and in 1952 with Litargirio, whom he also rode on the winning team in Aachen. The Italian team was again eliminated at the Helsinki Olympics (due to his brother's unfortunate misunderstanding) but Raimondo earned a creditable equal seventh place with Litargirio.

His partnership with Merano started in 1953, in the winning Nations Cup team in the Piazza di Siena, and with him Raimondo helped Italy to win again in Rome, Paris, Dublin and Pinerolo in 1955 and in Geneva, this time with The Quiet Man. After such an impressive list of Nations Cup victories in 1955 – and Italy also won in Belgrade without the d'Inzeos – the prospects looked good for the Stockholm Olympics in 1956.

OPPOSITE
Michael Whitaker (GB) – Team Silver Medals, Olympic Games 1984, World Championships 1986, Team Gold Medals, European Championships 1985, 1987, 1989 – Monsanta (Bob Langrish)
INSET: *Pierre Jonquères d'Oriola (France) – Gold Medal, Olympic Games 1952 and 1964, World Champion 1966 – Pomone B* (Findlay Davidson)

Like his brother, Raimondo lowered two fences in the first round, but Merano then jumped a faultless second round to earn the silver medal behind Hans Günter Winkler and Halla, and with Piero taking the bronze Italy were assured of the team silver medal.

If Piero scored a greater number of Grands Prix victories and achieved success in the European Championships, Raimondo was spectacularly successful in the World Championships. In 1955 in Aachen he and Merano had forced Hans Günter Winkler and Halla to a jump-off in which he took the silver medal. In Aachen again in 1956 Merano was well in the lead after the qualifying competitions, and in the final Raimondo was the only rider without jumping faults on all four horses, which secured him the gold medal.

The year 1960 was a busy and profitable one, with both the Olympic Games and the World Championship taking place in Italy. A Nations Cup win in Turin with Posillipo started the season well, and in the Piazza di Siena they were the clear individual leaders in the Olympic Nations Cup, in which Italy took the bronze medal behind Germany and the USA. In the two round individual event Posillipo jumped the only clear round of the competition, and though three fences came down in the second round this was good enough for the gold medal – one fence ahead of silver medallist Piero.

The scene then shifted north to Venice where the World Championship was held in appalling weather conditions. With Posillipo resting on his laurels, Raimondo rode Gowran Girl, and he finished the final sixteen points ahead of his nearest rival to take his second successive World Championship. To win an Olympic gold medal takes some doing, as does the winning of the World Championship; to win two successive World Championships, and to take the Olympic and World titles in the same year on two different horses implies a very high degree of horsemanship. And then in Buenos Aires four years later he took the bronze medal on yet another horse, Bowjack.

In the Piazza di Siena Raimondo won five Grands Prix, two with Merano and one each with Gowran Girl, Fiorello and Gone Away, and three Prix des Vainqueurs, with Merano, Bells of Clonmell and Fiorello. Indeed between them the d'Inzeo brothers won twelve Rome Grands Prix between 1956 and 1976.

Strangely enough for a country with Italy's history of success in international competition, she breeds relatively few top-class competition horses, and Italian riders have often had to look abroad for their mounts. Ireland has always been a favourite hunting ground, and the Irish breeders have every reason to be grateful to the d'Inzeos for the successes they have gained with Irish horses. And because of the difficulty of finding replacements, both Piero and Raimondo made their horses last. Typical of this care was the Irish gelding Bellevue, with whom Raimondo won the Grands Prix in Amsterdam and Vienna in 1968, and who won the Dublin Grand Prix in 1975 when he was not far short of twenty.

It is not surprising, therefore, to learn that Raimondo's horses meant much to him.

'I loved deeply all my horses,' he says, 'perhaps Merano a little more than the others,

OPPOSITE
Richard Meade OBE (GB) – Olympic Champion 1972, Silver Medal, World Championship 1970 – Kilcashel, Burghley 1980 (Bob Langrish)

Bruce Davidson (USA) – World Champion 1974, 1978 – J J Babu, Luhmühlen 1982 (Bob Langrish)

Raimondo d'Inzeo (Italy) – World Champion 1956 and 1960, Olympic Champion 1960 – with Merano, White City, London 1957 (Leslie Lane)

for he was the first that I trained to international level. I had no particular preference for Italian or Irish horses; Merano, Posillipo and Fiorello were my best Italian ones, and The Quiet Man, Gowran Girl, Bellevue, Bells of Clonmell and Stranger the best of the Irish and English.'

Raimondo's advice to a young rider is therefore 'To love his horse, and to be strongly dedicated to his training, and to be humble and persevering.'

Looking back on his years at the top, 'In my time we were fighting for an ideal, and my success was due to the fact that I strove for this. I took time over the training of my horses, which required patience, perseverance and sacrifice. Today there is not much "real" sport, instead there is an exaggerated professionalism. This could be, perhaps, the reason why there are so few Italian riders at the top in international equestrian sport today.'

Raimondo retired from the Carbiniere in 1981 as the Colonel commanding the Squadron Group of the mounted regiment, but he still rides every day. His record of seven Olympic appearances is bettered only by his brother, and his tally of six medals only by Hans Günter Winkler, with whom he shares the record of winning the World Championship twice. The world of show jumping misses not only his example as a rider, but also the twinkle in his eye that marked his love of horses and his obvious enjoyment of his sport.

DAVID BROOME, OBE MFH

In the competitors' stand at the Piazza di Siena in Rome in 1960 a young Welshman of twenty sat down to watch the second round of the individual competition of the Olympic Games. With a horse called Sunsalve, on whom he had sat for the first time only six weeks previously, he had picked up sixteen faults in the first round and seven in the second over a course which had eliminated twenty-six of the sixty starters. Not unhappy at having managed to complete the course twice, he watched as rider after rider, including some of the best and most experienced in the world, produced scores that made his total of twenty-three look more than just respectable. Then, with half a dozen left to jump, he realised that no one was going to overtake him for the bronze medal. With George Morris (USA), Hans Günter Winkler and Fritz Thiedemann (Germany) in fourth, fifth and sixth places, David Broome stood on the winners' podium with Raimondo and Piero d'Inzeo.

Twenty-eight years later on the other side of the world, there were some who thought that a rider two years short of his half century was perhaps a bit long in the tooth still to be taking on Olympic courses. The first round course for the individual competition in Seoul was huge, and only Karsten Huck for Germany had gone clear, though the ebullient Frenchman Pierre Durand and the fantastic little Jappeloup and dual World Cup winners Ian Millar and Big Ben for Canada had incurred only time penalties. David was one of thirteen riders with just one fence down, but another good round left him in fourth place equal with Anne Kursinski. He had, against all the odds, missed his third Olympic bronze medal by a whisker.

But two Olympic bronze medals, a World Championship, three European Championships, a haul of Grands Prix that includes six Irish Trophies in Dublin and five King George V Gold Cups in London, four Derbys, as well as over thirty winning appearances in Nations Cups testify to the consistency over four decades of this modest horseman from Wales.

Much of his success David considers he owes to his father, Fred, who started him jumping on ponies at the age of nine, and who has been his guide and mentor ever since. It was Fred's intuition and ability to spot a good horse that first set David on the road to stardom when he bought the ex-King's Troop, Royal Horse Artillery's Wildfire in 1958 for a mere £60. Wildfire had been ridden in horse trials by Christopher Morgan, until he fell and broke his rider's leg, and he was savage and almost unmanageable in the stable, but within a year David had turned him into the biggest money winner in Britain. In 1960 at the White City, London, he was second to David's first King George V Gold Cup winner Sunsalve, and at Ascot he won the first car, a Renault, offered as a prize in England.

Sunsalve was another example of Fred Broome's eye for a horse, for after Pat Smythe had won an Olympic trial on him at Cardiff, he had felt that they didn't suit each other, and sure enough at the next show they were eliminated. Only six weeks before the Olympics, Sunsalve arrived in the Broome stable, but it soon seemed clear that this horse with the huge but somewhat wild and erratic jump, who had won the Queen Elizabeth II Cup, the Ladies Championship, at the White City for Elizabeth Anderson in 1958, was unlikely to provide David with a mount for Rome.

At White City, however, the partnership was forged, and in Rome came the individual bronze medal. The course was one of the most severe ever seen, even at the Olympics, and to the twenty-year-old it seemed huge.

They talk about big courses today, but this was as big a course as I have ever ridden, and they broke seventy-two poles that day! The final combination of wall-triple-oxer was just about unjumpable, with one stride in and one and a half strides out. I said Sunsalve couldn't put in two strides, but I did as I was told, 'walked' into the first part, looking for two strides in the second. Of course he hadn't room, he took off in one and crashed through the oxer. We certainly made our contribution to the breakages! Then in the second round he stopped at the third fence. There's nothing like that for getting the adrenalin going, and with nothing more to lose I took the combination as I wanted to, and he was one of only two horses to come out in one stride.

In the Nations Cup David showed that his Olympic bronze medal had been no fluke by putting up the third best individual performance (behind Raimondo d'Inzeo and Hans Günter Winkler). In fact, after twelve faults in the first round, Sunsalve had been credited with a clear round in the second, the only one of the entire competition. This was later amended to four faults, but since the British team had been eliminated, they never discovered the reason. Another bronze medal at the World Championships in Venice a week later confirmed that here was a rising international star.

But in spite of victory in the Grand Prix in Dublin in August, when they arrived in Aachen for the following year's European Championship no one could quite believe that they would pose a serious threat to the likes of the d'Inzeos, and Winkler, Thiedemann and the other German riders on their home ground. In 1961 the Championship was decided on points gained in four competitions, two against the clock, a Puissance and a two-round Grand Prix over a Nations Cup course, at the end of which David found himself European Champion ahead of Piero d'Inzeo and Hans Günter Winkler.

In Tokyo in 1964, where there was no separate individual competition, David learned a lesson that was to stand him in good stead in Seoul twenty-four years later. 'A week before the competition Jacapo was jumping fantastically, then he went downhill. It's easy enough to get a horse to his peak, but terribly difficult to hold him there without competition. In Seoul it was a week before I jumped more than a metre.' The team just missed a medal, but Peter Robeson took the bronze after a jump-off.

By 1966 David had teamed up with Mr Softee, on whom David Barker had won the European Championship in London in 1962, and at the White City he brought Broome his second King George V Gold Cup. Victories in the Hickstead Derby the same year and in the European Championships of 1967 earned them a place in the team for the Mexico Olympics in 1968. In the relaxed atmosphere of the individual competition – it was, in David's words, 'Just like jumping on Clapham Common' – Mr Softee had one fence down, Bill Steinkraus and Marion Coakes having jumped clear. After the second round, over the biggest course he had yet seen, David lay equal third with Frank Chapot (USA), Hans Günter Winkler (Germany) and Jim Elder (Canada). In the jump-off all four went clear, with Mr Softee's speed earning David his second bronze medal, and in the Nations Cup he again showed his class by returning the second best individual performance.

In 1969 David took Mr Softee to Hickstead to defend their European title, now decided over three competitions, and as he entered the arena for the final round he knew that he was equal on points with Alwin Schockemöhle, but that by virtue of his better placings in the qualifying competitions he would retain his title if he went clear. This he did, and he looks back on this as one of his best performances.

The run-up to the 1970 World Championships was anything but propitious, for at a show at Alnwick ten days earlier both David and Harvey Smith were eliminated when neither of their World Championship horses would jump a ditch. But such a setback often acts as a spur, and in La Baule (France) Harvey won the first two qualifying competitions, David won the third, and they both qualified for the change horse final. Now the formula worked to David's advantage, for Douglas Bunn's Beethoven was known to be a difficult customer.

He really put the wind up the other three, Harvey, Graciano Mancinelli and Alwin Schockemöhle. I also had the advantage of following Harvey all the way through. I went clear on my first three rides, and was last to go on Alwin's Donald Rex, who had been clear for everybody so far. We had the third fence down, and then one of the moments I shall never forget was coming into the last, the water. As we cleared the tape I reckon we must have been six foot in the air. He was the best water jumper I ever sat on.

So David added the World Championship to his three European titles.

Munich in 1972 didn't have the happiest memories for many, as a result of the terrorist attack on the Israeli athletes, and for David it was disappointing, too. Out of touch in the individual competition, Manhattan produced a good first round for the team with one fence down, and as they entered the arena for the second round they could have three down and still the team would take the bronze medal. But it took about ten minutes to get from the warm-up area through the various controls and into the arena, and they had to pass all the national teams forming up for the closing ceremony. In a high wind the flags rattled like machine guns, and by the time Manhattan came to jump he was a nervous wreck.

When we came to the last line of fences we had eight faults, and Manhattan became stiffer and stiffer. He had the last but one down, and I thought, 'We've only got to jump the last to take home a medal'. But he hit the last about a foot from the top, and I think it was the most disappointing moment of my life. And the next week he jumped 2.2m (7ft 2in) in the Puissance at Rotterdam!

It was after these Games that most of the top British riders were made to turn professional. No other nation followed the British lead, and British teams were deprived of several of their best riders at the next three Olympics, until the distinction between amateurs and professionals was virtually abolished before the 1988 Games, and all riders became classified as 'competitors'. David, however, doesn't blame the authorities for this decision, as some do.

To be fair, we weren't really against it, because there was this guy going round saying that he could make us all fortunes, like the tennis players and golfers. But of course it never happened. About the only thing that did happen was a so-called World Professional Championship at Cardiff, which I won, but there weren't many foreigners. I suppose I should be in the record books as being the only Open and Professional World Champion!

In the mid-seventies David probably had his strongest team of horses with Sportsman, the ex-working hunter with whom he won his third King George V Cup in 1972, and Philco, the grey ex-racehorse from the USA, who won it in 1977; either of these would have given him the chance of success in the 1976 Olympics had he been eligible to ride. With Philco he won team silver in the 1977 European Championships in Vienna, and team gold in the 1978 World Championships in Aachen. Mr Ross brought his fifth King George V Gold Cup in 1981, team bronze in the 1982 World Championships in Dublin, and team silver in the European Championships the following year at Hickstead, as well as helping him to the top of the World Cup European league in 1979/80 – David was also third in 1978/79 and second in 1981/82.

After his creditable performance in Seoul, David has no immediate plans to retire. 'No one can beat Father Time,' he says, 'but at the moment I've got two top-class horses in Countryman and Lannegan, and I'll go on as long as I enjoy it and can do it. I'm probably about two good falls from retiring! You just don't bounce any more at my age.'

Strangely enough, considering the difficulty that so many young riders have in making the transition from ponies to horses, David considers his experience on different types of pony to have been the basis for his success.

I had three that were quite different, one galloped, one was a cob with a nice even stride, and the other went in the old-fashioned way – it gave me flexibility in the approach to a fence and a spread of experience. Also, in those days in Wales we never jumped off against the clock, we had to jump three clear rounds to win.

An interesting comment from the rider who came to be recognised as just about the best judge of pace in a timed jump-off in the world! How many times we have watched him go smoothly round a jump-off course without seeming to hurry, only to finish with those vital hundredths of a second in hand that bring victory and mark the difference between the good and the great rider!

His advice to the father of an ambitious young rider?

Buy him a tennis racket or a golf club! But if he's determined to ride, he must learn the trade, it's a hard school, and there are no short cuts. Then he must have a good horse. At novice level it's the rider who is the key to the combination, but at the top end it's the horse. There's not much to choose between the top riders of today, Nick Skelton, John and Michael Whitaker, Franke Sloothaak. But Milton is Milton, and they need another Milton to beat him.

David Broome, OBE (GB) – European Champion 1961, 1967, 1969; World Champion 1970; Olympic bronze medallist 1960, 1968; at home with one of his young horses (Bob Langrish)

When he does hang up his boots, David is unlikely to be lost to the sport. He is currently a member of the FEI Medication Control Committee, and much concerned with the problems that face the sport today.

First, we must look after the horse, and see that he's not over jumped. We're really the victims of our sport's success and of our own greed. Before we had the World Cup, our horses had three or four months in the winter to get over their aches and pains after a summer programme; now they're lucky if they get three weeks off. And the courses are now becoming very demanding. The poles are lighter and the cups shallower, but this means the horses must be sharper and jump more cleanly. In the big competitions, like the World Cup Final, for example, thirty-five to forty take part, but only half a dozen can really jump the course; the others are just there to make a class.

The key to the sport is in the hands of the course builders. There are some very good ones, but I'm worried about the trend of setting half-stride distances to combinations, asking the horse to be too athletic. The Jappeloups can cope, but the rest get buried.

On the question of medication:

I want to see everyone entering the ring under fair conditions. As long as we jump horses, we put them under stress just like any other athlete, and they're going to get the odd ache and pain. Most racehorses finish their careers at the age of four or five, but the jumper often doesn't start at international level till ten or eleven. By that time he's jumped a lot of fences. Now if we give him a little bute [Phenylbutazone, a drug mainly used to ease minor ailments, and whose use for competition horses is strictly controlled by the FEI] we're just making life easier for him; we're not making him jump higher or go faster, we're just making it easier for him to concentrate on jumping a course of a dozen fences. Again, if a horse knocks himself in the horsebox when travelling, there's no harm in giving a sachet of bute to help him over it. If we ban it altogether, some of our stars will disappear overnight. We have the rules, and our limits for a horse are more stringent than those for a human being.

Another cause for concern is stable security at international shows.

First of all, we must stop people doing things that are illegal. So no horse should be allowed out of his stable before a certain time, say eight o'clock in the morning, as in Dublin for the 1982 World Championships, and he should be booked in and out, and only permitted in certain areas. Next, we must tighten security within the stable; at present it's too easy if someone wants to get at a horse at night, or when the rider and his groom are out of the stable during a competition.

The FEI is aiming at racecourse security standards by 1995, and the employment of entirely independent doping control teams, who will test whichever horses they want, at any time they choose. That way we shall ensure our sport is clean, and that the horses are not abused.

The list of horses that David Broome has brought to the top, and kept there for long periods, is an indication of his own care for the horse over thirty years of competition at the highest level.

Germany

ALWIN SCHOCKEMÖHLE

In the heart of one of Europe's main horse breeding areas, between Osnabruck and Bremen in North-West Germany, lies the village of Muhlen. Here is situated one of the largest equestrian enterprises in the world, and here live two brothers who have each in different ways had an enormous impact on their chosen sport.

Alwin Schokemöhle was born in 1937 and when old enough to start work on the family farm decided that riding was preferable to other forms of manual labour. 'My father always kept horses, and I was happier to sit on a horse than to work in the barn with cows – in those days we had no machines and everything had to be done by hand.' Father had been a jockey and a jumper, and by the time Alwin was twelve he was winning jumping competitions and local races for half-breds, and it was not long before he came to the notice of Dr Gustav Rau, the architect of Germany's equestrian revival after World War II.

Dr Rau invited him to attend a course at Warendorf, now the Headquarters of the German Olympic Committee for Equestrian Sports, where he came under the influence of General Niemack, and found himself in the company of other young riders such as Reuber Klimke, Hermann Schridde and the Lütke-Westhues brothers, who were all at that stage considered as potential riders for the three day event team. In fact Alwin became a jumper almost by chance, when he was lucky enough to be offered a ride at Munich for an owner whose regular rider had allowed victory celebrations to get the better of him. He tied with Fritz Thiedemann for the Puissance, with the wall at 2.1m (just under 7ft), and returned to Warendorf as a jumper!

Alwin's first big opportunity came when Hans Freitag, owner of the Verden Biscuit Factory, asked him to ride his horses, and on the grey Bacchus he won the Hamburg Derby of 1957. But if this signalled the arrival of a new star, it certainly didn't bring any easing up of the strenuous schedule that Alwin had set for himself. In the same year, aged twenty, he took over the family estate, and came to a great decision. 'I'll make a million by the time I'm thirty and retire when I'm forty.' At this time he learned much from watching his two idols, Hans Günter Winkler and Fritz Thiedemann, and he progressed by buying young horses, making them and selling them, and by sheer hard work, often schooling his horses at the end of a hard day's work on the farm.

At the Rome Olympics of 1960 he found himself representing Germany alongside Winkler and Thiedemann, and his fifth place in the Nations Cup, with his team mates second and third respectively, helped to bring Germany the gold medal. The courses in Rome were severe and, with only three riders to a team, twelve teams were eliminated and the score of the remainder ran from 46.5 for the winners to 175 for the sixth. In the individual competition only thirty-four from a field of sixty completed the course, and Alwin and Ferdl were twenty-sixth.

From then on Alwin's career can be traced via the victories of half a dozen good horses. Bacchus won the Aachen championship of 1960; Ferdl took him to his first Olympics and won the Grand Prix of Rome in 1963; Freiherr won the German Championships of 1961 and 1963, the Grands Prix of Aachen in 1962 and Berlin in 1963; Wimpel took the Hamburg Derbys of 1969 and 1971 and shared the German Championship of 1969, and Donald Rex won the Aachen Grand Prix of that year. Donald Rex, whom Alwin considers the best horse he ever rode, won in Aachen, Berlin, Brussels, Dortmund and London, took team bronze at the Mexico Olympics of 1968 and was seventh in the individual competition; Rex the Robber won nearly every major Grand Prix in Europe, including the King George V Gold Cup in London, and the Irish Trophy in Dublin; and Warwick Rex took Alwin to his final triumph at the Montreal Olympics in 1976.

Of Donald Rex he says, 'He was so easy to ride, he just jumped like a machine, something like Milton today. He won fifteen Grands Prix in a row.' Rex the Robber, known as The Professor, was perhaps a shade too clever; certainly he had proved far too clever for his previous owners.

He knew too much, and was a little too careful. If the spreads got really big he would stop rather than make an error. It was at the time when Micky Brinckmann was building oxers that were 2.2m wide. He would sometimes say, 'Today we have only small oxers', and they would be 1.9m! The Robber would have been a much better horse today, when the poles are lighter, and the cups less deep. Freiherr was a very good horse, fast, but very careful.

Although he won so many Grands Prix, success in the European Championships and the Olympic Games eluded him for a long time, and in the World Championships he never actually won a medal, perhaps because it was not a competition that he particularly enjoyed.

At every other major championship it is a horse and rider combination that wins. But in La Baule, for example, my great friend David Broome became World Champion because he was brilliant at riding strange horses, while Beethoven was a difficult horse for a stranger to ride. Donald Rex, on the other hand, went well for everyone, though he was the only horse on which David had a fault.

It is perhaps surprising to discover that Alwin's determination was not always matched by his confidence, and he admits to having been nervous on several great occasions, which might well have cost him a title or two. Nevertheless in the European Championships, a fourth, two thirds and two seconds preceded his eventual triumph on Warwick Rex in 1975, which boded well for the following year's Olympics in Montreal.

Warwick Rex had originally been bought by Hartwig Steenken, who had not found

Alwin Schockemöhle (Germany) with Warwick Rex, winning the Olympic gold medal with the only double clear round in Montreal 1976 (Leslie Lane)

him easy and sold him to Dhr Melchior of Holland. He was then brought back to Germany by Hermann Schridde, who sold him to Alwin in 1974. (The 'Rex' prefix, incidentally, came from the firm owned by his partner, Otto Shuler-Frohlinde, to whom he sold a half share in some of his good horses.)

The Olympic selection procedure depended upon a series of trials, and with four riders in the team competition but only three in the individual, no one wanted to be the one to travel that far for only one event, let alone to be the fifth (reserve) rider. The trouble with trials is that to be sure of selection horses must be at their peak well in advance of the Games, and in the end the selectors chose Sonke Sonksen, Paul Schockemöhle, Hans Günter Winkler, Alwin and Gert Wiltfang. When it became clear that Warwick Rex was to go for the team event only, Alwin withdrew, but was persuaded to change his mind a week before departure.

Just two days before the team event in Bromont, site of the equestrian events, the Selection Committee decided in favour of Warwick Rex over Sonksen's Kwept. The first round course was big enough, and only Warwick could manage to jump it clear; the second round was massive, with a huge treble of heavy silver birch poles as the final obstacle. As Warwick, the last to jump, waited to enter the sand arena, the clouds descended and it seemed doubtful if the competition could be finished before the storm broke. But Warwick gave all he had, and Alwin took the gold medal with a zero score, three fences ahead of his nearest rivals.

After the first round in the team event in the Montreal stadium on the final day of the Games, Germany and France led with twenty-four penalties from Belgium on thirty-two, with Warwick equalling the best individual score of four. But as he approached the final combination, clear to that point, Warwick faltered and came down to a trot. Alwin kept him going but two fences came down, and though they still shared the best individual score, Germany had to be content with the silver medal behind France. Had Warwick's supreme effort over the huge Bromont fences taken its toll?

Apart from having achieved his ambition of winning an Olympic gold medal, Alwin had represented his country in fifty-eight Nations Cups, twenty-seven of which had resulted in wins. One factor made this seem a good moment to retire.

Those who had known Alwin Schockemöhle from the time that he had hit the headlines by winning the Hamburg Derby back in 1957 knew what his career in the saddle had cost him in terms of physical pain and suffering. The problem with the sciatic nerve had been with him since the age of nineteen and the falls, stresses and strains which are part of the competition rider's occupational hazard had inevitably made it worse. And as is so often the case, the only satisfactory cure would have been to have given up riding. Massage, physiotherapy, baths, plaster jackets, elastic bandages, surgical corsets, none could relieve for long the almost permanent pain.

It is hardly surprising, therefore, that Alwin developed a style of his own, since nature compelled him to sit back rather than forward on a horse.

Every rider rides differently. Style is a question of putting your personal stamp on all you have learned. In the early days my idols were Thiedemann and Winkler, but I wanted to ride like Raimondo d'Inzeo! He, I think, was the best in the world; and he kept his horses going for so long – he had to, for they didn't breed them in Italy, and they had to be bought from abroad. I have tried to mould all my horses to my own system, so that they obey me. When I watched Thiedemann I saw that he based his schooling on dressage, and that he had mastered the art of bringing his horse to the exact point of take-off.

Most of Alwin's horses were of the type bred in his native Oldenburg.

In the beginning I had no money, no sponsor, and the prize money was small, so I had to buy horses that had had problems with other riders, and I had to sell horses to keep going. If I had a good-looking horse he was the one that people wanted to buy, and I got left with the rather heavy ones.

Later, when buying a young horse, I would look first for natural jumping ability and technique, which can be assessed over a low jump, then for balance and a sound mouth – these are born, not made, though training can improve them – and finally I look for a good character.

Alwin's advice to a young rider reflects his early years.

He should grow up with horses. Young riders sometimes come to me today and the first questions they ask are: 'How many hours in the week do we have to work, and how many weeks in the year do we get for holidays?' And too many riders don't like to train their horses. If they have problems they just try changing the bit or changing their spurs – or they change the horse! I tell them it takes at least three years to train a horse, but they all want quick results. Even established riders don't train their horses enough. When I was riding at a show, I used to be out at six in the morning schooling my horses. Now, even half an hour before the class begins you see nobody. But even with a good horse, the morning after a timed jump-off you need to work him quietly for thirty or forty-five minutes to get his mind back to normal jumping, to make him relax and to put him in the hand again.

During his competitive days Alwin was never one to kowtow to authority if he thought they were mistaken, and he earned himself a reputation for being ready to stand up for the rights of riders. His views on the state of the sport today are equally forthright.

The sport today is very professional, but I think the FEI must do more to protect the horse. Firstly, there is still too much barring [rapping] of horses, as well as the use of applications to the horse's legs to make him jump more cleanly. This doesn't take place in the warm-up area, where there is a steward, but out of sight behind the stables or horseboxes. Second, on bute; used under control it is the best thing we have for the horse. It doesn't improve his performance; if he doesn't jump 2m without it he won't jump 2m with it, but it makes him happier and keeps him going. By the time a horse reaches international level he is probably not 100 per cent sound anyway, in the sense that if he was being vetted for sale there would be some reason for a vet to fail him if he wanted to.

But it must only be used under official veterinary control, the rules must be absolutely clear, and there must be much tougher sanctions for infringement – not just a fine, but suspension for a long period for both horse and rider, perhaps six months for the horse and a year for the rider.

If physical disability forced Alwin's retirement from competitive riding after his Olympic victory of 1976, it by no means signalled the end of his involvement with competition horses. This was partly due to the fact that, apart from his inclination to work hard, Alwin also developed a keen business sense. As he made money out of his horses, he invested in what was in Germany a booming business – the manufacture of steel mesh for reinforced concrete. His brother-in-law saw to the technical side, while Alwin visited clients. His sporting prowess undoubtedly helped to open doors, but success came from knowing the job. Recently he sold the three companies that they had built up, and now he has invested in agricultural products – pigs, chickens, and turkeys.

His success in business has enabled him to continue his involvement with horses. In his stable now are some two dozen jumping horses, and a team of three riders, led by Thomas Frühmann of Austria. But an interest dating back to his earliest days now occupies most of his time. He had always managed to keep one or two trotters; now he has developed one of the foremost studs and training establishments for this very popular German sport. In his paddocks are about thirty brood mares, many from the USA, and in the stables up to 120 trotters from yearlings upwards. His training facilities are impressive: for routine work, he has constructed an oval covered track just over a kilometre in length, cambered on the bends, ensuring perfect conditions whatever the North German weather can produce, while for fast work he has an 800m all-weather strip so that horses can be extended without straining their joints on bends.

In the mornings he can be seen on a sulky training and assessing his more fancied horses, and this compensates him for the end of his competitive riding days. And since he retired from riding he has won three German Trotting Derbys in Berlin, been leading trainer three times, and has won over a hundred stakes races.

Does he have other interests? 'No, just my horses and my family.'

Germany

PAUL SCHOCKEMÖHLE

As his elder brother Alwin was bowing out with an individual gold medal after the Montreal Olympic Games of 1976, Paul was preparing to take over as the mainstay of the German team. He had made his first winning appearance in the Prince of Wales' Cup in London in 1973 riding Abadir, had followed this up with victories in La Baule and Aachen the following year on Agent, and in 1975 and 1976 was successful in Geneva and Hickstead with Talisman, on whom he had won the first of his three Aachen Grands Prix in 1974. And at Montreal he rode Agent as a member of the silver medal team.

But it was the appearance on the scene of Deister at the European Championships of 1979 in Rotterdam that really set Paul on the trail to the top. That year they took home the team and individual silver medals, and at the next three Championships in Munich (1981), Hickstead (1983) and Dinard (1985) they proved unbeatable. In Munich Deister led from start to finish and ended with an unprecedented zero score, and indeed in the fifteen rounds jumped in those three Championships Deister had faulted at only three fences. At the International Festival in Rotterdam in 1980 (for the nations that boycotted the Moscow Olympics) they were fourth in the individual event, and in the World Championships of 1982 in Dublin they collected a team silver medal.

At Los Angeles in 1984 Deister produced the third best individual performance of the competition in the bronze medal team and was equal seventh in the individual event. In the World Cup Paul headed the European League in 1978/79 and again in 1986/87 and was runner-up in 1984/85, and has been second, third, fourth and fifth in the finals. He also has the distinction of having won three Hickstead Derbys, in 1982 and 1986 with Deister and in 1985 with Lorenzo. In Nations Cups Paul has helped Germany to victory more than twenty times, and he has won most of the important European Grands Prix as well as that in New York.

But successful as Paul has been in the saddle, he has recently had an even greater impact on the sport as owner, trainer, dealer and entrepreneur. At Muhlen in Oldenburg, north-west Germany, he and brother Alwin live and run their separate businesses on opposite sides of a small river. To the south, Alwin has his small but élite stable of jumpers and his huge establishment of trotters; on the north side Paul has built up his gigantic stable of over 400 horses of all ages. With three or four indoor schools, several outside jumping rings, and covered lungeing sheds, little is left to chance in the production of top-class jumpers.

In huge barns the young horses are herded together by ages, each with a halter bearing his identification tag. With so many to deal with, it is a wonder that the good ones can be separated from the others. 'Every three months or so we take them out and loose jump them in the indoor school. Their performance is recorded, and in this way we can keep track of their development.' And what of the failures? 'Our selection procedure from the breeders is now so well organised that we really don't have many failures. All our young horses are bred to jump from performance proven mares and stallions. Of course not all will make Grand Prix horses, but there is a high probability that they will jump.'

At the other end of the scale is the team of international jumpers, ridden by the 1988 Olympic team gold medallist Franke Sloothaak, winner of the 1989 Aachen Grand Prix with the great Walzerkönig. In between, some forty jumpers are sent out every weekend to shows around the country ridden by a team of young riders trained by Paul himself.

The showpiece of this great organisation is Performance Sales International, whose annual December sale of young competition horses is now in its tenth year. Prospective buyers come from all over the world to see young horses carefully selected and skilfully trained, and shown off in the best possible conditions.

But it is not only in the field of the production of competition horses that Paul is involved, for in 1989 he teamed up with Jon Tiriac, manager of German tennis ace Boris Becker, to promote the German Classics tournament in Bremen. With teams invited from six of the best nations in the world and £¼m in prize money, this provoked much comment, most favourable but some critical, and certainly set a trend for the indoor version of the sport for the future.

The Bremen show also saw the official retirement of the great Deister; if it also signalled the retirement of his rider from top class international competition, then we may be assured that the name of Paul Schockemöhle will continue to be in the forefront of show jumping news for the foreseeable future.

Paul Schockemöhle (Germany) – European Champion
1981, 1983 and 1985 (Bob Langrish)

Brazil

NELSON PESSOA

It is somewhat strange to discover that the records show that the silver medal at the European Championships of 1965 in Aachen went to a South American, and even more so to find that in 1966 in Lucerne no European rider managed to win a medal at all, gold, silver and bronze all apparently being swept off home across the Atlantic! But if the North and South Americans were confident of repeating their success at the World Championships in Buenos Aires later in the same year, their complacency was shattered when all three medals travelled back to Europe.

The World Championships are, of course, open to the world, and in 1966 the honours were taken, in spite of the arduous journey for their horses, by Pierre Jonquères d'Oriola (France), Jose Alvarez de Bohorques (Spain) and Raimondo d'Inzeo (Italy). Fourth came the Brazilian who has made Europe his home since 1961. It was this same rider, Nelson Pessoa, who won the European Championships of 1966 for Brazil, ahead of Frank Chapot (USA) and Hugo Arrambide (Argentina) – that year teams from the USA and Brazil were in Europe for the summer and the Championships were contested by nineteen riders from eleven nations, as against fourteen riders from eight nations in the World Championships in Buenos Aires.

Nelson Pessoa started riding back home in Brazil at the age of eight, but, though it seems hard to believe now, was terrified of horses, and especially of falling off. His father, who had a real estate business, and who rode at weekends, made him jump, but the boy who was one day to create the record for jumping the Puissance wall at 2.33m (7ft 8in) was afraid of jumping heights. 'If I jumped one metre it took me two hours to get to 1.5m. Then when I was twelve I used to ride my father's horse every day, and one day I took him out and jumped him by myself; from that moment I lost my fear.'

His father then bought him a good horse and at the age of twelve he started to compete, and, except for a six-month break for a broken leg, he has competed ever since. There were no junior classes, so from the start he was jumping against adults, and at the age of eighteen he went on his first team to Argentina and won his first Grand Prix. The Brazilian team of those days was based on the Cavalry School, and his father made him watch the best riders and copy them. In the 1952 Olympic Games in Helsinki the Brazilian team came fourth out of sixteen teams, and after five had jumped off for the individual medals one of them finished fourth too.

In 1956 Pessoa was selected for the Stockholm Olympics, in which the team came tenth out of twenty, and he finished in thirty-third position when twenty-one of the sixty-six starters failed to complete the course. Then after visiting Europe again the following year he returned to Brazil, ostensibly to finish his studies. And he did indeed start work in his father's real estate business, but his mind was far away in Europe. He

Nelson Pessoa (Brazil), European Champion 1966 and Puissance Wall record holder at 7ft 7¾in (2.33m) (Findlay Davidson)

had seen Winkler, Thiedemann and the d'Inzeo brothers, and, 'I wanted to be one of them.' In 1961 he married, and he and his wife came to settle in Europe.

For the Rome Olympics Pessoa had not yet found a suitable horse, and the entire Brazilian team was eliminated in a competition in which only six teams out of eighteen finished. But it was at this time that he began the partnership with the grey Gran Geste that was to last for nearly a decade. Between 1961 and 1968 this combination won a European Championship, the Grands Prix in Brussels, Aachen, Vienna, Dortmund (twice), two Aachen Championships, and five Derbys, three in Hamburg and two in Hickstead.

In Tokyo in 1964 Brazil didn't enter a team, and Pessoa should have represented Brazil with Gran Geste, who had won both the major competitions in Aachen, the German Championship on the Wednesday and the Grand Prix on the Sunday. But he arrived in such poor shape that Nelson had to ride his reserve horse, Mme Givaudin's Huipil, on whom he finished in a very creditable fifth place, and who shared the silver and gold medals of the 1965 and 1966 European Championships with Gran Geste.

One of the occasions that he particularly likes to remember is the Pan American Games of 1967 in Winnipeg, where Brazil was represented by Nelson and three young riders whom he had trained. The United States team was the hot favourite of six, and with Frank and Mary Chapot, Kathy Kusner and Bill Steinkraus they were indeed a formidable combination. But in the team competition two faultless rounds by Gran Geste helped Brazil to win the title, and in the individual final Gran Geste again went clear, and after a jump-off with Jim Day and Canadian Club, the only other combination to jump without fault in the team competition, they took the silver medal.

In Mexico in 1968 Gran Geste again fell victim to a virus, and Nelson rode his reserve horse Pass Op into sixteenth place, one ahead of double gold medallist d'Oriola. Brazil was unable to send a team to Munich in 1972, where Nelson finished down the line with Nagir, winner of Grands Prix in Amsterdam and Brussels, and in 1974 he turned professional, thus ruling out the Olympics until the change of rules reinstated him as a competitor in 1987. But the jinx that had dogged his Olympic forays plagued him again in 1988, when both of his intended mounts died of colic at home shortly before leaving for Seoul.

It could be said that Nelson's relative lack of success in the Olympic Games and World Championships precludes his inclusion among the great riders of the world; but let it be remembered that he has for the most part achieved what he has achieved without the backing of a National Federation such as has been behind the efforts of riders from Great Britain, the United States or Germany, for example, and that though he is the first to acknowledge his debt to his sponsors, Moët et Chandon, his has been largely a solo effort.

This effort has won him 135 Grands Prix around the world, over a hundred Puissances – seventy-two of them with one horse, the mare Miss Moët, (who broke that record for the Puissance wall in Paris in 1983), and six Derbys, four at Hamburg and two at Hickstead. His success he attributes more to dedication and patience than to his undeniable talent. 'Plenty of riders have the talent to win,' he says, 'but few have the dedication and the patience to reach the top.' And to young riders he says, 'You have to become a real horseman; jumping is only part of it.'

He feels that the sport today is in good shape, but thinks that its promotion needs a more professional approach. 'We need more shows like Aachen and Hickstead. We have the fourth biggest sport after racing, tennis and golf, but we don't exploit the potential for television as they do. Our horses cost a fortune, but we jump for peanuts.'

Nelson now lives with his family in Brussels, and has leased a farm just outside the city. 'My son is now sixteen, and wants to be a rider like me. So I will gradually hand over the reins to him, and eventually he will have the first choice of rides, and I will take second place.' It looks as though the name of Pessoa and the flag of Brazil will be prominent on the European scene for the foreseeable future. And it looks as though the handover from father to son will indeed be gradual, for in the autumn and winter of 1989 father was still winning the Grands Prix in Donaueschingen and Grenoble.

JOE FARGIS

Only on three occasions in the history of the jumping events at the Olympic Games has a rider won both team and individual gold medals at the same Games – Humberto Mariles Cortés for Mexico at Wembley Stadium in London in 1948, Hans Günter Winkler for Germany in Stockholm in 1956, and Joe Fargis for the United States in Los Angeles in 1984. But in the cases of Cortés and Winkler there were no separate individual competitions, and the individual medals were awarded on the results of the team competition. Joe Fargis is the only rider to have earned his medals as the result of two separate performances. (Since the advent of the separate individual competition in 1960, three individual gold medal winners have also produced the best individual performances in the team competition – Raimondo d'Inzeo in Rome, Pierre Jonquères d'Oriola in Tokyo and Alwin Schockemöhle in Montreal, and these performances netted them team bronze, silver and silver medals respectively.)

In the year (1948) in which Mariles Cortés was winning his medals in London, Joe Fargis was born in New York, to a family with no previous equestrian connections. In 1953 the family moved to Virginia, and Joe first became acquainted with horses two years later when a school friend whose mother had a riding school took him home. From that moment he became hooked on horses, and since the riding school was within walking distance of his own home, he spent all his spare time there.

This did not accord exactly with his parents' plans for him, which involved a college education. Joe did indeed complete three-and-a-half years of the four-year college course, but then realised that he wanted a career with horses. 'At that time I had no specific goals, I didn't dream about the Olympics or anything like that, I just had a good time riding horses.'

In the United States there is now an excellent system for the development and coaching of promising young riders, with equitation classes that stress the importance of the rider's seat. Joe's early instruction came from Jane Dillon in Virginia, who also coached Kathy Kusner, and at eighteen he started riding young horses and jumpers for Frances Rowe. At the age of twenty-one Joe was given a trial for the team, and as a result he spent three winters, from February to April, in training with Bert de Nemethy at Gladstone, New Jersey.

Jane Dillon started me off and taught me above all about being a good sport, about coping with the ups and downs and inevitable disappointments that go with horses. Frances Rowe taught me all about horses and about every aspect of horsemanship. Bert de Nemethy taught me the technicalities of competing and sophisticated my riding. He was a very serious teacher. We would start every day at seven in the morning, and we'd ride between six and eight horses a day.

In 1970 Joe came for the first time to Europe with the United States team. 'I didn't win much, but we held our own,' was how he described that trip. But he also has a less happy memory: 'I had one horse that wouldn't jump ditches, and I spent a lot of that summer in the bottom of them, dry ones, wet ones, deep ones, shallow ones. He never did really learn to jump them.'

At that time some of the long-established USET riders such as Frank and Mary Chapot and Bill Steinkraus were being replaced by a new young team, and in 1975 in the company of Michael Matz, Dennis Murphy and Buddy Brown, Joe won the team gold medal at the Pan American games in Mexico City, and later the Grand Prix at Spruce Meadows, Calgary. But his real break came in 1981.

By this time Joe was running a stable in partnership with Conrad Homfeld, and one day he saw a girl riding a new mare which she had recently brought to the stable. The mare's name was Touch of Class, and Joe soon realised that here was a horse of exceptional potential. Eventually he arranged for her to be bought for him to ride.

In 1982 a different sort of break interrupted Joe's career. With Touch of Class he was selected to represent the United States in the World Championships in Dublin, and they travelled to Hickstead en route for Ireland. News of this fantastic mare and her talented rider had preceded them to England, and much was expected of them. But when Joe entered the ring on his second horse in the opening class of the meeting, the horse slipped on take-off at the first fence, and Joe was on the ground with a broken leg.

'I just couldn't believe it. I had come to Europe full of expectations, and here I was holding up the show before it had even got started.' That was the end of their World Championship aspirations. However, the next time that Joe came to Hickstead, in 1989, he won the first big international class of the meeting and the Grand Prix with Mill Pearl. After the first class his reaction was simply, 'I was so pleased just to come out of the ring on my horse and not in an ambulance!'

In 1983 Joe joined Anne Kursinski, Katie Monahan and Melanie Smith in Rome, where they won the Nations Cup from a strong field of eight teams, and back in North America he and Touch of Class helped the United States to victories in Calgary, Washington and New York.

At Los Angeles in 1984 the United States team had everything going for them – a 'home' fixture, an impressive new arena, magnificent obstacles, and a course designed by Bert de Nemethy – he was not going to do his adopted country any favours, but at least they knew what his philosophy was and that he would build a course to test the best in the world. But in front of their own crowd the pressure on them was great too. They certainly rose to the occasion.

At the end of the first round of the team competition the United States with just one fence down from the whole team were already four fences ahead of their nearest rivals Germany. In the second round Touch of Class again went clear, as did Conrad Homfeld and Abdullah, and Melanie Smith and Calypso did not even have to jump to give the Americans the gold medal with a total score of twelve ahead of Great Britain on 36.75. In the individual competition, from fifty-one starters Touch of Class produced the only clear of the first round, with Abdullah and three others in close contention on four penalties. In the second round a fence down for Touch of Class and a clear for Abdullah led to a jump-off in which Touch of Class again went clear to give Joe his second gold

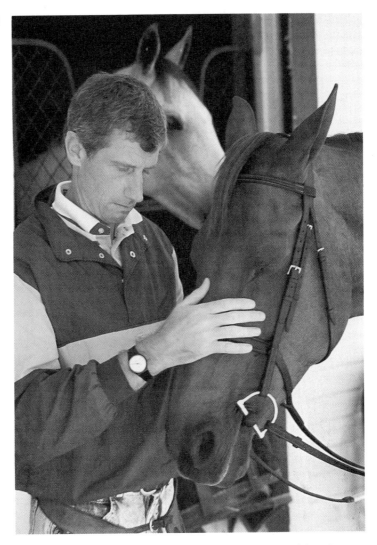

Joe Fargis (USA), Olympic Champion 1984, seen here with Mill Pearl
(Bob Langrish)

medal. In the five rounds of these two competitions this 16 hand Thoroughbred mare had jumped ninety-one fences, ninety of them clear.

To round off a great year, Touch of Class won the President's Cup at the Washington International Show and (with his team mates) the Nations Cup, and the World Cup qualifier Grand Prix at New York's Madison Square Garden. And in 1985 they were members of the winning Nations Cup teams in Aachen (from a field of fourteen nations), Washington and New York.

Meanwhile Joe had teamed up with another mare, Mill Pearl. Did he prefer mares? 'No. People always ask me that. But a good horse is a good horse.' In 1987 Mill Pearl won the qualifying class at Tampa, Florida, for the World Cup, in which Joe had headed the North American East Coast League in the two previous years, having come second in 1987.

Touch of Class had been lame in 1986, and though she went to Seoul for the Olympic Games in 1988, it was Mill Pearl who took part in both jumping competitions. In the team event, in which the United States took the silver medal, she returned the best individual performance (equal with Ludger Beerbaum of Germany) for a total of 4.25 penalties, while in the individual competition they finished equal seventh. The following year started well, with a Nations Cup win in Rome, where Joe rode his new horse, Chef, and with the Hickstead Grand Prix for Mill Pearl. In October Mill Pearl won the Grand Prix at the Baltimore World Cup qualifier, and in November she helped the United States to win the New York Nations Cup, held at the National Horse Show in New Jersey.

Much of his success Joe attributes to circumstance.

I believe that is how life develops. If it hadn't been for my school friend I might never have become involved with horses; if Touch of Class hadn't appeared in our stable I might never have won an Olympic medal; apart from my instructors, the outside influences on my life have been largely responsible for my success. I'm lucky enough to have been surrounded by good people. Then there are the horses; the horse is the athlete, and if you have a good horse, then you're on your way.

Care and consideration for the horse tempers his advice to young riders.

A lot of people don't put the horse first, but we have to create a partnership with a living, breathing creature. You can't treat him as a vehicle or just part of your equipment. A rider must obviously be prepared to work hard, but he must have resilience too, because more moments are average or bad than good. We wait so long for that one great round. So you must be patient. Set yourself goals by all means, but be prepared to take your time in getting there. With horses you can't hurry things.

In general Joe is happy about the state of the sport today, but has one reservation. 'Today there are just too many shows, which leads to the overworking of horses. With the World Cup there is now no winter break. We have to find some way to compel riders to look after their horses.'

He has amassed a host of happy memories.

I think that those moments in Los Angeles were the best of all, not just because we won the gold medals on a fantastic horse, but because the performances were good too. We didn't just 'leak by', we jumped clean and good rounds. Sometimes when you've won you know it wasn't really a good performance, but this was different. There was tremendous pressure on the whole team, the conditions were ideal, and there weren't going to be any excuses for a poor performance.

Joe is a bachelor, and one feels that his horses are his family. He has little time for other interests. 'If I had another interest it would have to be travel, because my friend the horse has taken me round the world.'

The world is likely to see quite a bit more of this quiet, stylish and successful rider in the years ahead.

France

PIERRE DURAND

Every so often a horse and rider hit the international scene and capture the imagination of the public by their particular idiosyncrasies or their sheer brilliance or a combination of both. Wilf White and Nizefella and John Whitaker and Ryan's Son provide examples from the distant and recent past; Pierre Durand and Jappeloup de Luze have been thrilling spectators around the world since 1982, when Pierre first acquired this five-year-old diminutive 15.2hh dark brown Selle-Français gelding, half Thoroughbred, half trotter, with an unpredictable and rebellious disposition.

Born near Bordeaux in 1955 into a family with no equestrian background, Pierre started riding at the age of ten, and since his first (and virtually only) teacher was Dominique Bentejac, an international three day event rider, he was initially aimed at that branch of the sport. Four years later he switched to show jumping, and quickly showed his aptitude here, being runner-up in the French Junior Championship of 1969, and taking part in the Junior European Championships in Cork (Ireland) in 1972. At sixteen he rode his first senior international competition at Biarritz, riding the mare Velleda, and in 1975 he first rode for France in the Nations Cup at Olsztyn (Poland) on Laudanum.

Though his father gave him every possible support, Pierre's progress now depended on his own natural ability and his observation of established riders, and in his own words 'Je suis un self-made rider'. At the same time he was pursuing his legal studies at the Bordeaux Institute for Political Studies from which he emerged with a law degree in 1982 and started work as a legal administrator specialising in bankruptcy.

But a couple of years earlier Jappeloup had come into his life. Aptly named (in ancient French) 'the Cry of the Wolf', he had been locally bred, but because of his diminutive frame and tempestuous temperament he seemed an unlikely prospect for international honours. For the next two years Pierre patiently trained him, and in 1982 they became French National Champions, won their first Grand Prix (at Fontainebleau), and represented France in Nations Cups in Madrid and Longchamp. The following year they helped France to win the Nations Cup at Hickstead and could now be counted established members of the national team.

But at the Los Angeles Olympic Games in 1984 Jappeloup was eliminated in the second round of the Nations Cup and could do no better than finish fourteenth in the individual competition. There were those who urged Pierre to sell this brilliant but not altogether reliable little horse, but he retained his faith in him, and third place in the World Cup Final of 1985 in Berlin, followed by second place in the 1985/86 European League and wins at the Olympia and Paris qualifiers resulted in sponsorship from the Bordeaux wine merchants de Luze.

As Jappeloup de Luze, the little horse won Grands Prix in Lucerne and Bordeaux in 1986, regained the French Championship, and helped France to win the Nations Cups in Rome, Lucerne, Hickstead and Fontainebleau, while Pierre finished in fourth place in the World Championships in Aachen, where Jappeloup surprisingly enough jumped clear in the final for both Gail Greenhough of Canada and Nick Skelton of Great Britain. In the team Championship Jappeloup turned in the best performance of any horse in the competition, in which France earned the bronze medal.

The year 1987 brought Grands Prix victories in La Baule, Amsterdam, Vienna and Brussels, and a Nations Cup win in La Baule, but the highlight of the year was at St Gallen, Switzerland, where Pierre became European Champion and the French team took the silver medal. The following year started well with second place once again in the World Cup Final in Göteborg and a Nations Cup win in Aachen, and Pierre went to Seoul full of hope but wondering how Jappeloup would react to the long journey and the utterly strange environment of Korea.

In the Nations Cup a fence down and time penalty in the first round were followed by one of only two clear rounds in the entire competition to give France the bronze medal. Would Jappeloup's temperament survive the ultimate test of the individual event? In the first round only Karsten Huck of Germany, Ian Millar of Canada and Pierre jumped clear, but the last two had ¾ and ¼ of a time penalty respectively. In the second round Big Ben lowered three fences to put Millar back down the line, and Jappeloup had to go clear to put the pressure on Huck's Nepomuk. Moreover Greg Best was already clear for the USA on Gem Twist for a total of four penalties. With nothing in hand, Pierre hoped that Jappeloup would keep his concentration. Concentrate he did, and with just one penalty for time a gold medal beckoned. Watch Nepomuk he could not, but as the German lowered the ninth fence, Pierre's team mates lifted the new Olympic Champion shoulder high. France had won her first individual medal for jumping since Pierre Jonquères d'Oriola won his second gold medal in Tokyo twenty-four years previously.

To round off a great year they won the Audi-Masters Grand Prix in Paris, and in 1989, after near misses in the Grands Prix in Cervia (Italy), Rome, and Stockholm, came to Rotterdam to defend their European title. A lapse of concentration in the first competition against the clock dropped Jappeloup to nineteenth place, but a clear round and eight penalties in the second brought them back into contention, and a faultless performance in the first round of the third competition found them in fifth position. The course for the final round was huge and the distance tightly measured. Jappeloup's jumping was as brilliant as ever, but half a time penalty dropped them back to sixth place. How expensive that lapse on the first day had been!

But horses are not machines, even the greatest have momentary lapses, and Jappeloup has thrilled crowds around the world with his sparkling performances, and Pierre has drawn their admiration for his handling of the difficult gelding who was once almost unridable. So what now lies ahead?

OPPOSITE

Pierre Durand (France), European Champion 1987 and Olympic Champion 1988, with Jappeloup de Luze and Narcotique (Team Renault)

After his Olympic victory, Pierre decided to set aside his legal career for the time being, and to concentrate on top level competition. French car makers Renault, already sponsors of jumping, formed Team Renault, consisting of Pierre Durand and Michel Robert, and Pierre, anxious to allay any suggestion that he was a 'one horse rider', bought (for two million French francs) a mare called Narcotique, on whom he has already won the St Gallen Grand Prix and been second in Luxembourg in 1989. He also has part ownership of a six-year-old stallion called Rock du Taillan, and rides the seven-year-old mare Quieva du Marais. 'My aim,' he says, 'is to prolong the competitive career of the fourteen-year-old Jappeloup, extend his already brilliant results, and bring my other horses up to his level of competition.'

As to advice to young riders: 'The young rider must learn to understand and respect the horse; he must set himself goals and define a path from which he deviates as little as possible; he must learn by himself in order to form his own opinions.'

As a lawyer, Pierre has strong opinions regarding the state of the sport today and the improvements that he would like to see in the future.

I think that our sport is judged differently in different countries; in general it is not sufficiently recognised by the media, and some of our competitors and officials lack the maturity and vision to realise the great potential of our sport in the future. I would like to see a greater respect for sporting ethics, a better definition of the rules and of the concept of competitions, a tightening up of the control of the running of events, and more respect for the horse.

One of the fascinating aspects of the jumping sport is the differing styles of the various nations, due in no small measure to the differing breeds of horses. The Germans, usually mounted on big strong, obedient horses, ride with the utmost precision, a style epitomised by Franke Sloothaak and the great Walzerkönig. From Great Britain, whose riders are among the most effective but seldom the most stylish in the world, we have the sheer poetry and perfection of Milton, ridden so quietly and sympathetically by John Whitaker. The riders of USET, with their big Thoroughbred horses, are not only among the most effective but exhibit a style that almost everyone would like to imitate. But for sheer brilliance none can match the ebullient little French horses, skilfully ridden with typically Gallic élan, who when they win, as they so often do, draw a bigger cheer than any others.

Horses like Jappeloup, and riders like Pierre Durand, thrill spectators around the world, indoors and out of doors, and it would surprise nobody if Pierre were to become the second rider, and the second Frenchman, to win two Olympic gold medals for jumping.

Great Britain

NICK SKELTON

Bob Langrish

The great horseman is likely to achieve success in which ever branch of horsemanship he enters, and Nick Skelton might well have been included in the section of this book devoted to National Hunt jockeys alongside John Francome and Peter Scudamore, for it was in National Hunt racing that his ambitions originally lay. His father, a chemist by profession, had served in the Royal Army Veterinary Corps in Egypt, and Nick received his first pony when a mere two years old. The family lived not far from Warwick racecourse, and it was there that Nick's interest in steeplechasing was aroused. But also not far away was the establishment of one of the most successful producers and trainers of show jumping horses and riders in England, and in 1974 at the age of sixteen Nick joined Ted Edgar's stable.

Ted is himself a former winner of the King George V Gold Cup, and with his instruction, with the example of his wife Elisabeth, one of England's most successful lady riders (and sister of David Broome), and with the sponsorship of Everest Double Glazing to ensure a supply of potentially top class horses, Nick could scarcely have found a better start. The partnership was to endure for twelve years.

In 1974 Nick rode for the gold medal team at the Junior European Championships, and the following year he won the individual title on Everest OK. His first chance to ride in a Nations Cup came in 1978, but that was the era of the Great British team of Derek Ricketts, Caroline Bradley, Malcolm Pyrah and David Broome, and he had to wait until December of the following year for his first Nations Cup win, at Zuidlaren in Holland. Since then he has ridden in over twenty winning teams.

In 1978 at Olympia he broke the British high jump record set by Donald Beard in 1937 at 2.29m (7ft 6¼in), when he cleared 2.32m (7ft 7¼in) on the grey German bred Everest Lastic, on whom he won the Geneva World Cup qualifier and finished in seventh place in the World Cup Final of that season. But he really hit the international headlines when at the substitute Olympics at Rotterdam in 1980 he was one of only three riders to jump double clear rounds (with Everest Maybe) in the Nations Cup, in which the team won the silver medal. In 1982 Nick was classified as a professional, and his next chance to ride in the Olympics did not come until 1988 in Seoul after the reclassification of professionals as 'competitors', and he finished in sixth place in the individual event.

In 1985 he had taken the bold decision to leave the Edgar/Everest establishment and set up on his own, and thanks to the solid grounding and international experience that those twelve years with Edgar had given him, and to his own determination and ability, his success continued.

In the World Championships Nick took the team bronze medal in 1982 with Everest

European League in 1982/83 and were third in the Final of 1982.

Having once established himself, it is not too difficult for a successful rider to find good horses; they tend to find him! But John was exceptionally lucky that as Ryan's Son reached the retiring age, another star appeared. And if the retiring star had endeared himself to the public as much for his idiosyncrasies as for his ability, the grey Milton was to capture the hearts of the fans through the sheer elegance and apparent effortlessness of his performance.

It is unfortunate that in Great Britain the breeding of show jumpers and other competition horses is not yet on a level with that on the continent, but Milton is an example of successful breeding with show jumping as the aim. His sire, the Dutch bred stallion Marius, combined his stud duties with a successful jumping career in the hands of the late Caroline Bradley, who also broke in the grey Milton and started him jumping. John took him on in 1985, and quickly had him ready to take over from Ryan's Son.

That year they won the World Cup qualifier in Bordeaux, and since then they have won Grands Prix in Birmingham, Calgary, Rotterdam, Stuttgart, Brussels, Cannes, Göteberg and Paris, as well as the Dinard Derby and World Cup qualifiers in s'Hertogenbosch, Paris and Geneva. At the World Championships of 1986 in Aachen they took a team silver medal and at the following year's European Championships they took team gold and individual silver.

If ever a horse deserved to start as favourite for the Olympic title, none had a better claim than Milton, and in Seoul in 1988, with the relaxation of the ban on professionals, or rather their reclassification as 'competitors', Great Britain had the opportunity of fielding her best possible team for the first time since 1972. It was unfortunate, therefore, both for the team and for John, that Milton's owners felt that they were not prepared to allow him to travel to Korea, and their presence was sorely missed.

But 1989 started well for John, with the Cannes Grand Prix for Milton and the Hamburg Derby for Gammon, and the combination arrived in Rotterdam for the European Championships in fine form. (Although John's name has come to be associated with two great horses, his success has by no means been confined to these two; Novelheiro, Clonee Temple, Hiliopolis, and Gammon are just some of the others he has taken to the top.)

The first competition of the Championships always involves something of a gamble for the best horses, for it is run under Table 'C' (with seconds added for a fence down) over a very big course, and there were plenty of speed merchants in the field, notably the ebullient little French horses, including the reigning Olympic Champion Jappeloup de Luze. But Milton's smooth flowing style conceals the fact that he can also cover the ground at speed, often taking out a stride between related fences, and John's performance in this opening competition must rank as one of his best. Without appearing to be in a hurry, they came home nearly three seconds ahead of Michel Robert of France!

The second competition involves two rounds over a Nations Cup course, and in the first round Milton never looked like touching a fence but, for the first time ever, he dropped a foot on the lath of the water. In the second round John became slightly anxious about the time (several riders incurred time penalties) and in cutting the corner to the penultimate fence they had it down. The team were assured of the gold medal, but

John had to surrender the individual lead to brother Michael, whose two clear rounds had pulled Monsanta up from tenth place to first.

In the first round of the two-round final for the individual title both Milton and Monsanta jumped clear but, over a course for which the time was very tight, Monsanta picked up half a time penalty, thus reducing the gap between them to less than three points. With the two brothers last to jump, the atmosphere was electric, but Milton produced a typically effortless performance for just half a penalty for time. Britain had secured the individual gold medal in addition to winning the team title, but which brother would take home the medal?

Monsanta lowered a fence, so John became European Champion. John has always been totally unflappable, and has displayed little more outward emotion after winning a Grand Prix than Lester Piggott did after winning the Derby. And on this occasion he was torn between joy at taking a major Championship after so many silver medals and sadness at depriving Michael of the title. However, on their present form the brothers will be fighting each other for titles for some time to come.

Although John acknowledges that much of his present success is due to Milton, nevertheless it is he who has made the horse into the star that he is, and Milton is a vastly different type from Ryan's Son. In the 1989 ranking list for British riders John accumulated more than twice the number of points as the second placed rider, who happened to be brother Michael. In John's hands Milton won four times as much prize money as the second horse in the table, and his winnings exceeded £¼m (approximately

US $400,000) in this year alone. In April 1990, John became only the second European rider to win the World Cup when he and Milton led from start to finish in the final at Dortmund.

John is reticent about the secret of his success, but it is evident that apart from his dedication and hard work, he has a natural talent and a deep sympathy with his horses. Totally unflappable, he not only trains his horses to perfection, but he also fills them with confidence in the arena. He has achieved much already; but maybe the best is yet to come.

John Whitaker (GB), European Champion 1989, with Milton (Bob Langrish)

MICHAEL WHITAKER

In the middle seventies the Libyans, having spent considerable sums of money in training a jumping team, spent even more on the construction of an equestrian stadium on a patch of desert outside Tripoli. Masses of concrete had been translated, by Italian architects and East European labour, into grandstands, offices and bars (though alcoholic drinks were barred), stabling for several hundred horses had been constructed, and special grass seed had been imported from America to ensure a green attractive arena.

The FEI had sanctioned a CSIO, and teams from several European nations were flown to Tripoli at their hosts' expense, including those from Germany and Great Britain. The Libyan riders, mounted mainly on expensively imported German and Irish horses, were keen to do well, and indeed their performance was extremely creditable. But in the speed competitions and in jump-offs they galloped so fast that it took them a considerable distance to make their turns, and it took them a while to realise why an unknown Englishman won most of their competitions.

This was Michael Whitaker's first CSIO, and he displayed that calm, smooth and economical style of riding that has since taken him to the top, and which has enabled him to get the best out of so many different horses. Born near Huddersfield, Yorkshire, he started riding almost as soon as he could walk, and was winning jumping competitions by the time he was eight. In 1976 when he was only sixteen he won both the Junior and the Young Rider Championships at Wembley's Horse of the Year Show, and two years later he was in the winning team at the Junior European Championships.

His first big win came in 1980 when he became the youngest ever winner of the Hickstead Derby on Owen Gregory, on whom he later won three Grands Prix including World Cup qualifier victories in Amsterdam and London. But it was the 1982 season that really sent him on his way, when he won the King George V Gold Cup in London and the Grand Prix in Tripoli with Disney Way, and as a result of further successes in 1983, including the Grand Prix in Barcelona and the World Cup qualifier in London, he was selected for the Los Angeles Olympics with Overton Amanda.

In the Nations Cup Amanda jumped one of only nine clear rounds out of just over a hundred in the entire competition to help Great Britain to a silver medal behind the United States – a creditable effort considering that many of her best riders were still barred as professionals. In the individual event only two riders (and two mares) went clear in the first round, Joe Fargis for the USA on Touch of Class, and Michael on Amanda. Could Michael, still only twenty-four, win the sport's highest accolade?

In the second round Touch of Class lowered a fence to finish on four penalties, and Joe Fargis was joined on this score by his team mate Conrad Homfeld, for whom Abdullah

Mark Phillips CVO *(GB) – Badminton winner 1971, 1972, 1974, 1981 – Lincoln, Badminton 1980* (Bob Langrish)

Ginny Leng MBE *(GB) – World Champion 1986, European Champion 1985, 1987, 1989, bronze medals, Olympic Games 1984, 1988 – Master Craftsman, Stockholm 1987* (Bob Langrish)

jumped a brilliant clear round. A clear would give Michael the Olympic title, and one fence down, would mean a three way jump-off. What happened at the combination of a wall and two oxers over ditches is now history, but in view of the mare's subsequent successes it is worth recalling her rider's views on what went wrong.

We had trained Amanda over ditches at home, and up to that point she had jumped them all in Los Angeles. But the first part of the combination was the wall at 1.68m (5ft 6in), and she never saw the first ditch with the oxer over it until she was in mid-air. She just hesitated for an instant, and as a result gave herself no chance of coming out the far end of the combination.

In the circumstances they did well to come out of it at all, and to finish twenty-eighth out of fifty-one starters.

And 1984 was in other respects not too bad a year, for Michael won the National Championship, the Aachen Championship and the World Cup qualifiers in Amsterdam and London. From 1985 onwards he became a regular member of British Nations Cup teams, and in that year he took a team gold medal in the European Championships with Warren Point, who in 1986 won the Dortmund World Cup qualifier and two Grands Prix at Hickstead, as well as helping Great Britain to a silver medal at the World Championships in Aachen. In 1987 Amanda won a team gold medal at the European Championships and Warren Point took the Grand Prix in Wembley.

The year 1989 looked like being a vintage one from the start, when Monsanta won the s'Hertogenbosch World Cup qualifier, and Didi the Grand Prix. Monsanta then won in Dortmund, Göteborg and Hickstead, while Didi won the Birmingham Grand Prix. It also led to the high point (so far) of Michael's career.

At the European Championships the first competition always involves a bit of a gamble, judged as it is under Table 'C' (with seconds added for a knock-down) over a big Table 'A' type course. Monsanta jumped clear, but had to be content with tenth place, one behind Nick Skelton and Apollo, with brother John in the lead on Milton at this stage. But in the second competition, over a Nations Cup course, Monsanta was the only horse to achieve two clear rounds, which gave Great Britain the team Championship and put Michael in the lead for the individual title, just a few time penalties ahead of his brother.

And in Rotterdam's picturesque arena time was to be an important factor in the final of two rounds over a huge course. In the first round Milton went clear, and so did Monsanta, but his half penalty for time reduced the deficit to less than three points. Milton's half penalty in the second round still meant that Michael had to go clear to take the title. Britain was now assured of the gold medal, but which brother was to be European Champion? Alas (for Michael) Monsanta lowered the penultimate fence, and he had to be content with the silver medal.

There was some consolation for this when three weeks later Michael and Monsanta won the world's richest show jumping prize. The Calgary Grand Prix was worth

OPPOSITE
World Champions in action – Lucinda Green MBE (GB), Regal Realm, Burghley 1985 (Bob Langrish)

Michael Whitaker (GB) congratulates brother John who has just deprived him of the European Championship of 1989! (Bob Langrish)

£87,000 (approximately US $135,000) to the winner, and even brother John was not altogether unhappy when Milton collected £21,164 for finishing fourth, deprived of another chance of beating his younger brother by a mere quarter of a time penalty.

His success so far Michael attributes to his mother, who taught him how to ride and who instilled the quiet style which has enabled him to get the best out of many different horses, to his father, who instilled the will to win, and to champion Horse Trials rider and trainer Lars Sederholm, who has helped him particularly with his work on the flat.

After a decade of international experience, Michael feels that the sport is in good shape. 'We need four things to keep the sport healthy: good organisation, good ground to jump on, good courses and good prize money, and by and large I think we have these.'

We are likely to see plenty more of the younger Whitaker, and if great horsemen are born rather than made, then there is every chance that the Whitaker name will be around in the twenty-first century, for Michael's wife Veronique was (before their marriage) a successful Belgian rider who won a team gold (1975) and two individual silver medals (1976 and 1977) at the Junior European Championships, and in 1984 she won the Queen Elizabeth II Cup at Birmingham's first Royal International Horse Show.

Part V

THE THREE DAY EVENT

 THE THREE DAY EVENT: hardly an inspiring name for perhaps the most demanding of equestrian sports; and not just uninspiring, but in these days not particularly accurate either, since most top-class three day events take place over four days. It embraces dressage, cross country and show jumping, and there was a time when its exponents were regarded as 'jacks of all trades and masters of none'. How is it then that Lucinda Green and Ginny Leng can take their place with Olympic athletes alongside Ian Botham (cricket) and Bill Beaumont (rugby football) on BBC's 'Question of Sport'? And how did New Zealand's Mark Todd put the name of his country into the forefront of equestrian sport when it had previously been mainly connected with rugby football?
of equestrian sport when it had previously been mainly connected with rugby football?

The three day event originated as a competition for cavalry officers of the European armies, and developed from the requirements of the cavalry charger. First, he was required to be obedient and steady on parade – hence the dressage test of the first day. Next, he had to be able to cross a considerable stretch of the countryside at varying paces, negotiating whatever obstacles might block his path – the roads and tracks, steeplechase and cross country. Finally, he was required to show that in spite of his exertions of the previous day, he was sound and fit to continue in service, and a relatively simple show jumping test was designed to demonstrate this.

Thus today's three day event starts with a dressage test, which may take two days to complete if there are more than about forty competitors. On what is normally referred to as cross-country day, competitors must complete up to almost 20 kilometres of roads and tracks, a steeplechase of up to 3½ kilometres, and a cross-country course of up to 8 kilometres with as many as thirty-two obstacles, and on the steeplechase and the cross country speed is a crucial factor. The last day's show jumping test is not too difficult, but the scores of the leaders are usually so close together that a clear round in this final test can be decisive.

Surprisingly enough, since British cavalry officers were in the early days more concerned with foxhunting than with competitions, the event became known as 'The Military', a term still used on the continent today, though in official FEI language it is the 'Concours Complet d'Equitation', a more accurate description of what it is all about than the English term 'three day event'.

The first Olympic competition was held at Stockholm in 1912, and the early events were dominated by Sweden and Holland, who between them took home fourteen of the thirty medals at the first five Games at which this event was staged. A record that was to stand for nearly half a century was set by **Charles Pahud de Mortanges** of Holland, who

The dressage arena at the Olympic Three Day Event, Seoul 1988 (Brian Hill)

rode Marcroix to victory at Amsterdam in 1928 and at Los Angeles four years later.

The format of the competition, apart from relatively minor modifications, has remained the same since the Berlin Olympics of 1936. Until 1960 teams consisted of only three riders, all of whom had to finish in order to produce a team score; from 1960 onwards a fourth rider was added, with the best three scores counting towards the team score, which enabled many more teams to complete the competition. In Berlin, where only three teams completed, the British team secured their first medal due to the tenacity of **Captain Dick Fanshawe**. After being submerged in the infamous Pond, he chased his horse across country on foot, and eventually returned to complete the course with a record penalty score. (Today, help is allowed in catching a loose horse, while there is a strict time limit within which each phase of the competition must be completed.)

Great Britain did not really become a force to be reckoned with until the events of the London Olympics of 1948 fired the imagination of the riding fraternity, and in particular of the 10th Duke of Beaufort, who offered his Badminton park as the venue for a British three day event. Four years later the British team might well have improved on their Berlin performance but for an unlucky technical elimination.

But if the British had been slow to take to what for them was a new equestrian sport, once they had started their experience of cross-country riding, both in the hunting field and on the racecourse, stood them in good stead. In 1953 they won the team gold and individual gold and silver medals at the first European Championships at Badminton, and in the following year they made a clean sweep of all the medals in Basle, repeating this feat in 1955 when the Championships were held by the invitation of HM The Queen at Windsor. Then in Stockholm in 1956 Great Britain won her first Olympic team gold medal together with individual bronze.

These medals were mainly won by the same three riders, and there can be little doubt that had they entered the sport at the age at which most riders do today, they would have dominated it for a very much longer period than they did. **Laurence Rook** was a major in the Royal Horse Guards who, like many cavalry officers of the time, was fortunate enough to compete in show jumping competitions in Germany after World War II on top-class German horses which had been taken over by the Allied Armies of Occupation, and he went into training at Aldershot in 1948 with the team for the London Olympics. After riding in Nations Cups in London and Dublin, Laurence turned to the new sport of eventing, and in 1951 he had his first ride round Badminton.

In 1952 he teamed up with **Reg Hindley** and **Bertie Hill** for the Helsinki Olympics, and as he neared the end of the cross-country course a team medal looked distinctly possible. But as Starlight sped round the edge of a cornfield, he slipped into a small ditch, and they were both on the floor; no penalties, and they were quickly reunited, but Laurence had been concussed, a turning flag was missed, and with it any hope of winning a medal.

At Badminton's European Championship of 1953, Starlight was dropped from the team because of his excitability in the dressage, whereupon Laurence proceeded to add his own gold medal to that of the British team by a margin of forty-four points! After collecting further Championship team gold medals with Starlight in 1954 and 1955, at Badminton in 1956, all set for the Olympics, Starlight jumped out of the dressage arena, and Laurence switched to Wild Venture for the Games, where the gold medal firmly established Great Britain as a major eventing nation. When Laurence retired from competitive riding, the FEI made use of his experience by appointing him as technical delegate at three Olympic Games, a Panam Games and a European Championship, and he spent some years as British delegate to the General Assembly.

Frank Weldon was commanding the King's Troop, Royal Horse Artillery when in 1952 he decided 'To have a go at Badminton', and though this first venture landed him in hospital, he became 'hooked' on the sport. In the spring of 1953 he won a one day event, as a result of which he joined the British team for the European Championships with the ex-racehorse Kilbarry, helping the team to their first major international success and taking the silver medal behind Laurence Rook.

In 1954 they were unlucky not to go one better at Badminton when the timekeeping system failed on the steeplechase, though they would still have won had not Kilbarry lowered two show jumps on the third day which relegated them to second place once again. But the next year they won the European Championship at Windsor and the autumn three day event at Harewood, and in 1956 they won Badminton and took the individual bronze medal as part of the gold medal team in Stockholm. Kilbarry was a great horse, but his boldness was ill-rewarded when at the first fence at a one day event he was brought down by a hidden pole in a brush fence and broke his neck.

Frank Weldon (GB), Olympic bronze medallist, European Champion, and for twenty-four years director of Badminton, with Kilbarry at Badminton 1956 (Desmond O'Neill)

Frank, who spent four years of World War II in the notorious Colditz prisoner-of-war camp, had started eventing at an age when most riders are considering retirement. But he still continued, and in 1959 he was fifth and ninth at Badminton on Samuel Johnson and Fermoy, and took team and individual silver medals at the European Championships at Harewood. In 1962 he was once again second at Badminton, this time on Young Pretender. But in 1965 came the opportunity to start rendering a service to the sport which few others have ever equalled – he became director of Badminton, combining this with the function of course designer. Over the next twenty-four years he raised the event to a level at which it became, with Burghley, one of only two 3-star events in the FEI calendar, and he was able to design courses that terrified riders, but seldom hurt horses. Under his direction Badminton became the one event in the world that all the top riders wanted to win.

Bertie Hill, the third member of this great team, entered the sport from a different direction. He successfully adapted his experience as a race rider to the requirements of cross country and dressage, and the theory that a natural horseman can successfully adapt not only to different horses but also to different equestrian sports was supported by one of the dressage judges at Bertie's first Badminton in 1952, who noted that here was a rider with a sound seat, good hands, tact and a sense of rhythm.

That same year Bertie rode Stella, owned by (Sir) John Miller, who later became the Crown Equerry, into eighth place at the Helsinki Olympics, where he and Reg Hindley were the first civilians to represent Great Britain in this sport, and but for Laurence Rook's unlucky fall on the flat a gold medal would have been possible. But he earned his reward over the next three years when the team won three European Championships in succession, with each member also winning an individual title, Bertie winning at Basle in 1954 on Ted Marsh's Crispin.

In 1955 he had taken the individual bronze at Windsor on Countryman, and here clearly was an Olympic horse. But the demands of farming in Devon meant that he had to sell him, and how fortunate it was for Great Britain and for Bertie when HM The Queen stepped in to buy him. At Badminton they came fourth, and at the Stockholm Olympics, in his final appearance for his country, Bertie's horsemanship was tested to the full. In appalling weather, Countryman slipped on taking off at the trakehner, and became straddled on the fence; British hopes seemed doomed. Countryman was pulled off the fence, but back onto the take-off side, and not many horses would have then jumped the fence as Countryman did. He won the first gold medal for Great Britain at the Olympic three day event, which was a fitting end to Bertie's career as a competitive rider.

But that was not the end of the story, for Bertie went on to become one of the country's greatest trainers of riders and horses, producing among others the grey Chicago, who with **Mark Phillips** (see p231) helped the team to victory in the 1970 World Championships at Punchestown.

The first five Badminton winners all held military rank, but in 1954 **Margaret Hough** gave notice that neither the military nor indeed the men were to have things all their own way when with Bambi V she snatched victory from Frank Weldon and Kilbarry. And in 1955 at Windsor no particular notice was taken of a horse called High and Mighty who finished in thirteenth place, 156 points behind the winner; but when at Badminton in 1956 he came second, less than two points behind Kilbarry, and forty-four ahead of

A. E. (Bertie) Hill (GB), European Champion 1954, team gold medal Olympic Games 1956, with HM Queen Elizabeth II's Countryman III (Leslie Lane)

anyone else, the name of **Sheila Willcox** forced itself into the headlines. It was to stay there for the next three years, for she won Badminton with High and Mighty in 1957 and 1958, on both occasions by huge margins, and after her marriage won it again in 1959 with Airs and Graces, the only rider to have won three times in succession. Second in 1959 was the present Duke of Beaufort, who now owned Countryman. As **David Somerset**, he lay fifty-seven points behind Sheila after the dressage, but in appalling conditions he and Countryman pulled themselves up into second place after the cross country, a position which they held to the end.

For good measure, Sheila won the Harewood Three Day Event in 1956 with High and Mighty, who then took the team and individual gold medals at the Copenhagen European Championships of 1957. Surely here was a rider whom any country would be happy to have in their Olympic team! But there was a snag: with only three riders allowed, it was felt for a variety of reasons (chivalry, kindness or male chauvinism!) that a lady rider should not be put under the sort of pressure to finish a competition that, for example, was to lead to **Bill Roycroft** discharging himself from hospital in Rome with a broken shoulder in order to win a team gold medal for Australia in 1960.

It was not until 1964 that the rule was changed, but by then Sheila had turned to the quieter fields of dressage. She did, however, return to Badminton in 1965 to be third with Glenamoy, and then in 1968 she became the first rider to win all three major British three day events of her time when she won Burghley with Fair and Square. This was to provide her with a link to the great lady riders of today, for Fair and Square was the sire of Be Fair, who won Badminton in 1973 for Lucinda Prior-Palmer (now Lucinda Green).

But if there was any undue optimism in Great Britain after recent Olympic and European Championship successes, this was shattered at Badminton in 1960. Nobody showed much more than a polite interest in the Australian team that had entered in preparation for the Olympics, until **Bill Roycroft** won it with Our Solo, and the others took second, third, fourth, tenth and eleventh places! But when rumours came out of Aldershot, where the Australians went into training for the Games, that they were working their horses for four hours or more each day, it was widely thought that they might well be leaving their medal hopes behind on the training gallops.

In Rome, sixth place for the team after the dressage looked respectable for a nation without a long history of participation in the sport, and when **Neale Lavis**, **Laurie Morgan** and **Brian Crago** all went clear on the cross country, while disasters had struck most of the other teams, gold medals looked almost a foregone conclusion. But for one thing: Brian Crago's horse had broken down. But the Aussies had not come from the other side of the world for nothing, and the fact that Bill Roycroft, though he had completed the course, was in hospital with a broken shoulder was not going to prevent the team and individual gold medals from going 'down under'. Bill discharged himself from hospital, jumped a clear round (on his Badminton winner Our Solo), and with **Anton Buhler** of Switzerland allowed just the bronze medal, the Europeans wondered what had hit them!

And if the British in particular thought that this triumph was just a one-off feat, another surprise lay in store for them in 1961, when the new Whitbread Trophy at Badminton also disappeared to Australia! Like many of his countrymen, **Laurie Morgan** was a true all-round horseman, and he returned to England to win the Foxhunters Steeplechase at Cheltenham in March with Colledge Master, and then in April Salad

LEFT: *Michael Plumb (USA) – silver medals at the World Championship 1974 and Olympic Games 1976 – with Blue Stone* (Bob Langrish). RIGHT: *Jack Le Goff (France), Olympic three day event rider and trainer of the USA teams to fifteen Olympic and World Championship medals* (Findlay Davidson)

Days, runner-up the year before and Olympic Champion in Rome, won Badminton.

Like Frank Weldon, Bill Roycroft and Laurie Morgan were both in their forties, both outstanding horsemen, and it was only the accident of geography that deprived the international circuit of their skill over a much longer period. Nonetheless, Bill Roycroft went on to ride in three more Olympics, and produced two sons and a daughter-in-law who have between them been the mainstay of Australian teams up to and including the 1988 Olympic Games in Seoul. Truly a great eventing dynasty!

If Great Britain had dominated the international scene during the fifties, the next decade saw the emergence of a strong USA team, of whom not much had been seen in Europe since their triumph at the London Olympics of 1948. With far fewer opportunities for competition than the Europeans, the United States Equestrian Team (USET) has had to rely more on the squad system, which depends on a nucleus of good riders and horses, and on a sound trainer. Their success has been largely due to two great riders, **Bruce Davidson** (see p225) and **Michael Plumb**, and to a great trainer, Frenchman Jack le Goff, who did for their three day event team what Hungarian Bertalan de Nemethy did for their show jumpers.

It is sad that **Michael Plumb** has not been seen riding more in Europe, for since he competed in Rome in 1960 he has been USET's most consistent team member. In the States he has been Rider of the Year ten times, and at the Olympics he has won an individual silver medal (in Montreal) and four team medals. He was a member of the winning US team at Burghley's World Championships of 1974, taking the silver medal behind Bruce Davidson.

The Swedes, not having been embroiled as combatants in World War II, were able to carry their pre-war supremacy over to the post-war period, winning team silver and gold medals at London and Helsinki, and individual gold at both Helsinki (**Hans von Blixen-Finecke**) and Stockholm (**Petrus Kastenmann**).

The only other country to feature consistently in the results has been West Germany. The Germans have for long been superb competitive riders, but their three day event team found it difficult to beat the British and the Americans because their highly organised breeding system produced horses more suited to dressage and show jumping. And they certainly had the riders: **Wilhelm Büsing** and **August Lütke-Westhues** in the fifties; **Fritz Ligges**, three day event bronze medallist in Tokyo and team gold and bronze for show jumping in Munich and Los Angeles; **Karl Schultz** and **Horst Karsten** in the seventies, and in the eighties **Helmut Rethemeier**, and the victorious team of the Seoul Olympics, **Claus Erhorn**, **Matthias Baumann**, **Thies Kaspareit** and **Ralf Ehrenbrink**.

After the doldrums of the early sixties, British fortunes began to revive towards the end of the decade, when gold medals at the Mexico Olympics, the 1970 World

Mary Gordon-Watson (Great Britain), European Champion 1969, World Champion 1970, team gold medal Olympic Games 1972, seen here with Cornishman V (Leslie Lane)

Championships at Punchestown, and the 1967 (Punchestown), 1969 (Haras du Pin), and 1971 (Burghley) European Championships culminated in further gold medals at the Munich Olympics of 1972.

This period saw the emergence of riders of the calibre of **Richard Meade** (see p219), and **Mark Phillips** (see p231), who were backed up by the veteran **Derek Allhusen**, who was winning Olympic (team gold and individual silver in Mexico) and European Championship medals long after he should have retired; by **Jane Holderness-Roddam**, who won Badminton in 1968 with the diminutive Our Nobby before going on to Mexico, and who returned to win Badminton again in 1978 with Warrior, who also won Burghley for her in 1976; and by **Mary Gordon-Watson**, who with Cornishman V won the Haras du Pin European Championship of 1969, the Punchestown World Championship of 1970, and who missed an individual medal by one place when a member of the Munich gold medal team.

And so we come to the four riders who have dominated the sport in the eighties – **Lucinda Green** (p246), **Virginia Leng** (p253), and **Ian Stark** (p258) of Great Britain, and **Mark Todd** (p238) of New Zealand. But before considering their careers in detail, we must pay tribute to the unique contribution to the sport made by the President of the FEI, **HRH The Princess Royal**.

To partake in any sport in the glare of publicity that accompanies the British royal family is difficult enough; to be successful in this most demanding of equestrian sports in those circumstances shows considerable talent. After a sound grounding in one day events, Princess Anne, as she then was, rode her mother HM The Queen's Doublet into fifth place at Badminton in 1971. Selected as an individual for Burghley's European Championship later that year, she led from start to finish to become European Champion. Fourth at Badminton in 1974 on Goodwill, she brought home team and individual silver medals from the European Championships in Luhmuhlen in 1975, and then became the first member of the Royal Family to ride for Britain in the Olympic Games. At Montreal, Goodwill fell when the bank gave way as he was taking off at the zigzag fence over a big ditch. Princess Anne was concussed, but nevertheless finished the course and completed the competition next day. In 1986 Princess Anne was elected President of the FEI in succession to her father, Prince Philip, and it is doubtful whether the FEI has ever had a President with more practical experience of the problems of international competition than The Princess Royal.

HRH The Princess Royal (GB), European Champion 1971, and President of the FEI (Bob Langrish)

RICHARD MEADE, OBE

There can be few horsemen better qualified to be presidents of their national federations than Richard Meade, President of the British Equestrian Federation, for during a riding career that has spanned a quarter of a century he has known both the ultimate disappointment and the ultimate triumph, and has earned his success by sheer determination to succeed. In two Olympic Games his team failed to finish; in one of them he had every chance of winning an individual gold medal; in the other he narrowly missed an individual medal after a masterly performance on a relatively inexperienced horse. In two other Games he won three gold medals, the only three day event rider to have done so.

His enthusiasm for the sport of horse trials was kindled in 1949 when he attended the first three day event held at Badminton as a spectator. His first serious competition was as a member of the Monmouthshire branch of the Pony Club, which came second to the Beaufort in the Pony Club Horse Trials Championship of 1954 which was held at High Grove, now home of HRH The Prince of Wales, and in the same year he scored an important win for a young rider when he won the Boys' Individual Championship at Tetbury on Sir Harry Llewellyn's St Teilo.

Called into the Army for National Service, Richard joined the 11th Hussars at Carlisle, where he hunted with the Dumfriesshire, and when the Regiment moved to Omagh in Northern Ireland he took the opportunity to hunt whenever possible in the South. Later he went on a course just outside Dublin with Colonel Joe Hume-Dudgeon, triple winner of the Dublin Show Jumping Grand Prix, and also received encouragement from Captain Harry Freeman-Jackson, who rode no less than twelve times at Badminton, coming second in 1961, and who won Burghley in 1963.

In 1960 Richard watched the Olympic three day event in Rome, and was inspired to try to reach the top in this sport, which he then saw as adding a new dimension to his enjoyment of riding, previously found mainly in the hunting field. He therefore went over to Ireland with the object of finding a potential Olympic horse. He saw several, amongst which was a horse called Barberry, owned by Miss Kitty Clements, but not in fact for sale. However, she was persuaded to lease the horse to Richard.

Barberry started eventing in the spring of 1962, won the military section at the Tweseldown one day event in the autumn, and then the intermediate class at Chatsworth, having also travelled to Holland to take part in the International Students Rally at Amsterdam. A win at Crookham in the spring of 1963, and second place in the one day event that replaced a waterlogged Badminton, was followed by his – and Richard's – first three day event at Munich, which although only a CCI, was in effect an unofficial European Championship. As part of the victorious British team they finished in fifteenth place, with Captain James Templer, European Champion of 1962, as the winner.

It was at this stage that Richard realised that the British idea that all that mattered was the cross country was a misconception, and that it was not very sensible to burden oneself with a heavy load of penalties in the dressage in the hope of picking up the necessary bonus points on the following day – this under the old scoring system of penalties and bonus points. The Germans were then slightly amazed when a member of the British team that had beaten them earlier in the year returned to Munich in the winter of 1963/64 for instruction! But Richard felt that with the lack of indoor facilities in England in those days, it was difficult to make progress here, and in Ottokar Pohlmann, winner of the Harewood Three Day Event in 1958, he had found a most capable and sympathetic instructor.

But Richard admits that he then allowed the pendulum to swing too much the other way. At Badminton in 1964 Barberry finished the dressage in third place but was not fit enough to cope with the holding going; having gone perhaps too fast on the steeplechase they fell in the lake on the cross country, and finished in thirteenth place. But at Eridge One Day Event in the autumn they won the advanced class, and then beat all the Olympic probables when winning their first three day event at Burghley, thus earning their trip to the Olympic Games in Tokyo.

Never before had a three day event been held in Japan, but the hosts had put an immense effort into the organisation. Laurence Rook, a former European Champion, told how, as Technical Delegate, he arrived to find that the Japanese had interpreted literally the FEI rule laying down the number of cross country fences per kilometre, so that fences had been planned at equal distances from each other all the way round the course regardless of the ground! To horse and rider accustomed to England's 'green and pleasant land', the volcanic ash on which Tokyo's cross-country course was laid out came as something of a surprise, and the torrential downpour on cross-country day, together with a couple of mountain passes on the roads and tracks, made it a real test of stamina. But Barberry responded to every question asked of him, and at the end of cross-country day they were in the lead.

'To have made it to the Games was something; to be in the gold medal position at our first Olympics was incredible,' said Richard, 'and for twenty-four hours I was on top of the world.' What, therefore, went wrong? 'The volcanic ash, though quite light, was very deep and also rather abrasive, and just not suited to a very free-going horse. Having said that, in those days the show jumping just didn't receive all that much attention, even though a knock down incurred ten penalties, and certainly it was my weakest point.' A clear round was needed for the gold; one down would have ensured silver. Two fences down dropped them to eighth place. And apart from Richard's individual disappointment, only he and Ben Jones of the British team completed the course, which meant the team's elimination.

Some compensation for the disappointments of Tokyo came on their return home in the form of victory at Burghley, where two years later they won the silver medal in the World Championships behind Carlos Moratorio of Argentina. Team gold at the European Championships at Punchestown in 1967 was a fitting end to the career of the horse that had launched Richard on his way to the top. For the following year both

Richard Meade (GB) on his way to winning Burghley in 1964 on the first of his four Olympic horses, Barberry (Sport & General)

Barberry and Richard's reserve horse Turnstone were injured during the preparations for the Mexico Olympics, and at the very last moment he took over the ride on Mary Gordon-Watson's Cornishman V.

If anyone thought that Richard's success thus far had been solely due to the brilliance of one good horse, they were now to be proved wrong. Before leaving England for Mexico, Richard and Cornishman had jumped just one cross-country fence together; when they waited in the starting box for the starter to send them off on the Olympic cross country, that was still the extent of their experience together! For instead of the expected three weeks in Mexico in which to get to know each other – little enough before facing the Olympic challenge – quarantine restrictions, lack of training facilities, and the unfortunate fact that Richard pulled a muscle shortly after arriving, meant that there was no opportunity for cross-country schooling.

To add to the difficulties, the daily rain storm became a monsoon on the day of the cross country itself – 4½in (11cm) of rain fell in an hour and a quarter! But perhaps because of the influence of the hunting field, it is often the case that in such conditions British horses and riders survive when others fall by the wayside. At the end of the day, the British team were in the lead, with seven jumping fences in hand to win the gold medal. This they duly did, with Derek Allhusen and Lochinvar taking the individual silver, with Cornishman just missing a medal in fourth place, and Ben Jones fifth on The Poacher. In spite of the success still to come, this is the moment in his career that Richard likes to remember best.

After the disappointments of Tokyo, where our team, though favourites, had been eliminated along with Japan and Korea, this was a tremendous moment. And it was a fascinating team. Derek, who won the silver medal, was a grandfather, Jane Bullen a twenty-year-old student nurse, and Ben Jones a sergeant in the Army. And in Bill Lithgow we had a marvellous Chef d'Equipe. Even after I had won Badminton in 1970, I thought, winning Badminton is terrific, but it doesn't compare with winning a team gold medal at the Olympics, where you have your friends to share it with.

It is noticeable, when comparing the careers of great riders, that once they have established themselves good horses seem to turn up whenever required. Cornishman went back to Mary Gordon-Watson, with whom he was to win the European Championships in Haras du Pin in 1969 and the World Championships in Punchestown in 1970, and now Richard was to team up with The Poacher, ridden so brilliantly into fifth place in Mexico by Ben Jones.

From 1959 to 1965 there were two sections at Badminton, in order to avoid two days of dressage, and in 1960 and 1965 the Little Badminton sections were won by Captain Martin Whiteley, the second of these on The Poacher. As Martin was now in the process of exchanging the sword (service in the Rifle Brigade) for the pen (house tutor at Eton College), he offered the ride to Richard Meade. In 1970 with The Poacher, Richard won his first Badminton (with a plus score on the last occasion on which the old scoring system was used), and helped the British team to a gold medal and took the individual silver medal at the World Championships at Punchestown. Then in 1971 came another team gold in the European Championships at Burghley.

If the team triumph in Mexico in 1968 is what Richard likes to remember best, his double gold in Riem Stadium four years later was a moment that the hundreds of supporters who travelled out to the Munich Olympics will never forget. The team consisted of Mark Phillips on Great Ovation, on whom he had won Badminton in 1971 and 1972, Mary Gordon-Watson on Cornishman V, former European and reigning World Champions, Bridget Parker on Cornish Gold, and Richard, this time on Derek Allhusen's home-bred Laurieston, on whom he had been second at Badminton earlier in the year, behind Great Ovation and in front of Cornish Gold.

An early fall on the cross country by Great Ovation put the pressure on the other team members, and it became essential for Richard to do a fast clear round to ensure a lead over the Americans and the Germans. This he did, and a clear round in the jumping on the last day clinched the gold medals for the team and enabled Richard to become the first and only British rider to win an individual Olympic gold medal.

After a team bronze medal on Wayfarer II at the European Championships at Kiev in 1973, Richard rode Jacob Jones at the Montreal Olympics of 1976. This was another occasion on which the team failed to complete the competition, but it was no mean feat to ride the inexperienced Jacob Jones into fourth place, and the only other team member to finish, in spite of a heavy fall on the cross country, was HRH Princess Anne. Great Britain was among those countries that boycotted the Moscow Olympics of 1980, and at the substitute event at Fontainebleau Richard's mount, Kilcashel, had to be withdrawn through lameness, but the following year this combination were in the gold medal team in the European Championships at Horsens (Denmark).

Nineteen years after winning his first international three day event (at Munich in 1963) Richard won Badminton again in 1982 with Speculator, and a year later won Boekelo for the second time, riding the former show horse Andeguy.

So what seems to have been the secret of his success? Dedication, tenacity of purpose and a determination to learn would seem to have been important in his development.

A rider must first of all school his horse to be responsive, and he must know just what his horse is capable of doing when it comes to a competition. It is the horse that has got to jump the fence, and it's not enough just to say 'It's a question of mind over matter, I'm going to get to the other side of that fence.' The horse must want to take you to a fence, but it is the rider's responsibility to present him correctly, and to instil in the horse trust in his rider, a trust that must never be betrayed. There's much more technical know-how around today; the eighteen- and nineteen-year-olds now competing know far more than I ever did at thirty.

What then would be his advice to a young rider wanting to follow in his footsteps?

First of all, find the right horse. Then take things stage by stage and really learn the trade. There are no short cuts, and if a potentially brilliant horse is taken too fast, then when it reaches advanced level it will just get caught out. Obtain as much experience as you can. I learned a lot from the hunting field; for many riders this is not possible, but it can be a tremendous help.

Finding the right horse, of course, is not too easy. First of all he must be sound, and this means that he can't have any glaring conformation faults, because it is a tough sport and any weaknesses will be found out, whereas in some sports you might be able to get away with it. You need an athletic horse, and he must have the right temperament. But nowadays he must be capable of doing a good dressage test, and for that he must have three good paces. As for breeding, I don't mind a horse that is not quite Thoroughbred, since he may be that little more amenable, but on the other hand if he hasn't got quality he won't be able to do the speed. I liken it to driving a car along the motorway; if it is going flat out, it won't last, whereas the car that's just ticking over at cruising speed will last that much longer.

In his position now as President of the British Equestrian Federation, Richard can take an overall view of the prospect for the sport in the future.

At home I think the sport is basically in good shape because it is successful, has a broad base and has a good image, and any changes must come because they are what the sport needs and not because they are what sponsors want. We must allow sponsors to obtain commercial benefits, but the sport must not become a circus for the élite. We must also ensure that it remains a sport in which anyone can enter and in which, if they have the talent, they can rise to the top.

Internationally, I think it very important that the sport is built up in as many countries as possible. It is not enough to have a few good nations at the top, and then at the Olympics or

World Championships to have nations competing who are just not up to it. The sport must not become élitist, either in the economic or the technical sense. It is good, for example, that before the Seoul Olympics we had riders from Korea and Japan competing over here. But that is only good provided they go back and build up the sport at home.

It is interesting that Richard, like John Francome, considers that a rider's ability to reap the highest rewards depends considerably on his ability to project his personality and sell himself, but he feels that on the whole three day event riders do better than most (in non-gambling sports) and that generally the top riders have been able to achieve good endorsements and sponsorship arrangements.

One of the problems that has to be faced today is the use of medication on the competition horse, and in particular the use of the anti-inflammatory drugs such as phenylbutazone, commonly referred to as 'bute'. Under current FEI regulations its use is permitted up to a certain level, but there are moves afoot to ban its use entirely. Richard's view is the practical one, which also considers the well-being of the horse.

I think that bute should continue to be allowed up to the permitted level. Apart from anything else, if it is banned it will be replaced by another drug which may not be as easy to detect and control. I know that a three day event horse must trot up sound on the third day, but how many steeplechasers would trot up absolutely level on the day after a hard race? And don't a lot of hunters come out stiff after a long day's hunting? We have to strike a balance between the theoretical view that the horse should be given no help whatsoever to keep going, with the competitive viewpoint that if we have an anti-inflammatory drug which neither stimulates nor depresses, and which cannot enhance performance, it should be permitted within certain limitations.

The present limitations were laid down by the FEI after extensive tests, and if there is to be a change there must be a good reason for it. And if bute were to be banned, then there would have to be a phasing-out period of at least three years, otherwise there would be a time when many of the top international horses could no longer compete, while their replacements were not yet ready to compete at the same level. And from the horse's point of view, isn't it better for him to continue to compete comfortably rather than to be turned out in a field?

On the question of the Olympic Games, Richard's experience of six Olympiads leaves him in no doubt as to what is best for the sport.

I am very strongly of the opinion that the equestrian events should be part of the Olympic games, because I think it gives great strength to the sport, and it is the one time that it gets major worldwide coverage. It would probably still do so if there were separate equestrian games like the winter Olympics, though not to the same extent. And from the competitors' point of view one of the attractions of the Olympics is the chance to meet competitors from other sports and other nations.

The British Equestrian Federation is fortunate to have a President who has achieved the highest honours as a rider, and one who so obviously has the interests of all equestrian sports at heart.

BRUCE DAVIDSON

Just once in every rider's life there is one horse that means more than all the others put together; one horse that really becomes a friend . . . Other horses may be more brilliant and may bring more success, but this one horse remains in the rider's heart for ever.

When Bruce Davidson used these words he was referring to the horse that he took to at first sight after months of fruitless searching; to the horse that failed the vet when he first tried to buy him; to the horse that took him two years to learn to ride; to the horse that made him Champion of the World: Irish Cap.

Raised on a farm at Millbrook, New York, Bruce rode ponies from an early age, and through the Pony Club gained all-round experience which included hunting, hunter trials, showing, jumping, and, at the age of fifteen or sixteen, combined training or horse trials. He then came to the notice of one of two great trainers who have between them been responsible for the almost legendary success of USET – the United States Equestrian Team – over the last two decades. Bertalan de Nemethy came from Hungary to develop the jumping team, and spent much time scouring the country for potential riders. Bert recognised his potential, and Bruce was screened for the jumping squad, and on Bert's advice he went to Ireland and spent the summer at Colonel Joe Dudgeon's Burton Hall establishment just outside Dublin.

But because he had always preferred cross-country riding, Bruce was transferred to the three day event squad, and so came under the aegis of the other great trainer, Jack Le Goff. Since the formation of the US Combined Training Association in the middle sixties, the production of teams had been fraught with difficulty; distances were so huge, the opportunities for international competition were so limited, and though team bronze and silver medals had been picked up in Helsinki (1952), Tokyo (1964), and in Mexico in 1968, only one rider, Michael Page, had achieved an individual medal, and the promise of the team gold medal of 1948 had not been fully realised.

Jack Le Goff was well qualified to put matters right. As a member of the famous Cadre Noir at Saumur, he was an acknowledged expert in the training of horses to the highest levels of dressage; as one of its instructors he had a reputation for toughness and single-mindedness that put, if not the fear of God, then at least a considerable element of respect into his pupils; and in the field of eventing he had himself earned a team gold medal at the Rome Olympics, over a horrendously difficult course, and had trained the French team for the Mexico Games, where one of his riders had won the individual gold medal.

Into this regime came Bruce Davidson, with a horse that he didn't seem able to ride, and it says much for his natural ability that Jack, whose immediate aim was to produce a team for the 1972 Olympics, recognised his potential. In 1971 Bruce won the Canadian National Championships on the team horse, Plain Sailing, owned by Raymond

Firestone, and in the spring of the following year they crossed to England to prepare for the Games. In Munich the team silver medal, and eighth place for Plain Sailing, was a satisfactory start for the new regime, and back at home in Gladstone, New Jersey, preparations began with a four year plan for the next Olympics.

The immediate objective was the World Championship of 1974 at Burghley, and the season started well when Bruce was third at Badminton with Irish Cap. There was surprise when, after an otherwise clear round, he was credited – perhaps debited is a better word – with time penalties on the roads and tracks, but in any case he could not have caught the winner, HM The Queen's horse Columbus, ridden by Mark Phillips. Then a disastrous run in the Osberton Three Day Event, just six weeks before the World Championships, did nothing for Bruce's morale, especially as Irish Cap finished up lame, but a win at Bramham on one of the younger horses restored his confidence.

At Burghley Bruce was to run in third position for the team, with the experienced Mike Plumb the last of the four to go. In the dressage Irish Cap responded magnificently, produced his best ever test, and finished second, only three points behind the brilliant Russian stallion Tost. Next day the team's first rider to go, Don Sachey, had a fall on Plain Sailing, but Denny Emerson had gone clear on Victor Dakin. On the steeplechase Irish Cap devoured the fences with his long stride, and came home fifteen seconds inside the time, slowing down!

On the cross country, apart from Bruce's anxiety as to how his bold jumping horse would cope with Capability's Cutting, and a peck on landing over the awkward drop at the Waterloo Rails, there were no anxious moments, and Irish Cap completed a brilliant clear round, as did Mike Plumb on Good Mixture. At the end of the day, Mark Phillips had gone into the lead with Columbus, with Bruce less than a point ahead of Mike, but the American team had a lead of thirty-eight over the British.

But the whole point of the third day of the three day event is to show that the horse is still fit to continue in service, and he has to show this first by passing inspection by the Ground Jury, and then by completing a jumping course in the main arena. The scenes in the stables that night were dramatic; Plain Sailing had a painful and swollen bruise on his stomach, Victor Dakin had a suspicious-looking tendon, and Good Mixture had a badly bruised leg. But across in the British team stable the hopes of a World Champion for HM The Queen to follow her European Champion of 1971, Doublet, ridden by Princess Anne, were fading as Columbus appeared to have slipped a tendon off the hock.

After much work with ice packs, the Americans passed inspection on the final morning, but though the withdrawal of Columbus had taken pressure off the team, Bruce now found himself with just a dozen fences in the main arena between him and the World Championship. But Irish Cap had performed like a champion on the previous day, and he wasn't going to throw it all away now. Team gold and individual gold and silver medals were reward for Goff's planning, and Bruce was World Champion.

The next objective was the Montreal Olympics in 1976, but before that came the Pan American Games of 1975 in Mexico, where Bruce took the silver medal behind Tad Coffin, and the team took the gold. It was not the simple victory that it sounded.

Bruce Davidson (USA), World Champion at Burghley 1974 and Lexington 1978 (Brian Hill)

The competition was a complete fiasco. Just as I entered the penalty zone in front of a huge oxer, a soldier dashed out and seized my horse by the bridle just as we were about to take off. There was a hold-up on the course and he'd been told to stop me at his fence. We all landed in a heap in the middle of the oxer. My horse was pretty shaken, but we finished the course. Then the ground jury said, 'That shouldn't have happened, we'll take your penalties away'.

Some medals, even when the opposition is not very great, are tougher to win than others! He also remembers riding a dressage test at Radnor when a dog fight started in the dressage arena. 'Then a little old lady ran in with a stick, screaming and beating the dogs, then someone else dashed in and the arena seemed quite full. We just continued with our test and eventually it all quietened down!'

Montreal was another triumph for the USET system of training and selection. While the British, as holders of the Olympic title, staked their hopes on horses that were experienced but whose soundness was questionable, the Americans, who put the emphasis on fitness and soundness, romped away with the medals – gold for the team, individual gold for Tad Coffin and silver for Mike Plumb. In spite of a fall in the water Irish Cap still finished in tenth place.

Bruce's victory at Burghley in 1974 gave the United States the right to hold the World Championships of 1978 at Lexington, Kentucky. He hoped to defend his title with Irish Cap again, but a week after being selected he went lame, and so Bruce switched to Might Tango, on whom he had won the US National Championships the previous year, but who was only seven and not very experienced. Kentucky in September can be almost unbearably hot and humid, but in spite of protests at the choice of site and date, the event went ahead, and no expense was spared either on the technical side or on the arrangements for competitors.

First of the American team and fifth overall to start, Might Tango produced a respectable dressage test to lie in eleventh place, with the United States leading from Germany by a single point, and with Great Britain third. Mike Plumb took the individual lead from Jane Holderness-Roddam and Warrior.

Shortly after 10 o'clock on the morning of cross-country day, Bruce set out on Phase 'A'; it was humid but not yet oppressively hot. The steeplechase course was more testing than usual, because of the undulating ground and the variety of obstacles, which included a water and a bullfinch; it was also very slippery. With a couple of anxious moments they survived, but when they arrived back in the box at the end of Phase 'C', no one had yet completed the cross-country; the first two had been eliminated and the next two were still out on the course.

At Fence 3, the Park Pavilion, Might Tango was distracted by the crowd and scrambled through it; at the Sinkhole (9 and 10) Bruce chose the safer route, but at the Fort Lexington complex (13 to 15) Bruce was nearly shot into orbit as his horse banked the first part. The Head of the Lake, a water ditch followed by a Normandy Bank into the lake, was a really testing fence that Might Tango took in his stride, and then they came to the notorious Serpent – best described as a zigzag of zigzags over a water ditch. The only horse to have got this far, Lucinda Prior-Palmer's Village Gossip, had fallen here, and Might Tango hit the third element but made a miraculous recovery to finish the course without further trouble.

It had been a severe course with obstacles of true World Championship status; but now the true problems were to become apparent. As Bruce was being debriefed by Jack Le Goff, Might Tango staggered and nearly collapsed; the heat and humidity had taken their toll of a great young horse that had given his utmost. It took all the efforts of the team vet, with ice packs, glucose, oxygen and intravenous injections to revive him.

Out on the course the disasters accumulated. For the American team Jim Wofford and Carawich, winner of Burghley with Aly Pattinson three years earlier, fell at the Serpent, Tad Coffin and Bally Cor, Olympic Champions, fell twice, and the dressage leaders Mike Plumb and Laurenson were eliminated at the Serpent after two stops at the Footbridge. The Serpent alone had accounted for two refusals, seven falls, six eliminations and three retirements. At the end of the day the stables looked like a horse hospital.

Might Tango was now in the lead, and the Canadian team, the only one to get four riders round, were way out ahead of the United States and Germany, the only other teams left in the competition. And the final day produced a 90°F (32°C) temperature with 90 per cent humidity. One of the strange conditions of the three day event is that, in order to maintain the relative influence of the three tests, the tougher the cross-country course, the tougher must be the jumping course on the final day, and the Lexington course was long, tough and containing several obstacles more usually found on the cross country, including a pond and a Devil's Dyke.

Second to go, Might Tango could knock two fences down and still win, but needed to jump clear to stand a chance of keeping the silver medal position for the team. Considering the state he had been in the day before, he did well to knock just two down. So Bruce retained his World Championship, a feat that no other rider has done before or since. The Canadians surprised everyone, as they had done in the Olympic show jumping ten years earlier, by taking the gold medal ahead of Germany and the USA.

Bruce was now top of the world, but the world of eventing had been shocked by the damage done to the image of the sport by the trail of disaster in Lexington. But it often takes a disaster to bring about reforms, and from now on those responsible for the sport were to start putting the welfare of the horse at the top of their list of priorities.

The World Champion of the seventies is still very much in contention today. To the substitute Olympics in 1980 USET sent a young team, but in Los Angeles in 1984 Bruce was a member of the gold medal team, finishing eleventh on J J Babu, on whom he had been runner-up at Badminton the previous year, less than one point behind Richard Meade and Speculator. In 1985 he won the hotly contested Boekelo Three Day Event in Holland with Dr Peaches, whom he then took to Gawlor, Australia, the following year to attempt the defence of his double World title. But it was not to be, for Dr Peaches was spun at the first horse inspection.

But in other respects 1986 was not a bad year, for J J Babu was sixth at Badminton, won the British Open Championship at Gatcombe, and was second by less than a point to Ginny Leng and Murphy Himself at Burghley. The following year Bruce won in Stockholm, where the Swedes were laying the foundations for the 1990 World Equestrian Games, and in 1988 he had a most successful season at home, continuing in the same vein in 1989. Not surprisingly, the World Champion has been Leading Rider in the States eight times, and has won the National Championship on six occasions.

It is perhaps surprising to hear one of the sport's most successful exponents say that individual success is not all that important to him.

I don't really set out for individual achievement. I love horses and I love the way of life that involvement with the sport brings. If a young rider wants to succeed he must know why he's doing it, and what he wants out of it, and understand that he will only get out of it what he puts into it. Our sport requires a complete horseman. Therefore he must start at the bottom, and learn all about horses, including the menial tasks like mucking out. Unless he really understands horses, when things go wrong he won't know what to do.

His priority when selecting the potential three day event horse, apart from the prerequisites of soundness and natural ability, lies in the gallop. 'The kind of gallop that you want must be natural and not something that you have to ask for; if you have to ask for it then he'll probably break down.'

Bruce has strong views about the state of the sport in general.

There have been many improvements in recent years, and there is room for more. But we must not change the character of the sport, which requires a complete horseman. If you reduce the endurance factor, for example, you reduce the need for horsemanship; you could coach someone through the event, because the rider's judgement wouldn't be so important. I would like to see better trot-up surfaces for the horse inspections; some are gravel, some cobblestones, some asphalt. But on the last day we are only seeking to ensure that the horse, who may be a bit footsore after the rigours of the cross country, is fit to jump twelve fences on grass. The non-slip surfaces at Seoul and at Burghley are good.

The horse inspection system, with a holding pen for doubtful cases, is now good, but in the ten minute box at the cross country start we must not let the vets take over, unless a horse is obviously in distress. Sometimes eight of the ten minutes are taken up with vets checking the horse, his temperature and heart rate, leaving no time to prepare him for the cross country.

We have a problem in the dressage judging. Too often you see someone judging who you know never rode a good test on any horse he ever sat on, so how does he know a good or a bad test when he sees one? But I don't know what the solution is, because in Seoul the straight dressage people were even less satisfied than we were.

On the question of medication, I think we must realise that by the time a horse reaches international level at the age of nine, ten or eleven, he inevitably shows signs of wear. And after he has exerted himself on the cross country, he may be a bit sore or stiff next day, just like the human athlete. I think it is wrong therefore to ban the use of bute, which isn't going to cover up any serious injury.

Some successful event riders have come into the sport from racing. One of Bruce's remaining ambitions is to ride round Aintree, and he has recently ridden in point-to-points and hunter chases in England, and has won a steeplechase at Cheltenham. His other interests include skiing, sailing, water sports and cross country running, and if it didn't conflict with his riding he would even like to run in a marathon.

Bruce is not just a complete horseman; he is not far from being a complete sportsman as well!

MARK PHILLIPS, CVO

If Mark did not actually ride before he could walk he must have come perilously close to doing so, for he apparently won his first rosette, on the leading rein, before his second birthday. He eventually joined the Beaufort Branch of the Pony Club, which was lucky enough to have two Olympic medallists to help with their instruction – Colonel Alec Scott (team bronze at the Berlin Three Day Event in 1936), and Lt-Col Frank Weldon (individual Olympic bronze in Stockholm and a member of the team that won the Olympic gold medal and three successive European Championships).

Neither the Junior nor the Young Rider programmes had been started by then, but the expert instruction that Mark received in the Pony Club, and the experience that he gained from competing in the team with older riders stood him in good stead when he progressed to eventing at senior level. His first horse was Rock On, with the reputation of being almost unrideable, and certainly uncontrollable across country, but with an otherwise admirable temperament. Mark was then lucky enough to come under the wing of another member of the British gold medal team, Bertie Hill, who very soon realised that in his new pupil he had a rider of considerable natural talent, with a horse who, if his courage and ability could be channelled in the right direction, could go to the very top.

By the autumn of 1967 Rock On had qualified for the Burghley Three Day Event in September. There was, however, just one snag: Mark was due to enter Sandhurst one week before Burghley, and cadets were confined to barracks for their first three weeks (until they were considered smart enough to be seen in public). But one of the fascinating things about the horse in life is that he very often opens doors that are closed. Serving at Sandhurst at the time was Lt-Col Bill Lithgow, former Commander of the King's Troop RHA and the 10th Hussars, who was later to become chef d'équipe of the British Team.

After a telephone call from Bertie Hill, Bill Lithgow ensured that Mark was posted to his college, and then took the decision to grant him leave to ride at Burghley without reference to the Commandant. These days a rider at a three day event reckons to spend the whole week there; Mark not only arrived at Burghley the night before the dressage test, but also had not ridden his horse for six weeks, Rock On having been down in Devon with Bertie Hill. But since after the dressage he was lying second to last, at least he was not going to hit the headlines and bring his absence to the notice of the military authorities.

But a spectacular cross-country round, by far the fastest of the day, brought them up into tenth place. Even this seemed fairly safe, but a clear round on the third day took them into fourth place, and people began to take notice.

'Bill Lithgow had told me to keep a low profile, and even finishing fourth we might have got away with it if the Commandant's daughter hadn't mentioned to him at breakfast how well one of his cadets had gone at Burghley!'

Fortunately the Commandant took an enlightened view of Bill Lithgow's initiative, and over the ensuing years the uniform of the Queen's Dragoon Guards was to keep the Army in the public eye on many important sporting occasions. Luckily Badminton came during Sandhurst's Easter break, and from twentieth position after the dressage, Mark and Rock On climbed to third place after the cross country. A mistake in the show jumping cost them a place, but fourth at Badminton was no mean feat, and brought their inclusion on the short list for the 1968 Olympic Games in Mexico, for which the Army was now quite happy to give him leave!

Mark was now to learn that three day eventing was a high risk sport, for Rock On broke down during a gallop in preparation for the final Olympic Trial at Burghley. But it says much for the selectors' regard for Mark's ability that they decided to take him to Mexico, without a horse of his own, as reserve rider. The success of the team in winning the gold medal fired his enthusiasm for the Olympics, though the ill fortune that had struck before Mexico was to pursue him occasionally over the next twenty years.

Meanwhile Mark had passed out of Sandhurst as the second best cadet of his year, and been commissioned in the Queen's Dragoon Guards; and his parents, his grandmother and his aunt, Flavia Phillips, had bought him a new horse, the four-year-old Great Ovation. Rock On had by now recovered and had been selected for the 1969 European Championships in France in September, with the proviso that he successfully completed the Punchestown Three Day Event three weeks earlier – a somewhat drastic preparation for a major event! However, with only a technical refusal at Punchestown the selectors were satisfied, and Mark was chosen to ride at Haras du Pin as an individual.

His first appearance with a Union Jack on his saddle cloth was not particularly auspicious, for in the dressage it slipped further and further back until it eventually fell off! On the second day Rock On's boldness and exuberance resulted in a fall at one of the easier fences on the stiff cross-country course and a refusal elsewhere, but still enabled him to return the fastest time of the day. His seventh place in his first European Championship was highly satisfactory, after which he set off to join his Regiment in Germany.

His hopes for 1970 rested on Rock On for Badminton, and then hopefully for the World Championships at Punchestown later in the year, and it was disappointing that after several weekends spent driving through the night in order to ride in England and return to duty by 9 o'clock on Monday morning, Rock On broke down again. But good riders find good horses, and Bertie Hill offered Mark the ride on the grey Chicago, and in spite of an injury to his back when Great Ovation fell just before the final trial, Mark and Chicago duly made the team for the World Championships.

Punchestown 1970, like Lexington 1978, is a date that brings back unhappy memories for officials, spectators and competitors alike. The size of the cross-country course was well up to championship standard, but the timber and the presentation of the obstacles were not, and there is nothing more dangerous than a course of large fences built of flimsy material. Chicago was in fifteenth position after the dressage, well in contention when faced with a stiff cross country, but heavy overnight rain turned the second day into a battle for survival.

The thirteen horses before me had all been eliminated, and I was held up for half-an-hour in the box, and three times on the course. All went reasonably well until we got to the bogey fence, a 2ft high and 6ft wide parallel with a drop of about 7ft on landing. Because of the number of falls at this obstacle, they had filled in the middle with brush – during the competition – and Chicago tried to bank it, and fell right in the middle of it. We could have walked out underneath the back rail, but unfortunately someone led Chicago out through the side of the fence, which meant that we had to jump the whole thing again.

Not only that, but we had to wait five minutes while they rebuilt the obstacle. When we eventually set off again, Chicago sailed over it, but by then a crowd had collected on the landing side, and inside the penalty zone. Either we ploughed into them or turned, and in turning we slipped and fell again, on the flat but inside the penalty zone. I think that jumping the last three fences knowing that another fall would eliminate us was my worst moment in a three day event.

But they finished without further incident, and on the third day the British team were so far ahead of the French, the only other team to complete the cross country, that they really only had to get their remaining three riders round the show jumping in order to win. The team gold medal and eleventh place for Chicago even after his two falls were compensation for an unhappy event.

At Badminton in 1971 Mark intended to ride Chicago, whom he hoped to partner in the European Championships later in the year. By now Bertie Hill had decided that he could no longer afford to keep and run Chicago, but since a syndicate had been formed to buy him for the British team, this did not matter. But when Chicago failed to satisfy the team vet and was sold to Germany, whom he was later to help to a silver medal at the Munich Olympics, it certainly did.

Great Ovation had not been in consideration for Badminton as yet, but a win at Rushall and third at Liphook decided Mark to let him take his chance – and when he led the field after the dressage it looked a pretty good chance! But in view of the waterlogged state of the course and his horse's relative lack of experience, Mark decided to take it fairly easily. This was until they were held up because an Irish horse had fallen at the Normandy Bank. 'This gave us a breather, and I realised that I could ride the rest of the course as if it were a one day event.'

At the end of the day they found themselves still in the lead by twenty points, and a clear round in the show jumping gave Mark his first Whitbread Trophy. After that their selection for the European Championships at Burghley was almost a foregone conclusion, and they won the final trial at Eridge too. At Burghley Princess Anne, riding as an individual on Doublet, led from start to finish, and but for chancing a corner at the penultimate fence, where Great Ovation ran out, Mark would have followed her into second place. As it was he was fifth, with a team gold medal.

He was then despatched, this time with Rock On, to Munich for the pre-Olympic three day event, where they arrived at the last obstacle in the show jumping arena on the final day, needing only to jump it to win even if they knocked it down. But as so many riders have learned to their cost, a moment's lack of concentration by horse or rider can turn triumph into tragedy in a few short seconds. Rock On took off miles from the fence and they landed in a heap in the middle of it. He suffered a heap of penalties too and was down to fifth place!

However, Mark and Great Ovation were entitled to start as favourites for Badminton in 1972, but this time it was an excess of caution by two experienced riders that determined the final result. Great Ovation led after the dressage, but picked up 8.8 time penalties on the steeplechase, something that no experienced rider should normally do, and as a result of which he was overtaken by the end of the cross country by Richard Meade on Laurieston, who had incurred 2.4 penalties on the steeplechase. With half a penalty between them, both went clear in the show jumping, and Mark prepared to accept the runner-up's prize; but Laurieston had picked up 1¼ time penalties, and Mark and Great Ovation had won their second Badminton.

It certainly now looked as though Mark would have a crack at his first Olympic event, and he did, but at Munich, third after the dressage, Great Ovation fell at the big spread fence at No 4 on the cross country, and though they jumped faultlessly the next day, theirs was the discard score for the British gold medal team.

It was at this stage that Columbus appeared on the scene – but with Princess Anne. But HM The Queen's 17.1hh grey was really too strong for her daughter, and he ran away with her on the steeplechase at Burghley in September. Princess Anne considered Mark the rider most likely to get to terms with him, and asked him to ride him for her at the Chatsworth One Day Event in October. Columbus went lame and never even set foot in the dressage arena, but Mark won with Mrs Elaine Straker's George, beating Princess Anne into second place on Goodwill.

For several years now the press had been speculating on the possibility of a royal romance, and in May 1973 the engagement of Mark and Princess Anne was announced from Buckingham Palace. Mark suddenly found himself to be front page news, and there were now more important things to be attended to in the immediate future than riding. But when Bertie Hill asked him at very short notice to ride Maid Marion at Burghley, because she had fallen with his son at Osberton, Mark agreed, and led the Championship event from start to finish.

The royal wedding took place in Westminster Abbey in November, followed by a honeymoon on board the royal yacht *Britannia* in the West Indies, after which Mark had his first taste of royal duties during a two week official tour. He and his wife had a taste of the less palatable side of royal life the following March when they were victims of an attempted kidnapping only half a mile from Buckingham Palace. Returning from an engagement with Riding for the Disabled, of which Princess Anne was Patron, their car was stopped in The Mall. The bodyguard and chauffeur and a policeman who came to investigate were shot before the gunman was arrested in an incident in which there was no loss of life but which could have ended disastrously.

Badminton 1974 was perhaps the peak of Mark's competitive career, and was a truly royal event. Princess Anne on her mother's Doublet led after the dressage from Mark on

Great Ovation, with Columbus third and Goodwill twenty-seventh. Princess Anne's hopes suffered a setback when Doublet made a mistake at the open ditch on the steeplechase, and then Great Ovation retired at the bullfinch on the cross country. But Columbus flew round the course without problems, as did Goodwill, to end the day in first and fifth places, and clear rounds on the final day enabled them both to finish on their dressage scores, and Goodwill to move up a place. A great day for HM The Queen with her horses first and fourth, ridden by her son-in-law and daughter.

The World Championship at Burghley should have been the crowning moment of a royal eventing year. Only tenth after the dressage, Columbus set a scorching pace round the cross country to put him in the lead by nine points. But at the penultimate fence Mark had felt that all was not quite well, and back in the stables it was evident that Columbus·had slipped the tendon off his hock, a most painful injury for a horse. A night of non-stop attention produced him sound in the morning, but as the team vet entered his box he kicked out and the tendon slipped again. There was no option but to withdraw him from the competition.

In 1975 Badminton was abandoned in torrential rain after the dressage, but Mark was offered the ride at Burghley on Janet Hodgson's Gretna Green, Janet having been severely concussed in a fall at Luhmuhlen, and although he sat on the horse for the first time only two days before the event started, he once again showed his class by finishing in second place.

Another Olympic year, 1976 found Mark with a strong hand for Badminton and hopes for the Games themselves. He had entered three for Badminton, but owing to a misunderstanding found that his best horse, Persian Holiday, had to go 'hors concours', not counting for the prizes. His first ride Brazil was retired after a fall, but the grey mare Favour finished third. Since Persian Holiday was running 'hors concours' and was in Mark's view his best hope for Montreal, he was not pushed unduly and did well to finish in what would have been sixth place, and the Olympic short list included Favour, Persian Holiday, and Goodwill. But after the final trial at Osberton, where Favour incurred a refusal, and where Percy went clear and won, the selectors named Goodwill for the team, and Mark with both his horses as reserve.

So once again Mark sat on the sidelines at the Olympics, though he had an important role with Princess Anne riding for the team. With two fit and sound horses of his own, it must have been disappointing to see two of the team horses out of the competition after the cross country; Hugh Thomas' Playamar broke down, and Lucinda Prior-Palmer's Be Fair, after a medal-winning performance, suffered a replica of Columbus' misfortune at the World Championships. Goodwill seemed to be going as well as ever until the bank on the take-off side of the zigzag fence over a ditch gave way just as he was taking off. But although Goodwill was winded and lost a shoe, and his rider was slightly concussed, they completed the course and the next day's show jumping to finish in twenty-fourth place.

The following year was slightly disappointing, for after winning the Open Championship at Locko Park in August and the final trial for the European Championship at Burghley, Persian Holiday developed a last minute virus that robbed him of a tilt at the title.

But if 1977 was a disappointing year as far as eventing was concerned, Mark established his reputation as an all-round horseman by earning a place on the British show jumping team with Trevor Banks' Olympic veteran Hideaway, and riding in the Nations Cups in La Baule and Calgary. And in 1978, in spite of not being able to ride the horse regularly, he came fourth in the King George V Gold Cup, the Grand Prix, at the Royal International Horse Show, and helped to win the Nations Cup in Calgary.

By now Mark had decided to retire from the Army. Since the government was unlikely to agree to the sovereign's daughter living in either Germany or Northern Ireland, the prospects for further service with his Regiment looked slim, and he did not relish the idea of sitting behind a desk in Whitehall. The Gatcombe Park estate had to be farmed, and Mark therefore attended a course at the Royal Agricultural College at Cirencester. He also acquired a new horse called Lincoln.

Columbus was now (in 1979) back in service after a season's hunting, and in March he and Mark completed one circuit of the Grand National course at Aintree in a friendly match with former Champion Jockey Richard Pitman. This evidently didn't do much for their dressage at Badminton, for they were twenty points behind the leaders, but Columbus had lost none of his spark across country, and they finished in third place. Lincoln came second at Windsor and in the autumn was second again at Boekelo.

The Range Rover Team was formed in 1979, and from then on Range Rover sponsored Mark's horses, and also awarded training bursaries and scholarships for promising young riders to train at Gatcombe. Mark certainly kept their name to the fore during the eighties. In 1981 he won his fourth Badminton, this time on Lincoln, and three years later he won the Novice Championship with Distinctive, who in 1985 won the first Chatsworth Three Day Event. A virus caused their withdrawal from the World Championship team of 1986, but meanwhile the ex-working hunter champion Cartier was working his way to selection for the Seoul Olympics of 1988.

It would have been a fitting end to a long career in the saddle if Mark could have bowed out with Olympic honours, and indeed he came home with a team silver medal. But Cartier was lame on returning to the box at the end of phase 'C' and had to be withdrawn.

Mark will be remembered for his dash across country, and it is not therefore surprising that this phase is uppermost in his mind when selecting a three day event horse.

My first priority is four good feet. Next I would place temperament; you can usually succeed with the less talented but rideable horse, whereas the brilliant but temperamentally difficult horse is seldom reliable. Movement is important, because unless you finish in the first three or four in the dressage you don't stand a chance of winning – the best finish on their dressage scores. Finally, I always choose the horse that shows cross-country ability, and work on his dressage, never the reverse.

As well as running the Range Rover Team, Mark travels the world as a trainer, and in 1989 he designed the cross-county course for Burghley's European Championships, producing a course that met with universal approval, tough enough to test the best, but with well thought-out alternatives to enable the less experienced to negotiate it safely. His influence on the sport is likely to be considerable for some time to come.

New Zealand

MARK TODD, MBE

In the history of the Olympic Games only three riders have won individual gold medals twice, and only two of them have done this at successive Games on the same horse. Pierre Jonquères d'Oriola won the show jumping for France on Ali Baba at Helsinki in 1952, and again on Lutteur B in Tokyo in 1964; Charles Pahud de Mortanges won the three day event for Holland on Marcroix in Amsterdam in 1928 and in Los Angeles in 1932. Both of these, however, came from countries with long histories of success in international equestrian sport. But if, as the nations departed from the Montreal Olympics of 1976, it had been suggested that a New Zealander would win the three day event gold medal at the Los Angeles Games, and moreover return four years later on the same horse, by then aged sixteen, to retain his title in Seoul, he would have been accused of delving into the realms of phantasy.

Prior to 1980, the year in which the Moscow Olympics were boycotted by most of the Western nations because of the Russian occupation of Afghanistan, no New Zealand rider had ever even competed in the Olympic three day event. Since then New Zealand has won two Olympic individual gold medals, a team bronze medal, and World Championship individual silver and team bronze medals, largely due to Mark Todd, who has also won Badminton and Burghley, the only 3-star three day events in the FEI calendar, as well as a host of other international competitions. Not only that, but Mark has also joined the ranks of the select few who have represented their countries at the Olympic Games in more than one discipline.

Indeed prior to 1980, mention of the Kiwis brought to mind either an increasing number of racehorses imported from New Zealand that were successful on English racecourses, or the all-conquering All-Blacks rugby football team. Mark Todd has changed all that.

Mark came from a family with no competitive equestrian background, though horses were in constant use for stock work on his grandfather's dairy farm, where he used to ride ponies during school holidays and at weekends. But there are over eighty branches of the Pony Club in New Zealand, and from the age of nine he took part in gymkhanas, show jumping and one day events, eventually acquiring a horse called Top Hunter,

OPPOSITE
Mark Todd MBE (New Zealand) and Charisma – Olympic Champions 1984, 1988 (Bob Langrish)

OVERLEAF
Ian Stark MBE (GB) silver medal, Olympic Games 1988, Badminton winner 1986, 1988 – Sir Wattie, Seoul 1988 (Bob Langrish)

who, although he became a Grade 'A' show jumper, seemed more suited to eventing. Switched to this sport, he went to advanced in one season, and his rider became hooked on this particular discipline.

Mark was then pitched into international eventing at the deep end, for they were selected to represent New Zealand in the 1978 World Championships in Lexington, Kentucky, where the intense heat and humidity compounded the difficulties of a severe cross-country course. At his first international event, and only his second three day event, he was astonished to find himself in sixth place after the dressage, but Top Hunter was eliminated on the cross country, and was afterwards found to have broken down, the damage probably having occurred on the steeplechase.

The horse recovered, and was sold in England, and when Mark brought him over here he was offered the chance of riding young horses for Jurg Zindel. He returned to New Zealand, and came back in the spring of 1979 with Jocasta, with whom he completed Burghley and was seventh at Boekelo. Now fired with enthusiasm, the following winter in New Zealand he bought a horse called Southern Comfort, a ten-year-old who had had a thorough grounding via the Pony Club, the hunting field and horse trials, and who had completed two three day events.

At Badminton Southern Comfort lay about half way down the field after the dressage, but a sparkling cross-country round pulled them up into third place. At what is arguably the greatest three day event in the World, at which he had hoped perhaps to finish in the first ten, this was no mean feat, and he made sure of his position with a clear round in the show jumping. Still to go were Lucinda Green on Killaire and Helen Butler, in the lead with Merganser II. Mark was fairly astonished when Killaire had a fence down and let him into second place, but when poor Helen lowered four fences and he realised that he had won Badminton he could scarcely believe it.

Just to prove that this success was no fluke, he went on to be second at Punchestown on Jocasta, but then events took a turn for the worse. Before the substitute equestrian Olympics in Fontainebleau, Southern Comfort fell ill, and in the three day event itself Jocasta was eliminated at the penultimate fence on the cross country. Then in the following spring Southern Comfort succumbed to a virus two weeks before Badminton, where Jocasta was retired at the Quarry. Eager to ride in the 1982 World Championships in Luhmühlen, Mark leased the promising Milton Tyson, but after completing Burghley with a fall he decided this was not the right horse. It was an understandably despondent Mark who returned to the dairy farm in New Zealand at the end of 1981.

It was not until the spring of 1983 that he resumed eventing, on a horse called Felix II that he had ridden for Tom and Mimi May back in 1981. Angela Tucker had been all set to ride him at Badminton when she broke a collar bone a couple of weeks before. A telephone call brought Mark back in time to ride Felix into ninth place. It was a call in the reverse direction, however, that really set Mark back on his path to the top, when he was asked to return to New Zealand to ride a horse called Charisma in the three day event in June. His first impressions were not great.

Here was a sort of small, hairy, black horse, and I nearly got in the car and went straight home. But I decided I might as well sit on him, and as soon as I did I liked him. We then won four one day events, the New Zealand One Day Championship, and the Three Day Championship, and finished the season by winning the Olympic Selection Trial.

This was really the turning point in Mark's life. He sold his dairy herd, and returned to England in the spring of 1984 with Charisma and Night Life, who was by the same sire. The run-up to Badminton, however, was far from smooth, for Charisma ran out at the first one day event and fell at the second. But at Badminton itself they were second to Lucinda Green and Beagle Bay.

The Olympic course at Los Angeles was very different from Badminton, with mainly artificial fences set up on a golf course. The track was twisty and undulating, and Charisma, being small and nippy, was able to save time; he also liked the firm ground and was not worried by the heat. In fourth place after the dressage, they pulled up to second after the cross country. In the show jumping a clear round put the pressure on Karen Stives, in the lead for the host nation (USA) with Ben Arthur, and when they had a fence down Mark became Olympic Champion, and New Zealand had won her first equestrian Olympic medal.

At Badminton in 1985 a brilliant cross-country round put Mark and Charisma into the lead for the first time before the show jumping at a major three day event. Last to go, all went well until the final fence, and a pole down relegated them to second place for the second year running.

The World Championships were held at Gawler, South Australia, in 1986, and with Charisma preparing for the championships, Mark rode Any Chance and Michaelmas Day at Badminton, and although both horses deposited him into the Coffin, they finished fifth and eighteenth in a field of over sixty.

The Gawler World Championships themselves were every bit as dramatic as those of Lexington in 1978. At the first horse inspection horses from the Australian, New Zealand and US teams were eliminated, one of them the mount of the USA's double World Champion Bruce Davidson. In the dressage arena the atmosphere had its effect even on the experienced Charisma, but his test nevertheless put him in second place at the end of the day. But more surprising was the lead that the New Zealand team held at the end of this test. A tough cross-country course was made more difficult by the torrential rain that fell overnight, and Mark took an unaccustomed ducking when going for the bold route at the water, though he still managed one of the quicker rounds of the day. But his team-mates had ridden brilliantly. Tinks Pottinger and Volunteer had completed the only clear round within the time to lead from Ginny Leng and Priceless, with Trudy Boyce and Mossman in third place. In spite of Mark's fall, both individual and team gold medals looked probable for New Zealand.

But how quickly triumph can turn into disaster in this sport! Volunteer had knocked his knee on a comparatively straightforward fence on the cross country, and failed the final horse inspection. But this still left Trudy Boyce with the silver medal after the jumping, and most of those present considered that the moral team victory was New Zealand's. Certainly it had been shown that the New Zealand team was no 'one-man band'. As a consolation prize for his lapse at Gawler, Charisma ended the year by winning at Luhmühlen after a dressage test that included four 'tens'.

In 1987 Badminton was cancelled due to the wet weather for the third time in its history, and Charisma's first serious objective was the Stockholm CCI in June, though he had earlier won at Saumur, France. After taking the lead in the dressage, and holding it after the cross country, Charisma then had four fences down in the show jumping to put him in sixth place, but it was some consolation that Tinks Pottinger finished in third place for New Zealand.

The next target was Burghley, and Charisma took his now customary place at the head of the table after the first day, with Mark's second string Wilton Fair third. Cross-country day dented a number of established reputations, but reinforced that of New Zealand, for four of her horses stood in the first six. With Charisma first and Wilton Fair second, could Mark become the first rider to be both winner and runner-up at Burghley? And could the fifteen-year-old Charisma end his career in England with a major victory? Jumping out of order, Wilton Fair had already made sure of second place when Mark entered the arena on Charisma. But again his show jumping let him down, though with first and second places Mark still could not complain! To round off the season Mark won the French three day event at Le Lion d'Angers on Lizzie Purbrick's Pedro the Cruel, with his own Peppermint Park in third place.

And so to another Olympic year. While the North Americans were ruining their chances of medals in a series of trials at home, and with the British hopefuls required to run at Badminton, where Tinks Pottinger kept the New Zealand flag flying in fourth place despite what was generally agreed to be a harshly marked dressage test, Mark had decided to concentrate solely on the defence of his Olympic title with Charisma.

To win any major international three day event is difficult enough; to win an Olympic gold medal, then to keep the same horse fit and winning over the next four years, and to come back and successfully defend the title when the horse is aged sixteen is quite remarkable; one could be excused for thinking that a considerable element of luck in this extremely risky sport would be necessary. And yet, reviewing Mark and Charisma's progress back to Seoul, it seems that nothing was left to chance, that a gold medal was almost inevitable.

In the dressage arena Charisma performed with the sparkle of a four-year-old allied to all the experience of his sixteen years, and produced what many, including his rider, regarded as his best test ever. Across country he made the fences look easy, and galloped so effortlessly when others were struggling that Mark was able to ease him up towards the end – and they were still fastest of all. Before the show jumping Charisma had two fences in hand from Ginny Leng and the relatively inexperienced Master Craftsman, who had to go clear to stay ahead of Ian Stark and Sir Wattie. Charisma entered the arena as though he owned it, and though he rolled off one pole the issue somehow never seemed in doubt, and the sixteen-year-old retired from the competitive scene in a blaze of glory.

New Zealand took the team bronze medal, with Tinks Pottinger and Volunteer being the only other partnership to finish on their dressage score. But Mark could not relax, for while others were celebrating, he had two more days of Olympic competition ahead!

In his early days Mark had done plenty of show jumping, but as he himself put it, 'Show jumping is as different from eventing as eventing is from racing', and a different approach is required. From a field of seventeen teams, New Zealand finished in twelfth place in the team competition, one behind Ireland, and Mark on Bago, whom he had only been riding for four months, was the best of the team by a considerable margin. In the individual jumping they had only one fence down in the first qualifying competition, and after the second were among the thirty-seven starters in the final in the Olympic

Stadium, where they finished in twenty-sixth place with some well-established international show jumping riders below them.

But to stay at the top requires dedication and hard work, and less than a month later Mark was separating the Olympic silver and bronze medallists, Ian Stark and Ginny Leng, when coming second at Boekelo on Peppermint Park. It was perhaps at Badminton in 1989, however, that Mark showed above all what a supreme horseman he is. With only a young horse of his own to ride, he accepted an invitation to ride Rodney Powell's The Irishman when Rodney suffered an injury when schooling another horse.

The Irishman was one of the fancied runners, but normally it takes a considerable time to forge the partnership between horse and rider necessary to compete at Badminton; Mark sat on The Irishman for the first time on the Tuesday of Badminton week. On Friday he rode a very respectable dressage test to lie in seventh place; on Saturday over what was acknowledged to be a difficult course even for Badminton, they were one of only three combinations to achieve a clear round without time penalties, and so found themselves in the lead. The last to jump on Sunday, they had a margin of 0.4 over Ginny Leng and Master Craftsman. Mark was no stranger to pressure of that sort, but he had little idea how The Irishman would jump, and it was no fault of his that the horse dropped a hind leg on one of the simplest fences on the course to finish third.

So what accounts for the phenomenal success of this quiet, modest man?

I've always been absolutely dedicated, and I learned a lot from watching the top riders in action, and I took whatever training was available. Fortunately, I always had good balance, which is essential if you're as tall as I am. In my early days I used to ride work on a lot of racehorses, and I rode in point-to-points, show jumping and rodeos, and I worked a lot with vets. As far as the dressage is concerned, I was half way down the field after the first day when South Comfort won Badminton. Then I realised just how important it was, and I really worked at it. Charisma had done a fair bit before I got him, and he was so elegant and such a good mover, as well as having the right temperament. It's a phase that you've really got to keep working on, though in the end you're only as good as the horse you're on.

His advice to a young rider is to get out and compete as much as possible.

You'll learn more from competing than you will from training, though of course you need training as well. Learn all you can by watching top riders, and broaden your knowledge and experience as much as possible. It's not just a question of dressage and jumping, it's the whole broad spectrum of horsemanship, of being able not only to ride, but also to understand horses. To get the best out of a horse, you must understand him – they're all different, and you have to adapt yourself to each one.

And don't be impatient. If things don't go right, question yourself: what are you doing wrong? If a horse doesn't go in the way you want, it's usually your fault. This where you need help from a trainer.

Mark's views on selecting a potential three day event horse are equally clear.

He must be an all-round athlete. He must have good limbs, a good head and a nice eye. But as far as conformation is concerned I'm more concerned about the overall picture, he must be a neat package. I prefer a Thoroughbred or something very near it, though Wilton Fair was about 1/4

Thoroughbred and ¹/₂ Irish Draught. He must move well, have a good attitude to life and an even temperament, and he must have a reasonable style of jumping. Remember that you can train and improve a horse, but you can't change him or alter his basic way of going. You can improve an adequate mover, but you can't change a bad mover into a good one. He must be able to gallop, by which I mean that when you ask him to go he must lengthen his stride and not just move faster. But the ideal is hard to find, so usually we must end up with a compromise.

And on the state of the sport in general:

I think the format of the three day event is about right, and I wouldn't like to see it changed. But important events shouldn't go to unsuitable places, like Lexington in 1978, for example, where the heat was too much for the horses. I think the prize money in three day events is a long way short of what it should be. This isn't an amateur sport any more and it's no good trying to pretend that it is. You just can't win unless you dedicate yourself to it full time. I don't think more money would be detrimental to the sport, because it involves such hard work and so much can go wrong. What we can win in a year, for example, is peanuts compared with what the show jumpers can win. But our horses can only do two major competitions a year, and we put in as much effort for those two as the jumpers do for a whole season. And if we try to remain amateur, you can bet the other nations won't, and they'll beat us.

Shortly before we met, Mark had ridden round one circuit of the Grand National course at Aintree on the second leg of the Barbour Seagram Challenge. Six of the leading National Hunt jockeys had first ridden round the British Open Horse Trials Championship course at Gatcombe Park on horses provided by the eventers. Mark's Aintree mount had been the ex-Irish eventer Mr Todd.

The National fences weren't as big as I had expected. I didn't mind the Chair or Bechers because we're used to jumping big fences, big ditches and drops – mind you, I might have given a different answer to the question before we'd ridden round! I think the real problems at Aintree are the other forty horses and the speed at which they go. The jockeys went well at Gatcombe because they are all basically good horsemen, and they'd succeed in any sphere. You can't grab someone off the street and make him into a champion rider. It's like horses, you can improve him to a certain extent, but he must have the basic talent naturally, by instinct.

This natural horseman's basic talent has been assisted by several trainers; in New Zealand, Ken Brown; in England, Bill Noble, with help from all directions as far as jumping – Ted Edgar (GB), George Morris (USA) and Jeff McVean (Australia).
So what of the future?

I'll go on competing as long as I enjoy it and as long as I have the will to win. The most difficult thing will be to keep motivated. It's very hard work and there's a lot of travel, and if your heart's not set on it, you won't win. For both the Olympics I decided at the start of the year that my sole objective was to prepare my horse to win there. I don't think I'll ever go back to dairy farming. I love the farm life, but in 1984 I had to make up my mind, farming or horses, and I think I'll always be involved with horses in some way.

LUCINDA GREEN, MBE

Records, so the saying goes, are made to be broken. If that is so, then those set by Lucinda Green will take some breaking. In the opinion of most riders, Badminton is *the* three day event par excellence, and though nothing quite compares with an Olympic gold medal, no other course quite compares with Badminton's. To win Badminton, therefore, is a considerable feat in itself. To win it six times against the sort of opposition that exists there suggests a great partnership between an outstanding rider and one or two wonder horses. To win six times on six different horses implies a truly great rider.

Add a couple of wins at Burghley, another at Chatsworth, a long list of CCI victories which includes Boekelo and Punchestown, a Junior European Team Championship, eleven Senior European medals including two individual championships, a World Championship (team and individual), and an Olympic team silver medal and we have a record that is indeed hard to beat.

Daughter of a Cavalry general, Lucinda Prior-Palmer started riding at the age of four, and was a member of the Royal Artillery Salisbury Plain Branch of the Pony Club, but at that stage had no particular ambition as a rider.

Every schoolgirl has her dream, and I always dreamed of doing something glorious, but I was never sure whether it was going to be dancing, acting or something else. But horses became a tremendous love, to the point where I found school very difficult, and left at fifteen! But I never aspired to enormous heights, because I couldn't stand the disappointment of not making it. When I was given Be Fair on my fifteenth birthday, I thought, well, he could be a Badminton horse, he might get to a novice event, but he probably won't get further than that. That's really the way I have woven my life, thinking it would be lovely if it happened but it probably never will, and that way if it doesn't happen I'm not too disappointed.

It was Be Fair that started the ball rolling, and of all her horses he was perhaps the one most likely to reach the top, for his sire was Fair and Square, who won Burghley for Sheila Willcox in 1968. A present from Lucinda's parents, Be Fair and his young rider had to learn together.

'Be Fair,' says Lucinda, 'took me into the world of eventing. He was inexperienced, and we made mistakes and had our share of falls and refusals. But he became the most brilliant of all my horses, and I don't think I would ever have got to the top without such a brilliant horse to start with.'

In 1971 they won a team gold medal at the Junior European Championships at Wesel (Germany), and in 1972 he gave Lucinda her first taste of success at Badminton when he finished fifth (with three members of that year's Olympic team ahead of her and the other well behind). The following year's course was considered one of the most difficult, but by this time they had really got their act together. After a brilliant dressage test which left them only a couple of points behind the German leader, the second fastest clear round on the cross country put them firmly in the lead where they remained to the end. Lucinda won her first Badminton by twenty-two points from the runner-up and forty-five from the third.

A team bronze medal in the European Championships in Kiev (USSR) followed, but a fall at Badminton in 1974 was something Lucinda would prefer to forget. The following year promised better, but the deluge that fell throughout the dressage resulted in Badminton being abandoned as Be Fair left the arena in the lead at that stage. Compensation came, however, in the shape of victory in the European Championships in Luhmuhlen, together with the team silver medal. European Champion at the age of twenty-one, and all set for the Montreal Olympics!

As we waited in the box, stop watches poised, as Be Fair galloped towards the end of the cross country course at Bromont, it really seemed as though they were heading for a medal. But as they landed over the last fence something seemed not quite right, and back in the box it was apparent that Be Fair had suffered the same injury as Columbus had done at the Burghley World Championships of 1974. As he hobbled away, with a tendon slipped off his hock, it was a sad end to the competitive days of a great horse, though he did in fact recover sufficiently to enjoy his last years in the hunting field.

Meanwhile Lucinda had suffered the most extraordinary combination of triumph and tragedy. Wideawake, a tough, workmanlike, but seemingly accident-prone gelding had arrived at Appleshaw back in 1973. His first escapade involved escaping and galloping headlong into a van on the road, and when eventually put into work he proved himself to be unco-operative both in and out of the stable. And when his patient rider did start to make progress with him, he escaped again and lamed himself, and then damaged a leg sufficiently to put himself off work for months.

Eventually, with some help from Bruce Davidson, who schooled him when Lucinda broke her collar bone falling in a point-to-point, Wideawake progressed sufficiently to finish fourth at the Wylye Novice Three Day Event. Then at Tidworth he led after the cross country, but dropped down the order by lowering three fences in the show jumping. As Lucinda had had a few exciting moments with him due to his propensity for skimming over his fences if he was right, but clouting them if he was wrong, she decided that a season's hunting might do him good. But far from being enthused by the thrills of the chase and the company of other horses, Wideawake simply 'froze', an embarrassing predicament for his rider in the middle of a hunt!

But eventually tact, persuasion, determination and patience won the day, and in the autumn of 1975 Wideawake won the prestigious Boekelo Three Day Event in Holland – in thick fog. And with Be Fair excused on account of the forthcoming Olympics, he became Lucinda's hope for Badminton in 1976. The same stable as Be Fair's when he had won in 1973 seemed a good omen, dressage tuition from David Hunt had brought about sufficient improvement for him to be third at that stage, and he flew round the cross country and into the lead. When he jumped clear on the final day Lucinda had won her second Badminton.

This popular and well deserved victory was being cheered as Wideawake completed his lap of honour in front of Her Majesty The Queen, who had just presented Lucinda with her trophy. In an instant there was complete silence. Wideawake stopped in his tracks, reared up, and died.

The cause of his death was never established, and it was hardly a promising run-up to the Olympic Games three months ahead. And when, having overcome this setback, and having apparently done what was necessary to achieve a medal in Montreal, she suffered a second tragedy with Be Fair, it must have seemed as though the Fates were well and truly against her. But a good rider attracts good horses, and Lucinda was not out of action for long.

When George arrived at Appleshaw just five weeks before Badminton in 1977 his past record did not suggest a very good horse. But although he had fallen five times at major events in four seasons, he was the true three day event type, and Lucinda found little difficulty in coming to terms with him, winning the advanced class at Brigstock on their first outing.

Badminton in 1977 was one of the wettest, but George's dressage left him handily placed in fourth position, though he seemed unlikely to hold this when he clouted several fences on the steeplechase and removed the guard rail from the open ditch! On the cross country everything seemed to fall into place, and one of only two clear rounds within the time put George into the lead, with three fences in hand for the show jumping. The previous year he had lowered three on the last day, but this time it was St George's Day, and he made no mistake. It was Lucinda's third Badminton, and the second in succession.

A week later Lucinda broke her collar bone again in a fall at Locko Park, and though she was by now well used to the ups and downs of her chosen sport, nothing so far had prepared her for what was to happen in the European Championships at Burghley. Lying third after the dressage, George began to hang to the left as he galloped round the steeplechase, and at the end of the first circuit he became entangled with the ropes, and Lucinda was thrown over his head. She then found herself being dragged by the reins under George's legs as he thundered on. Somehow she eventually managed to attract his attention and haul him to a halt, and to this day she doesn't really know how she found the strength to vault back into the saddle, let alone complete the course.

Back in the box the unbelievable was confirmed: no time penalties on the steeplechase! But had George taken too much out of himself to cope with the cross country? Certainly his rider was so exhausted that he was unlikely to receive the customary instructions from the saddle. But great horse that he was, he overcame several anxious moments, and galloped home with 5.4 time penalties to put the British team in the lead and himself in second place, nine points behind Karl Schultz of Germany and Madrigal.

Before the show jumping George seemed to have given his all on the previous day, and to have nothing much left. But because of the team classification riders jumped in programme order, and when Madrigal knocked the penultimate fence Lucinda's spirits rose – there were still ten penalties for a knock-down then. Last minute encouragement from Dick Stilwell, who over the years has done much to raise the morale of riders at moments such as this, boosted Lucinda, and the applause as they entered the ring did the same for George. Two minutes later, Lucinda was European Champion for the second time, and Great Britain had won another Championship.

Of all the horses she rode, Lucinda rates George as the most talented, with the ability to excel in any of the three phases. What might they have achieved together if their partnership had been a longer one? But at twelve years of age George had won both Badminton and Burghley, and what better note on which to retire than as European Champion?

But meanwhile George had not had all the glory to himself. Three weeks before Burghley in 1976, Lucinda had been asked to ride Charles Cyzer's Killaire. He arrived, like George, with a most unimpressive record. There the similarity with George ended, for Killaire was not Lucinda's idea of the ideal three day eventer. He was in show condition (ie much too fat!), and anyway seemed unable to gallop. On further acquaintance he seemed unable to jump, either. He was hardly the hope for the future after the tragedies of Wideawake and Be Fair.

The combined efforts of his rider and David Hunt produced a dressage test that left them in a respectable fifteenth place, and when an overnight downpour caused the removal of the steeplechase fences to a rotovated field, it appeared that the conditions might just slow everyone else down to Killaire's pace. And he was nothing if not a trier, and, pushed all the way, he scuttled round the cross country, recorded the third fastest time and climbed to fifth place. The next day he crept over rather than jumped the fences, but a clear round brought the horse that nobody thought had a chance up into second place behind Jane Holderness-Roddam and Warrior.

The following year at Badminton was George's year, but when he won he was not alone on his lap of honour. Killaire's dressage had by then so improved that he ended the day in third place in spite of being the first to go. On the steeplechase it was hard work all the way; on the cross country he gave all he had, and on the final day just one error landed him in third place overall. Few realised what a feat of horsemanship had been involved in riding two such different horses into first and third places in the world's toughest three day event.

Lucinda's sponsorship by Overseas Containers Ltd started in 1978, and their hopes rested solely on Killaire and Village Gossip, bought from Lord and Lady Brookeborough a couple of years earlier, and second at Boekelo in 1977. The new sponsors were delighted when Gossip was the only horse at Badminton in 1978 to finish on his dressage score – on the cross country he was forty-five seconds inside the time. He was second again, and again to Jane Holderness-Roddam and Warrior.

There are few of those involved in the 1978 World Championships in Lexington, other than the winners, Bruce Davidson and Might Tango, who wouldn't prefer to draw a veil over the whole event. A tough course, temperatures around 90°F (32°C) coupled with 90 per cent humidity, combined to exhaust many of the horses, Village Gossip among them, and to damage seriously the image of the sport.

Perhaps Killaire was lucky to have been chosen only as reserve, for in the following year he came to Badminton ready to gallop for his life. Second to Judy Bradwell and Castlewellan after the dressage, he managed the steeplechase without penalty, incurred 6.8 on the cross country, and jumped clear on the final day. With Sue Hatherley and Mark Phillips finishing close behind, Lucinda won her fourth Badminton.

Lucinda Green, MBE (GB) – World Champion 1982, European Champion 1975, 1977, Badminton winner 1973, 1976, 1977, 1979, 1983 and 1984, with Regal Realm (Bob Langrish)

It just didn't seem possible, she said at the time, to have been granted the opportunity of riding four horses to victory in the world's toughest event. And of Killaire: 'His honesty shone through his lack of natural ability.' But just to confirm his rider's ability too, Lucinda at that same Badminton rode Village Gossip into seventh place. Then in 1980 Killaire was second again, and became the only horse to have been first, second and third at Badminton.

If Killaire had seemed to be an unlikely champion, then Regal Realm appeared even less likely to achieve the highest honours. But what Lucinda described as 'that brilliant little upside-down Australian cattle pony' was to need all her artistry, determination and tact, and her brilliance as a horseman, not just as a rider, is nowhere better demonstrated than in the results that she achieved with him.

SR Direct Mail had now taken over Lucinda's sponsorship from OCL, and in 1981 she and David Green, the Australian Olympic rider, were married. (David lost no time in establishing the rightful pecking order when in 1982 he beat his wife and Village Gossip by 0.2 points to win Punchestown with Botany Bay!) Regal Realm had come second at Boekelo the previous autumn, but their record together from then on was little short of incredible – World Champion at Luhmühlen in 1982, winner of Badminton (Lucinda's fifth) and runner-up in the European Championships at Frauenfeld (Germany) in 1983, a team silver medal in the Los Angeles Olympics of 1984 and team gold in Burghley's European Championships of 1985.

Lucinda had now won Badminton more times than any other rider. Surely even she could not continue to find, train and ride horses that were capable of beating the world's best. But at Burghley in 1981 she suffered an early setback when Village Gossip failed the first horse inspection. And when Beagle Bay survived mistakes at the last steeplechase fence and at the Trout Hatchery, only to pull up with severe bruising that seemed likely to put him on the sidelines on the final day, there was little prospect of anything to celebrate at the end. But the efforts of the support team – without the use of drugs – produced Beagle Bay sound, and he brought Lucinda her second Burghley victory, and in 1984 he recorded her sixth win at Badminton, testimony enough to the talent of a remarkable rider.

Lucinda's advice to young riders is forthright.

Don't do it unless you really, really enjoy it. It's a lot of hard work and it requires tremendous dedication, and any other life just goes by the wayside, which doesn't matter if you really love doing it. Nothing makes me sadder than to see people competing for reasons other than that they adore it. In a rider's development two things are important: the seat over a fence across country and temperament. I think temperament is very important, because eventing is, I think, a more severe test of character than other equestrian sports.

The seat is not easy to explain, the rider must be just a fraction behind the horse's movement, with the lower leg giving security. It's not just a question of not falling off, though Ginny Leng's seat over the fourth fence at Seoul illustrated this; it's more a question of balance and of giving the horse confidence. The rider who gets a bit in front of the horse's movement just as he is taking off at a difficult combination like a coffin isn't helping him.

Her ideas on selecting the potential three day event horse are equally precise:

I have an exact idea of what I want, which is probably why I never seem to find it; roughly 16 hands, Thoroughbred as near as makes no difference, though I prefer one that just isn't quite Thoroughbred to keep him really sober; but sharp as anything, wicked, naughty but dead sensible, which is a hard combination to find in any horse, and with legs like iron posts. I would always go for a sharp, difficult horse rather than an easy, lazy horse. And it's not enough that the rider loves it, the horse has got to love it too, that's what I mean by sharp.

And as for movement:

I think we all went through a phase when Charisma appeared on the scene of thinking that we must never buy or train another horse that can't move. We did this for three or four years, and as a result we came out at the end with horses that couldn't jump! Now we have reverted, first of all we're going to have a good time out there and not be scared to death or eliminated, and we're going to buy a horse that can really jump. And he's going to have to walk well and have a balanced canter, then the trot should come with work. I think movement is important if you want to win a gold medal, and if you want to win, win, win, you must have a horse that jumps really cleverly and sharply and can move; but he is really so much one in a million that I'd rather have a horse that will get round and be fourth or fifth in preference to the one that leads after the dressage and then gets eliminated. Movement is important, but it's not as vital as we used to think. What is vital is that he has natural balance, as then he can go much quicker across country and he will still do a decent dressage.

Lucinda is not only a member of the Horse Trials Committee at home, she is also a member of the FEI Three Day Event Committee. Her main worry concerning the sport at home concerns breeding, and she feels very strongly that unless a serious breeding programme is developed, the 'Great British event horse' is going to die out. Another worry concerns finance.

I would like to see the prize money in three day events going as high as it wants. The three day event is so hard to win, and it's the culmination of three to five years' work. An increase in prize money wouldn't be detrimental to the sport because so much hard work and dedication are required to win, at least at two and three star level. And the big money should be well spread down through the lesser placings, because you only really get the chance to compete twice a year – if you keep your horse sound.

As one of the world's leading riders, she is only too well aware that one of the problems they face from the highest level to the lowest is to satisfy the demands of those who control their destinies in the only section of the three day event competition that relies entirely on human opinion for its results.

If only the dressage judges themselves could agree on what they are looking for, it would make things easier for competitors. Some of the variations in judging at Seoul were ridiculous, though fortunately the right people won in the end. But I'm not sure that having specialist dressage judges for that test would cure the problem, because at Seoul even the pure dressage competitors had a meeting to complain about their judging. I'm afraid it's just a matter of variations of human opinion, and I can see no solution to the problem apart from reducing the influence of the dressage.

As for the future of the sport, Lucinda feels it is very important that a big effort is made to encourage the lesser countries. Although the number of nations affiliated to the FEI and the number of equestrian teams competing in the Olympic Games has increased, the numbers competing in the three day event have dwindled.

Great Britain is the Mecca of the sport and we should encourage riders from other nations to come over here to compete. It is sad that the Eastern European countries have not been able to produce teams, and perhaps the idea of a World Cup, which is being considered in the FEI, though no one quite knows what form it should take, will help the lesser nations.

Lucinda and David now have two children. Lucinda herself lacks a really top-class international horse for the first time since the days of Be Fair, so what of the future?

I don't think I shall be hitting the lights for a year or two, as I've actually run clean out of horses, and not for lack of trying. I should love to have another Olympic Games, because there is nothing quite like it in the sporting world. But we're all worried in case the equestrian events won't be at Barcelona because the real fun is in being in that Olympic Village. Separate Equestrian Olympics, and certainly not World Equestrian Games, could never replace what for me is a wonderful experience.

Whether Lucinda makes it back to the very top or not, she has over a period of fifteen years made the greatest contribution to the sport, and her influence will doubtless continue to be felt, if not from the saddle, then from elsewhere. In addition to the demands of her family, she writes regularly for the equestrian press, enlivened the television coverage of Seoul's three day event with her erudite and amusing commentary, and is a much respected member of national and international committees.

VIRGINIA LENG, MBE

Virginia Leng, MBE – with Nightcap
(Bob Langrish)

The first lady ever to win an individual Olympic three day event medal started riding – and, so she tells us, jumped her first fence – at the age of three! As the daughter of an officer of the Royal Marines, her early memories are mainly of travel – Malta, Singapore, the Philippines, Canada and Cyprus are a few of the places in which she lived. After school in Kent from the age of thirteen to sixteen, during which time she was able to ride, she acquired her first horse, Dubonnet. But her initial efforts in the world of horse trials gave little indication of what was to come, for at her first event she missed out three fences on the cross country, and at the Pony Club Area Trials she eliminated her entire team by starting before the bell in the show jumping!

But then things began to improve, and she well remembers the purple rosette she won at the Wylye One Day Event for being tenth. She caught the eye of the Junior selectors, and with Dubonnet she won a team gold medal at the 1973 Junior European Championships at Pompadour, France, and completed her first Badminton in 1974.

Meanwhile she had acquired Jason, part Russian Arab, part Thoroughbred and a complete run-away, whom she had tamed sufficiently to finish second at the French Championships at Haras du Pin, and with whom she burst upon the senior international scene by winning the Canadian pre-Olympic three day event at Bromont, near Montreal, in 1975. She had arrived! She was selected for the 'long list' for the 1976 Olympic Games at Montreal, but in the run-up to Badminton her career was not just interrupted, it looked for a time as though it might have come to an end. In a fall at Ermington she jarred and twisted her arm, breaking it into twenty-three pieces, so badly in fact, that amputation was seriously considered.

As if this was not enough, on the very day that Jason was to leave for Badminton, where he was to be ridden by John Kearsley, he broke a blood vessel, and never competed in three day events again. But far from being disheartened by two setbacks that might well have quenched her enthusiasm for the sport altogether, Ginny announced her intention of competing at Burghley in the autumn. The horse on which she aimed to make her come-back was Tio Pepe, and when they ended the second day among the top dozen it really looked as though the tide had turned. On the final day they were eliminated for missing a show jump!

There seemed little more that could go wrong, but at Badminton in 1977 Tio Pepe broke down in the steeplechase – on both front legs. Even Ginny's spirit could hardly survive this fourth setback, but fortunately she had at home two horses that were to take her to the very top. A couple of years earlier she had bought the five-year-old Priceless from his breeder Mrs Diana Scott, who still stands his sire, Ben Faerie, and she liked him so much that she returned to Devon to buy Night Cap, who was by the same sire and the same age.

When Priceless was six, having progressed to intermediate level, and was about to go to the Bramham Three Day Event, Ginny decided that he would have to be sold to raise money. But this time, although Fate seemed to be being cruel once again, perhaps it was only to be kind, for Priceless failed the vet – not because he was unsound but because the vet thought him unsuitable as a three day event horse – and he promptly won Bramham; not bad for an unsuitable six-year-old! And Ginny now regards Priceless as having been one of the major contributing factors to her subsequent phenomenal success.

Although without Dubonnet we'd never have got started, Priceless was really the turning point. The right horse for the rider is really important. Take Murphy Himself, for example; although we won Burghley, I was just not strong enough to get the best out of him. Then I think patience and determination are important too. I suppose I'm considered a bit of a perfectionist, I'm never satisfied with anything but the best. And I think being humble, and not getting conceited about anything, because we can all ride, it's just a question of who rides better on the day.

Soundness is a big factor, too. We've been very lucky; certainly neither Priceless nor Night Cap ever had any trouble whatsoever. And I'm sure it was because they were never pushed, particularly at one day events, and they were never run in bad ground. And they were never run if they had the slightest small problem like a sore knee or a stifle that wasn't quite right. If you run horses when they're not right, then they start favouring a leg, and then trouble starts. And we never give our horses drugs. Bute doesn't exist in our yard.

I'm not against someone giving a horse one sachet of bute to make him more comfortable if he has an injury, but not for anything else. On the third day of a three day event, for example, the object of the show jumping is really to show that the horse is sound and fit to continue after the second day; is he sound and fit if he has to have bute to enable him to jump? I agree with the idea of banning bute for competition horses, but the only thing that worries me is that it will then be replaced with something else that is not detectable, and which may be more damaging to the horse, so I accept that it can be used under supervision for minor ailments.

Having had her share of triumph and disaster on the way up, Ginny has sound advice for the ambitious young rider.

He, or she, must start with something like a pony in the Pony Club. Then when he gets onto a horse he must progress through a riding club or through hunting and hunter trials and on to show jumping and eventing, with the aim of getting selected for the Juniors. I would never have got where I am without the Juniors. If he is successful he can start to try for small local sponsorship, such as free petrol from the garage in return for a bit of advertisement.

The story of Ginny's involvement with her sponsors since the early eighties illustrates both her determination and her patience.

When my father died it was a question of getting a sponsor or giving up. So I got myself a little portfolio, and went on the train to London about once a week for six months. I selected firms from the Yellow Pages, and knocked on doors, which was quite embarrassing. Most people were charming, and would pat me on the head and say, 'Sorry we can't help, but have a cup of coffee'. In the end it happened through a friend who had heard that British National, as they then were, had sponsored a chap sailing. I managed to persuade the managing director to meet me for lunch, at the end of which the prospects didn't look too hopeful, though he said he would mention it to the chairman. In the end the only reason I suceeded was because the chairman's wife was fond of horses! And through various changes of name, Citybank Savings have looked after me ever since.

And certainly from that moment on Ginny began to put her sponsor's name in front of the thousands who support horse trials and three day events. In that same year, 1981, Priceless was sixth in the European Championships at Horsens, Denmark, and the British team won the gold medal, and over the next seven years she was to amass an astonishing collection of major international victories.

The list is a long one!

Badminton
1985 Priceless
1989 Master Craftsman

Burghley
1983 Priceless
1984 Night Cap
1985 Priceless (EC)
1986 Murphy Himself
1989 Master Craftsman (EC)

European Championships

		Team	Indiv.	
1981	Horsens	Gold		Priceless
1983	Frauenfeld	Silver		Night Cap
1985	Burghley	Gold	Gold	Priceless
1987	Luhmühlen	Gold	Gold	Night Cap
1989	Burghley	Gold	Gold	Master Craftsman

World Championships

1982	Luhmühlen	Gold		Priceless
1986	Gawler	Gold	Gold	Priceless

Olympic Games

		Team	Indiv.	
1984	Los Angeles	Silver	Bronze	Priceless
1988	Seoul	Silver	Bronze	Master Craftsman

Apart from these major successes, Ginny has won a considerable number of other international three day events, and the fact that she managed to keep Night Cap and Priceless in winning form for so long is a tribute to her own care for her horses, and to the dedication of her back-up team.

Her mother, Heather Holgate, gave her every encouragement from the age of three onwards, but wisely has never sought to instruct her, but rather to let her learn from her own mistakes. But now she takes charge of all the feeding of the horses, and takes a great load off Ginny's back by doing most of the road work and exercising, leaving Ginny free to do the schooling. The familiar figure of 'Dot', alias Dorothy Wilson, completes the team, and though she too does not instruct Ginny, it is her watchful eye that oversees the preparation of the horses for each phase of an event. (Dot does, however, put her experience to good use by instructing a number of other riders.)

In dressage, Ginny's trainer has been Pat Manning, with additional coaching from Ferdi Eilberg when abroad with the team. For show jumping, it has been Pat Burgess, with lessons also from Nick Skelton. In her early days she learned the basics of cross-country riding from Sally Strachan, whose sister Clarissa won team gold medals at the World and European Championships. Sally was evidently a hard taskmaster.

She wouldn't let me ride a cross-country course until I had walked seven correctly, taking the right line. Later I had a lot of help from Lady Hugh Russell. I learned a lot, too, from watching Lucinda Green. I used to play videos of her riding across country over and over again, and in slow motion. I studied her through all the phases of the jump and noted her position and balance. I watched all the good riders, and asked a lot of questions, and I realised that I had to change my style. I think I'm more of a flat work rider as far as the seat is concerned, it's not natural for me to put my feet forward, and I have to work on it even now.

No one who saw her survive Master Craftsman's blunder at the fourth fence on the cross country at the Olympic games in Seoul could doubt the security of her cross country seat now! In fact few other riders would have achieved a medal on a horse as relatively inexperienced as Master Craftsman, who became her choice for the Olympics when she parted company with Murphy Himself. Murphy had gone brilliantly for Ginny when winning Burghley in 1986, but when he shot her into orbit at the Ski Jump at Badminton the following May, she realised that he was really too strong for her, and that he was a man's horse. What better man than Ian Stark, who just happened to have available for exchange the fast improving Griffin, on whom he had won an advanced section at Gatcombe in 1987. At Gatcombe in 1988 Griffin duly won again for Ginny, while Murphy, who seemed to have met his match in the 'Flying Scotsman', came third in the Championship. Two horses, two riders, and two sponsors all seemed happy, and at Boekelo in October Ian won on Murphy, and Ginny and Griffin were third, with Olympic Champion Mark Todd and Peppermint Park splitting the two.

Nevertheless, Ginny thinks that Murphy was probably the most talented horse she has ever ridden, even if he was not the horse for her.

But after Murphy I rather changed my mind about the sort of horse I want. He must be not too big, reasonably short-coupled, and Thoroughbred or seven-eighths. And he must have the right temperament, otherwise he'll let you down in the end. Movement has become less important to me, because you can improve it with flat work; the trot is important, the canter will look after itself. Beneficial moved like a pony when he was five, now he moves like a horse. So I go first for the jump, then for movement at the trot.

Ginny is no stranger to serious injury, and her fall at Badminton in 1988 seemed not too serious at the time, and it did not prevent her from riding Master Craftsman into third place behind Ian Stark's Sir Wattie and Glenburnie on the following day. It clearly didn't impede her too much at the Olympics either, but during a winter visit to the States she was still not quite 'sound', and a visit to an American orthopaedic surgeon revealed a broken ankle! So, nine months after the fall she underwent an operation for the removal of a chip of bone, recovering in time to start the 1989 season at home.

At home Ginny feels that the sport faces problems.

At an advanced one day event, the cross-country speed required is faster than that required for a championship three day event, which is the same as the speed for an intermediate one day event. The result is that horses are taken too fast during their build-up period, with risks to their confidence and soundness. In the advanced class at Weston Park I maintained a good rhythm across country, and my time penalties equalled my dressage score – rather depressing! But if the speed were slower, then competitions would be won solely on the dressage. The trouble is that we're catering for two different types of competitor, those who want to get to the top and win Badminton, and those who just want to have fun going fast across country and to win one day events.

Internationally, I think the sport will go down the route that suits sponsors and spectators. Three day events will stay as they are, but I think there will be more events like Gatcombe and Chantilly, France, where they run a one day event over three days with big prize money, which is good for sponsors and good for competitors. After a horse inspection, there is dressage on the first day, cross country (Phase D only) on the second, and after another horse inspection, show jumping on the third. The ordinary one day event is still essential to cater for those who compete just for fun and to bring on young horses, but top horses could do several events each year on the lines of Chantilly, as well as their three day events.

Whatever the formula for the future, Ginny's international record, especially in European and World Championships, will be hard to beat, though she herself is likely to improve upon it, for two major factors in her success appear to be her care for her horses and her saving of them for the big occasions.

This was never more clearly demonstrated than by her preparation for and performance in the 1989 European Championship. The selectors, in their wisdom, had chosen to ignore the form book and had insisted that all horses in contention for the Burghley team, including that year's Badminton winner and the Olympic bronze medal holder, ridden by the current World and European Champion, should prove themselves by competing at the British Open Championships over the demanding Gatcombe Park course just three-and-a-half weeks before Burghley. After a hot dry summer the ground was 'firm', and, as we have already seen, it was against Ginny's principles to run a horse if the conditions were unfavourable. (A misunderstanding there might have been, but her principle remained.)

Master Craftsman did not run, other contenders ran under protest, and the selectors acknowledged a misunderstanding. In the European Championships Master Craftsman performed an exemplary dressage test, marred only by a break in one extended trot, galloped round the very testing cross-country course to a three fence lead over his nearest rivals, jumped a smooth clear round on the final day, and Ginny notched up another record – a hat-trick of European Championships – at the same time leading Great Britain to another gold medal.

IAN STARK, MBE

The first rider ever to be first and second at the same Badminton came into the sport from a somewhat unconventional direction; not for him the path of steady progress via the Pony Club, Junior and Young Rider selection until finally making the grade on the senior team. Ian Stark burst upon the scene from a most unlikely background – the Scottish civil service. And since leaving the civil service in 1982 he has won Badminton twice, and has accumulated three Olympic, one World Championship, and five European Championship medals in the space of five years!

Coming from a totally unhorsey family, Ian started to ride occasionally at the local riding school at the age of ten or eleven, which was enough to make him sure that all he ever wanted to do was to ride horses. He managed to hunt with the Duke of Buccleuch's Hunt, where, in his own words, 'I was known as "the out of control child on the unmade horses", but at least it taught me how to hang on.' Leaving school at eighteen, he knew what he wanted to do, but wasn't quite sure how to set about doing it, especially as he didn't particularly want to go and work with horses for somebody else.

He decided to register at his local employment office, just in case a job came up in which he might be interested, but was fairly amazed when they rang up three days later and offered him a temporary job in their own office for six months. He kept the job for ten years.

I didn't like the work much, but they were very good to me, letting me take all my holidays in single days and half days when I wanted to ride, and I even took my allowable two weeks' sick leave in order to go hunting. When I eventually handed in my notice after ten years I don't think they minded much because I wasn't there all that much anyway!

In those days Ian rode any horse he could find; 'Now,' he says, 'they find me,' and today he attributes his success partly to the fact that he rode so many different horses. There was a local dealer who used to bring loads of young horses over from Ireland. No one knew for certain which ones had been backed and which were unbroken, and it was Ian who had to get on board and find out, an experience which he describes eloquently as 'weathering the storm'. Ian used to buy young horses, make them, and then sell them on in order to go out and buy more; 'If I got a good price, I would go out and buy two cheap ones'.

He rode in his first three day event in 1979 at Wylye, where he finished in eleventh place on a mare called Woodside Dreamer, whom he hoped to take to Badminton the following year. But she banged a leg, so it was back to novices again. Then in 1982 he was given the ride on two horses that were to take him to the top in double quick time.

Oxford Blue had been bought by Polly Lochore as a three-year-old, and had done a couple of novice events when he came to Ian at the age of six. Sir Wattie was sent to him at the same age as a problem child. The problems evidently didn't take long to sort out, because in June 1983 Sir Wattie won the Bramham Three Day Event, with Oxford Blue in third place.

In the autumn Ian went to his first international event at Achselschwang in Germany, where Sir Wattie came second, and then Oxford Blue took sixth place at Boekelo, results that so impressed the selectors that although he had never been to Badminton or Burghley they placed him on the 'long list' for the 1984 Olympic Games. But at his first Badminton in April, Oxford Blue was third and Sir Wattie sixth, and Ian was on his way to his first Olympics.

It all happened so quickly that I hardly had time to take it in. I had watched Badminton a couple of times, and everyone had seemed intimidated by the whole set-up. but I thought that since it had taken me so long to get there I might as well have a go. I treated it just like an intermediate three day event, and I was lucky in that because of the Olympics Frank Weldon had shortened the course. When we got to Los Angeles, I walked the course for the first time with the other three who were all experienced team riders – Lucinda, Ginny and Tiny Clapham; but when we got to the end they all thought it was the biggest they had ever seen, and in some places almost unjumpable. I thought, heavens, if that's what they think, what on earth am I doing here?

The fences were all artificial, because they were built on a golf course and they all had to be taken away after the event, but, like Badminton, they were imposing, solid and well built. My only problem on the day was that Oxford Blue hit the second fence hard and I dropped my whip. As he was a bit spooky, and sometimes needed the odd reminder on the way round, this was a bit of a worry. But we got round all right.

They certainly did, for Ian finished in ninth place and the team brought home the silver medal. In 1985 he won Bramham on Deansland, and Burghley's European Championships in the autumn proved a triumph for the home team, who took the first three places. (A fence down in the show jumping dropped Oxford Blue from a silver to a bronze medal, but at least Ian was happy that his error had elevated a fellow Scot, Lorna Clarke!)

Badminton 1986 will be remembered as the year in which it *wasn't* cancelled. With Oxford Blue earmarked for the World Championships, Ian rode his new rising star the grey Glenburnie, and Sir Wattie. In the rain and mud several riders with two horses elected to ride only one across country, and when the time came for Sir Wattie to start Ian knew that a clear round with less than twenty time penalties would put him in the lead. This he duly achieved, though not without anxious moments. The cross country had played havoc with the placings after the dressage and lying in second and third places were Rachel Hunt and Rodney Powell, who had pulled Piglet and Pomeroy up from forty-seventh and thirtieth to second and third respectively. So bad were the ground conditions by this time that the public were denied access to the park for the show jumping, but the dearth of spectators in no way dimmed for Ian the excitement of winning his first Whitbread Trophy.

Ian Stark, MBE (GB), holding the Whitbread Trophy at Badminton in 1986, with Sir Wattie (Bob Langrish)

There was not long to celebrate, for two days later Ian was off with the rest of the team to join Oxford Blue for the World Championships in Gawler, South Australia. Not at his best for the dressage, Oxford Blue set out to redeem himself across country, and that he did not quite manage to do so was no fault of his own. Heavy overnight rain had made the course extremely slippery in places, and in turning on the flat between two fences he slipped and very nearly fell. From an unpromising position somewhere under Oxford Blue's neck Ian desperately tried first to swing back into the saddle and then to cling on long enough to clear the penalty zone. In the end he lost his grip and picked up those sixty penalties.

'If only' is a phrase heard often enough at three day events, but even with this delay they completed the course with the second fastest time of the day, and without the cost of the fall they would have gone into the lead. As it was they helped the team to another gold medal which, added to individual gold for Ginny Leng and bronze for Lorna Clarke, made the whole trip worthwhile, even if the final horse inspection probably robbed New Zealand of team and individual gold.

One incident at the Championships nearly shattered the camaraderie of international riders, if not the 'entente cordiale' itself. 'We were driving to a party in a convoy of cars which had been lent to us by our hosts, and Ginny was driving a car at the back, and trying to change her clothes at the same time. We had to slow down, and Ginny crashed her car into the back of the Germans' Mercedes, which crashed into the back of the French, and we all landed in one great pile-up!'

Back in Europe, Ian had a busy autumn; with Glenburnie, fourth at Le Touquet and Burghley, where an easier course than usual allowed the first six in the dressage to maintain their positions right through to the end; with Sir Wattie, fourth again at the first Gatcombe Park British Championship and third at Bialy Bor in Poland, and with the young Yair, third at Le Lion d'Angers in France.

With the weather causing the cancellation of Badminton in 1987, the main objective was the European Championship in Luhmühlen in September. In August Ian won an advanced section at the Open Championships at Gatcombe on Griffin (about who more later), and at Burghley he survived a horrid fall on Yair. At Luhmühlen Sir Wattie, after the usual final help from team trainer Ferdi Eilberg, produced an excellent dressage test to lie in third place. The cross-country courses at Luhmühlen are always imposing, and this was reckoned to be a true Championship course, with alternatives for the less experienced nations.

By the time that Ian was due to start, Lucinda Green had fallen with Shannagh but completed the course, and Ginny Leng and Rachel Hunt had both gone clear. The words 'slow and careful' do not belong in Ian's cross-country vocabulary, and he set off at his usual cracking pace. All seemed to be going well, until Ian was stopped because a horse had fallen in front of him towards the end of the course. Although this gives a horse a breather, it destroys the rhythm of the round, and there is always the worry that the time of the hold-up may not be accurately recorded. However, all was well, and Ian and Ginny were the only two riders to finish within the time, and clear rounds on the final day enabled them to finish on their dressage scores, and to bring home team gold and individual gold (for Ginny) and silver (for Ian).

One of the problems facing British team selectors and riders in an Olympic year is how to treat Badminton, usually regarded as the sternest test of any year's calendar, and certainly in 1988 Frank Weldon seemed to have made few concessions to those with their sights set on Seoul. Having walked the course, Ian's response was, 'Up to the lake it's big; after the lake it's very big!' After the dressage he found himself in the highly satisfactory position of being in second and fourth places with Sir Wattie and Glenburnie. The cross-country course was to eliminate the dressage leaders (Angela Tucker and General Bugle) and drop the combination in third position (Robert Lemieux and The Poser) down to thirty-third.

At the end of the day Ian's two horses remained on their dressage scores, and in the final test, jumping out of order, Glenburnie assured Ian of a second successive Whitbread Trophy with one fence down. Sir Wattie kept his sheet clean, and Ian went into the record book as the first rider ever to be first and second at the world's most prestigious three day event.

A few weeks later he won at Windsor with the piebald Mix 'n' Match, and in Breda, Holland, he came fifth on Ginny Leng's Bally Hack – and thereby hangs a story! They had talked, not very seriously, about swapping the big grey Murphy Himself, on whom Ginny had won Burghley in 1986, and Griffin, a chestnut on whom Ian had won at Gatcombe. When Ginny broke her ankle at Badminton, she asked Ian to ride Bally Hack for her at Breda, and after his success there, she jokingly suggested that perhaps he'd better ride Murphy Himself as well. In fact her mother, Heather Holgate thought Murphy had tremendous potential, but after Badminton she preferred her daughter not to ride him again. Ian takes up the story.

Griffin was on the small side for me, so I went and tried Murphy in Ginny's manège, and I couldn't think how she had managed to win on him. She wasn't there when I tried him, so I rang her next day, and Dot told me that he never went well at home. So we agreed to meet with our two horses at Weston Park. On the cross country course I thought, 'This is more like the Murphy I've seen on TV', and Ginny seemed to get on well with Griffin. So we changed horses and drove home, with the idea that we would have three weeks in which to get to know each other's horses, and would then ride them at Witton Castle.

But when I got home I hadn't had a rest since November, so I put Murphy in the field. Then Ginny rang to say she wanted Griffin, and was I ready to clinch the deal? So I quickly had to start riding Murphy, and after a couple of days I agreed, and so the deal was done. No money changed hands, and Murphy then won the Scottish Championships, and was third in the British Championships at Gatcombe, where Griffin won an advanced section for Ginny.

Since Murphy and Griffin were clearly such different types, it is interesting to hear Ian's views on the ideal three day event horse.

First of all I go for temperament, and his attitude to work. I like good workmanlike paces, definitely not extravagant ones, because if things do go wrong in the dressage they are so much more obviously wrong if the horse is an extravagant mover. He must of course have a nice way of jumping and a desire to get to the other side of the fence. Thoroughbred or very near it. I wouldn't, for example, go out and buy a horse like Murphy from scratch, I prefer the old-fashioned steeplechasing type like Glenburnie. But probably a touch of Irish Draught or Connemara is ideal. But I think we've become more and more fussy when choosing horses, and we turn down a horse today because of little things we would have accepted some years ago. But then I always look at the good points, and I have to take my wife Jenny along to point out the bad ones! [Jenny has always been a key part of the team from the moment that she encouraged Ian to forsake his steady job and dedicate himself to the perilous sport at which he has risen, with her help, to the top – author.]

The team horses for the Olympics flew to Seoul over the North Pole, and arrived in good shape in the utterly strange surroundings of South Korea. In the dressage arena in front of the huge empty stands on Kwach'on racecourse, Sir Wattie was very full of himself but performed as well as he has ever done to end up in fourth position – and little did they know then that the first four after the dressage would fill the first four places at the end of the competition, though not in quite the same order.

As is so often the case when the Olympic Games are allocated to a country without previous equestrian experience, the cross-country obstacles were stiff enough, but it was the going and the heat that worried competitors most. An early blow for the British team was the withdrawal of Mark Phillips' Cartier on arrival at the start of the cross country, which left a team of three, one of them young Karen Straker at her first major international championship. Karen, after a very respectable dressage test, rode like a veteran, until at the second water obstacle Get Smart pitched on landing, and it was doubtful if even the likes of Ian or Ginny could have stayed in the saddle. A typical Leng performance restored British morale somewhat, and then it was all up to Sir Wattie, who duly obliged with the third fastest round of the day, to put them in third place behind Ginny, with the reigning Olympic Champion out in front. In the team classification West Germany led from New Zealand and Great Britain.

No one could catch Mark Todd, but Ginny took the bronze medal when the relatively inexperienced Master Craftsman had two fences down in the show jumping, while Sir Wattie rose to the occasion and clinched the silver for himself and the team with a clear round, giving Ian his third Olympic medal. Then, back in Europe, to round off a great season, Ian won the big autumn three day event at Boekelo with Murphy Himself, with Ginny on Griffin in third place behind Mark Todd on Peppermint Park.

At Badminton in 1989 Ian once again demonstrated his consistency by finishing fourth and fifth on Glenburnie and Murphy Himself. But soon afterwards his luck changed, and a bad fall in a one day event put him out of action for a period and affected him for much of the season. Nevertheless at the European Championships at Burghley Glenburnie finished in eighth place after being the only horse to negotiate the straight route through the 'S' fence in the arena during the cross country.

In the space of five years Ian has reached the top through sheer dedication and hard work, allied to that instinctive natural ability which Mark Todd considers indispensable. During that five years the sport has changed much:

Since I've been involved there have been many changes. Sponsorship has increased enormously. We must continue to encourage more sponsors, and more prize money. Sponsors are not always looked after as they should be. I've just been to an event in Arizona, not an area much involved with eventing, but they managed to attract twenty-nine sponsors, and they gave them a really good time. They let them have their names on the saddle cloths of the horses they sponsored, they entertained them, and as a result these new sponsors have pledged themselves to the future of American eventing.

Ian has certainly done his own sponsors proud. David Stevenson, managing director of Edinburgh Woollen Mill, was himself an Olympic pole vaulter (and his wife a long jumper,) but when Ian approached him after his first ride at Badminton he probably did not foresee the success that lay ahead. And for the 'Flying Scot' there is likely to be much success still to come.

WHAT MAKES THE 'GREAT HORSEMAN?'

We have examined the careers of some three dozen riders from five equestrian sports, and at the start of this enterprise we determined that a great horseman was someone who had achieved outstanding success over a considerable period of time on several different horses. And it has been a privilege to meet so many great riders, and to discuss their careers, their attitudes to their sport, and the secrets of their success. Throughout our discussions several themes have emerged, which may perhaps indicate what it is that makes the great horseman, why he is more successful than others with the same opportunities.

The first is an obvious one, is common to most forms of human endeavour, and can be summed up in the phrase '**dedication and hard work**'. The idea of the 'gifted amateur', someone who was so brilliant that he could achieve success without working at it, went out the window long before concepts of amateurism and professionalism were even considered. The successful horseman has always had to work hard to achieve success. But the hard work has been not so much in the race or in the competition itself as in the preparation, on the gallops, over the schooling fences, or in the manège.

Love of the horse as an animal is something without which few riders would achieve success. It is a theme that recurs less in the case of jockeys, since their lasting partnerships are for the most part formed with humans, owners and trainers, rather than with horses, of whom they may ride hundreds in a season and thousands in a career. Even in the case of National Hunt racing, where the partnership between horse and rider is more crucial than on the flat, two of our greatest riders expressed no particular affection for the horses they rode, though the likes of Mandarin, Arkle or Desert Orchid could hardly fail to raise a spark of affection in those who were lucky enough to ride them. But in dressage, jumping and the three day event, 'Don't do it unless you love horses' has been a recurring theme.

The recognition and the seizing of **opportunity** when it presents itself is something that was emphasised by Bill Steinkraus as being of great importance in the development of a rider's career. It was clearly exploited, for example, by Steve Donoghue, Lester Piggott, Jonjo O'Neill and Steve Cauthen from the world of racing, by show jumpers Nelson Pessoa, Pierre Durand, and Nick Skelton, and by Mark Todd and Ian Stark among the three day eventers. Had they not recognised and seized opportunities that offered themselves at crucial moments in their careers, they probably would not have achieved the success that they did.

Several riders mentioned how much they had learned by observing closely the most successful riders when they themselves were starting. Ginny Leng, for example, studied replays of Lucinda Green (or Prior-Palmer as she then was) in action; Nelson Pessoa watched the leading European riders when he came to Europe; Alwin Schockemöhle watched Hans Günter Winkler and Fritz Thiedemann. Power of **observation** would seem to play an important part in the successful rider's development.

Something without which no rider can become a great horseman is **natural talent**. 'You can't take someone off the street and make him into a great rider if he hasn't got it' are words that have been repeated again and again during interviews with riders. But the talent emerges from different directions; some, like Lester Piggott, Peter Scudamore, and the d'Inzeo brothers, were almost literally born into the sport; others, such as Sir Gordon Richards, Bill Shoemaker, Bill Steinkraus himself, Jo Fargis and Ian Stark, were born into families with no equestrian background; all were blessed with natural talent without which they would not have succeeded.

Natural talent seems to have expressed itself in various ways. Without **balance**, separation from the horse in those inevitable awkward moments that occur in competition becomes an alarming probability. Mark Todd considered it essential for someone of his height; John Francome was probably endowed with it, but certainly developed it through bareback riding on ponies.

An **eye for a stride** is something that can be improved with experience, but few riders who are not born with it will reach the top in those sports in which jumping plays an important part. For whether a horse is approaching the Chair in Aintree's Grand National or bearing down on the last fence of a three-mile chase at Cheltenham, or a rider is coming to the Lake at Badminton, or setting his horse up for the 2.20m Puissance wall, the closeness of the take-off to the optimum point will determine whether or not the jump is successful.

But the better a rider is, the less he seems to be doing about it. The Winters, the O'Neills, the Francomes and the Scudamores of this world do not appear to be doing much more than balancing their horses and sitting still; but then nor do the d'Inzeos, the Broomes, the Todds or the Greens. And the only reason that they don't appear to be doing much is that they all possess what is probably the most important single attribute of the horseman whose sport involves the jumping of fences – and eye for a stride.

How each of them uses it depends upon his sport. But they share one thing in common: they all see their stride to a fence very much further away than lesser mortals. And therefore the adjustments that they have to make to ensure that their horses arrive at the optimum point of take-off are so small as to be almost unnoticeable. Not for nothing did Fred Winter describe his stable jockey John Francome as the best presenter of a horse at a fence in the business; and it is interesting to reflect on Peter Scudamore's views on what it takes to become a successful steeplechase jockey.

An eye for a stride is a question of **judgement**, but there are other factors involving judgement too. Judgement of pace is essential in a jockey, very important for a three day event rider, and important too for a show jumper in a timed jump-off. Equally important is judgement of what the horse is capable of in competition. The three day event rider must judge whether he can take the quickest route at difficult obstacles or whether he ought to make use of easier but more time-consuming alternatives. It is relatively easy for the dressage rider to obtain the utmost brilliance of which his horse is capable in the outside arena before a competition; but how much can he afford to demand in the test itself in front of an expectant crowd and in an electric atmosphere?

Today, with overcrowded competition schedules, judgement is also required concerning the frequency with which a horse can be asked to compete. For the jockey this is normally taken care of by others, and they are generally more skilful at it then those in show jumping and eventing. But the great riders save their horses for the big competitions, and the really great ones keep their horses going for considerable periods of time – Raimondo d'Inzeo was winning Grands Prix on Bellevue when the horse was in his late 'teens', and Mark Todd won his second Olympic gold medal on Charisma when he (Charisma) was sixteen.

Peter Scudamore mentioned that he heard Lester Piggott say that **concentration** was the greatest asset of any sportsman. Certainly the lack of it, even if only momentary, has often been the deciding factor in the losing of a major competition, and it must therefore be true that it is something that everyone who aims to be successful must maintain.

Another hallmark of the great rider is **adaptability**. For the jockey it is essential, since many of his rides will be on completely strange horses. Richard Meade displayed it when winning a team gold medal in Mexico on Cornishman V, on whom he had only jumped one cross-country fence prior to the Olympic competition, and Mark Todd showed it when riding The Irishman into third place at Badminton in 1989, having sat on the horse for the first time only a couple of days previously. And the World Show Jumping Championship is decided (for better or worse) in a final in which the four finalists jump each other's horses.

And what of **style**? Does it matter, is it the forerunner of a better performance, or is it just 'nice to have' but not really necessary? The answer would seem to lie in the observation that a rider with style is doing nothing to impede his horse, and is himself balanced and therefore well placed to respond to any unforseen situation. But in the three FEI disciplines of dressage, show jumping and the three day event style also implies something else: the training of the horse so that only the very lightest of aids are necessary to achieve a required response. The dressage rider whose aids are almost imperceptible is a joy to watch; the jumping rider whose horse appears to lengthen or shorten with no obvious pushing or pulling has certainly done his homework. Though we may sometimes catch him (or her) in an-inelegant position, style is one of the hall marks of the great rider.

Finally, few great riders would deny that good **luck** has played its part in their success; the good horse that became available at the right moment, the opportunity or the opening that arrived to be seized, even the ill fortune that put a rival out of contention. No great rider owes his success to luck alone, but few would deny that it has helped.

So we seem to have arrived at about a dozen factors which when combined are likely to result in a great horseman. One question remains. Would the great horsemen of the past have maintained their positions today? The answer is that they probably would have done so. What made them great in their own times would still have worked to their advantage in the changed conditions of today. The riders of today may be more 'professional', but it is the conditions of their sport that have enabled them to be so.

As to the future, much will depend upon the extent to which those responsible for the development of equestrian sport remember that there will be no great horsemen without great horses, and that the sport will only continue to flourish so long as priority is given to the well-being of the horse.

BIBLIOGRAPHY

Part 1 Flat Racing

Bailey, Ivor. *Lester Piggott* (Arthur Barker Ltd, 1972)

Donoghue, Steve. *Donoghue Up* (Collins, 1935)

Donoghue, Steve. *Just My Story* (Hutchinson & Co, 1923)

Duval, Claude. *Lester* (Stanley Paul & Co Ltd, 1972)

FitzGeorge-Parker, Tim. *Flat Race Jockeys – The Great Ones* (Pelham Books, 1973)

FitzGeorge-Parker, Tim. *Jockeys of the Seventies* (Pelham Books, 1980)

Francis, Dick. *Lester Piggott – The Official Biography* (Joseph, 1986)

Mitchell, Derek. *Steve Cauthen* (Partridge Press, 1987)

Morris, Tony & Randall, John. *Horse Racing – Records, Facts & Champions* (Guinness Publishing Ltd, 1988)

Richards, Gordon. *My Story* (Hodder & Stroughton, 1955)

Seth-Smith, Michael. *Steve: The Life and Times of Steve Donoghue* (Faber & Faber, 1974)

Shoemaker, William & Smith, Dan. *The Shoe* (Rand McNally & Co, 1976)

Wellcome, John. *Fred Archer* (Faber & Faber Ltd, 1967)

The Benson & Hedges Racing Year (Pelham Books, 1989)

The Illustrated Encyclopedia of World Horse Racing (Marshall Cavendish Books Ltd, 1989)

Pacemaker Directory of the Turf (Pacemaker Publications Ltd, annual)

'89 Flat Racing Special (ACG Publications, 1989)

Part 2 National Hunt Racing

Francis, Dick. *The Sport of Queens* (Michael Joseph, 1957)

Francome, John. *Born Lucky* (Pelham Books, 1985)

Hedges, David. *Mr Grand National – A Biography of Fred Winter* (Pelham Books, 1969)

Herbert, Ivor. *Horse Racing* (William Collins & Sons Ltd, 1980)

Pitman, Richard. *Great Horses Make Great Jockeys* (Pelham Books, 1976)

Pitman, Richard & Others. *The Guinness Guide to Steeplechasing* (Guinness Superlatives Ltd, 1979)

Scudamore, Peter. *Scudamore on Steeplechasing* (Partridge Press, 1988)

Smyly, Patricia. *The Encyclopedia of Steeplechasing* (Robert Hale & Co, 1979)

O'Neill, Jonjo with Richards, Tim. *Jonjo* (Stanley Paul, 1985)

Part 3 Dressage

Ammann, Max. *The Nashua Dressage World Cup Media Guide 1989/1990* (BCM Editions Hippiques/Zuidgroep, 1989)

Kidd, Jane. *Horsemanship in Europe* (J. A. Allen & Co Ltd, 1977)

Klimke, Reiner. *Ahlerich – The Making of a Dressage World Champion* (Merehurst Press, 1987)

Littauer, Vladimir. *The Development of Modern Riding* (J. A. Allen & Co, 1961)

Williams, Dorian. *Great Riding Schools of the World* (The Macmillan Publishing Co Inc, 1975)

Wynmalen, Henry. *Equitation* (Country Life Ltd, 1938)

Part 4 Show Jumping

British Equestrian Federation. *Olympic Handbook* (Threshold Books Ltd, 1988)

Draper, Judith. *Show Jumping – Records, Facts & Champions* (Guinness Superlatives Ltd, 1987)

Kaiser, Ulrich. *Alwin Schockemöhle* (Copress Verlag, 1978)

Llewellyn, Harry. *Passports to Life* (Hutchinson/Stanley Paul & Co Ltd, 1980)

Media Guide – FEI European Jumping Championship 1989 (BCM/Equestrian Communications, 1989)

Part 5 The Three Day Event

O'Connor, Sally & Others. *Bruce Davidson, World Champion of Eventing* (Houghton Mifftin, 1980)

Foster, Carol. *Badminton Horse Trials* (Barrie & Jenkins, 1980)

Green, Lucinda. *Four Square* (Pelham Books, 1980)

——. *Regal Realm* (Pelham Books, 1983)

Leng, Virginia. *Ginny and Her Horses* (Stanley Paul & Co Ltd, 1987)

Rippon, Angela. *Mark Phillips: The Man and His Horses* (David & Charles, 1982)

Wathen, Guy. *Horse Trials* (Partridge Press, 1989)

Eventing Year Book Vol I (Barn Owl Associates, 1989)

INDEX

N.B. Horses (p269) and personalities (p271) are listed separately.
Italic entries refers to illustrations

GENERAL

Aachen, 111,207
Achselswang, 259
Aintree, 70,73,79,84,86-8,96,107, 200,230,237,245,265
Aix-les-Bains, 28
Alexandra Palace, 38
'Amsterdam, 111,173,190,197, 204,207,210,219,238
Angouteme, 28
Antwerp, 110,145
Apprentice Plate, 37
Aqueduct, 9,16,60
Arc de Triomphe, Prix de l', 8,11, 13,17,19,45,48,55,58,71
Arlington, 60
Arlington Million, 17,53,66
Ascot, 9,11,*11*,*15*,19,22-47,*32*,*34*, *41*,*46*,*47*,55-66,*62*,*65*,66,100, 108,175
Ascot Stakes, 31
Auteuil, 86,88,100
Ayr, 13,64,77,97

Bad Harzburg, 158
Bad Hersfeld, 158
Bad Lippspringe, 155
Badminton, 146, 210-66,*212*
Baltimore, 194
Balve, 125
Bangor, 20,103
Barcelona, 166,167,204,252
Basle, 211,213
Bath, 31,38,39
Becher Chase, 86
Bedford, 70
Belgrade, 170
Belmont Park, 29,61,87
Belmont Stakes, 16,17,52,61
Benson and Hedges Gold Cup, 13, 17,45
Berlin, 119,125,182,185,195,210, 231
Bessborough Stakes, *66*
Bialy Bor, 261
Biarritz, 149,195
Bilbao, 155
Birmingham, 28,38,146,202,207, 208
Blue Grass Stakes, 52
Boekelo, 223,229,237,241,244, 246,247,249,250,256,259,263
Bordeaux, 55,153,195,197,202
Bradstone Mandarin Handicap Chase, 99
Bramham, 226,254,259
Breda, 262
Breeders Cup Classic, 54,66
Breeders Cup Turf, 56,57
Breeders Cup Turf Mile, 17,56
Bremen, 62,124,181,187
Brighton, 39
British Horse Trials Championship, 229,236,245,256,257,261,262
British Equestrian Federation (BEF), 141,219,223
Bromont, 129,183,184,253

Brussels, 115,132,144,150,182, 189,190,197,202
Buenos Aires, 152,173,188
Burghley, 148,*173*,*207*,213-59
Buttevant, 70

Cadre Noir, 150,225
Calgary, 192,200,202,208,237
Cambridgeshire Handicap, 10,20, 26
Cannes, 202
Cardiff, *140*,176,178
Carlisle, 73,100,103,219
Castleford Chase, 97
Cedar Valley, 130
Cervia, 197
Cesarewich, English, 20; Irish, 28, 78
Champion Chase, 84
Champion Four Year Old Hurdle, French, 87
Champion Hurdle, English, 31, 70-3,78,79,83-5,88,89,95,96, 98,100,105; French, 100; Scottish, 97,98; Welsh, 98,*100*
Champion Stakes, 43,45,55,57
Chantilly, 9,27,56,257
Chatsworth, 219,234,237,246
Cheltenham, 22,31,*53*,54,69,*70*, 70-4,*72*,74,76,83-8,91,95-100, 105,108,215,230
Cheltenham Gold Cup, 70-4,77-9, *80*,*81*,81-90,95-9,103,104,265
Chepstow, 38,84,88,91,92,105
Chester, 27
Chester Cup, 29,38
City and Suburban Handicap, 22, 23,31
Combined Training Association (USA), 225
Copenhagen, 123,130,215
Cork, 70,96,144,195
Coronation Hurdle, 84
Cotswold Chase, 84
County Handicap Hurdle, 86
Coventry Stakes, 28
Craven Meeting, 22,28
Craven Stakes, 45
Crookham, 219
Curragh, The, 9

Daily Mail Cup, *141*
Deauville, 29,31
Derby, Dressage, Hamburg, 111, 115,119,*120*,127
Derby, Jumping, Dinard, 202; Hamburg, 143,146,148,181, 182,184,189,190,200,202; Hickstead, 90,*139*,145-8,175, 176,186,189,190,200,201,204; Millstreet, 200
Derby, Racing, Epsom, *14*,8-63, 95,203; French (Prix du Jockey Club), 10,55,56,64; Irish, 11, 13,*14*,19,29,31,32,45,48,55,57, 64; Kentucky, 15,16,17,54,61, 63; Santa Anita, 52,53,54,61
Derby, Trotting, German, 185
Derby racecourse, 25
Derby Trial, 63
Deutsche Olympiade Kommittee für Reiterei (DOKR), 154
Diadem Stakes, 19
Dinard, 186,200,202
Doncaster, 13,22,64,91,98,99
Dortmund, 125,144,167,182,189, 203,207

Dublin, 31,78,142,145,159,167, 170,173,175,176,178,180,182, 186,192,200,201,211,219,225

Eclipse Stakes, 13,43
Embassy Chase Final, 91
Epsom, 17,19,32,48,53,54
Eridge, 220,233
Ermington, 253
Essen, 130
European Championship, Dressage, 111,113,*114*,115,122, 124,129-31; Jumping, 141-207; Jumping, Junior, 90,144,195, 199,204,208; Three Day Event, 211-63; Three Day Event, Junior, 246,253

Federation Equestre Internationale (FEI), 109,111,115,158,160, 164,180,185,204,209,211,*218*, 218,220,224,238,251,252,266
Fighting Fifth Hurdle, 100
Flemington, 9
Folkestone, 39
Fontainebleau, 195,197,223,241
Fontwell Park, 83
Foxhunters Steeplechase, 215
Frauenfeld, 250,255
Fred Darling Stakes, 45
Free Handicap Hurdle, 91
French Grand Prix, 24,26

Gatcombe Park, 107,229,237,245, 256,257,261,262
Gatwick, 80
Gawler, 229,242,255,260
Geneva, 170,186,199,202
Goodwood, 37,63,115,*116*,124, 125,129,131
Goodwood Cup, 24
Gothenburg, 143,197,202,207
Grand Annual Challenge Cup, 84
Grand International Chase, 84
Grand National, English, 8,20,25, 42,70-104,*87*,134,200,237,245, 265; Irish, 78,79; Welsh, 84,105
Grand Sefton Chase, 84
Grand Sefton Trial, 83
Grand Steeplechase de Paris, 81,86
Great Metropolitan, 22
Guineas, 1000,10,15,17,19,22,26, 29,32,48,55,63,*66*; 2000, 13,15, 17,19,22,24,26,29,30,32,38,39, 45,48,55,57,61,*62*; 2000, Trial, 63
Guineas, Irish 2000, 19,45,57

Haras du Pin, 218,222,232,253
Hardwick Stakes, 24
Harewood, 122,123,211,213,215, 220
Harringay, 121
Harrisburg, 145,159,161
Haydock Park, 37,57,82,84
Helsinki, 111,139,140,143,150, 155,158,161,166,170,188,211, 213,217,225,238
Hickstead, 90,*137*,*139*,141,143, 145,152,157,177,178,186,192, 194,195,197,200,201,207,*234*
Hollywood Park, 52
Hong Kong, 9,19,58,59,66
Horsens, 223,255
Horse of the Year Show, 111,121, 200,204

Horse Trials Committee, 251
Huntingdon, 91,100
Hurst Park, 83,84,85
Hyères, 28

Imperial Cup, 83,92
Indianapolis, 120
International Festival of Dressage, 124,125; Jumping, 186
International Olympic Committee (IOC), 141
Irish Trophy, 175,182

Jeres de la Frontera, 200
Jockey Club, 40,42,43,49,52,58, 70,91,95,103
John Player Championship, 161
July Cup, 55

Keeneland, 52
Kempton Park, 74,82,83,86,98,99
Kennel Gate Novice Hurdle, 108
Kiev, 222,247
Kim Muir Memorial Challenge Cup, 85
King of Cambodia Trophy, 155
King Edward VII Stakes, 43
King George V Gold Cup, 132,140, 143,149,150,157,161,167,*166*, 175,178,182,199,201,204,237
King George V Stakes, 34
King George VI & Queen Elizabeth Stakes, *11*,13,*15*,19,45,55,57, 58,63,65
King George VI Steeplechase, 83, 84,85,92,95,99
Kwach'on, 263

La Baule, 141,144,177,182,186, 197,237
Lambourn, 90,94,95
Laurel Park, 45
Lausanne, 126
Laxenburg, 126
Le Touquet, 261
Le Tremblay, 55
Leicester, 37,84,88,100
Lewes, 24,26,37
Lexington, 228,229,241,242,245, 249
Lincolnshire Handicap, 25,31
Lingfield, 29,42,63,86
Lion d'Angers, Le, 243,261
Liphook, 233
Lisbon, 146
Little Badminton, 222
Liverpool, 28,38,83,88
Liverpool Hurdle, 87
Locko Park, 236,248
London, 111-217,*147*,*151*,*168*, *174*,254
Longchamp, 66,195
Los Angeles, 111,114,115,124, 127,144,146,148,186,191-259
Lucerne, 132,144,146,150,167, 188,197
Ludlow, 84, *85*
Luhmühlen, *173*,218,236,241, 242,247,250,255,261
Luxembourg, 198

Mackeson Gold Cup, 97
Madrid, 54,134,145,150,155,195
Madison Square Garden, 161,193
Manchester Cup, 23
Market Rasen, 97
Maryland Hunt Cup, 80,89
Meadowlands, 16

Mecca Dante Stakes, 63
Melbourne, 110
Merrill's Marauders, 160
Mexico City, 134,192
Middleham, 27
Mildmay Course, 98
Mildmay of Fleet Steeplechase, 91
Millbrook, 225
Millstreet, 200
Mondorf-les-Bains, 127
Montreal, 90,111,*113*,114,124,
  129,131,145,146,148,157,182,
  183,186,191,201,216,218,222,
  226,228,236,238,247,248,253
Moscow, 114,124,126,186,201,
  223,238
Munich, 111,114,115,124,130,
  132,143,144,146,157,161,177,
  181,186,190,217-20,222,223,
  226,233,234

National Hunt Committee, 70
National Hunt Festival Meeting,
  70,76,91
National Hunt Flat Race, 94
National Hunt Handicap Chase,
  71,91
Newbury, 42,*45*,71,84,85,88,92,
  99,105
Newcastle, 72,100
Newmarket, 9,19,20,22,24-9,39,
  40,45,48,49,55,66,*66*,82,121
Newton Abbot, 82,95
New York, 60,87,143,145,159,
  186,191-3,225
Nice, 132,145,150
Normandy, 73
Nottingham, 31,38,58,74

Oaks, English, 10,11,13,15,17,22,
  26,32,38,43,48,55,57,63; Irish,
  11,57,63; Yorkshire, 11,22
Olympia, 32,195,199
Olympic Games, 9,90,110-262,
  113,*145*,*157*,*223*,*231*,*260*
Olsztyn, 195
Osberton, 226,234,236
Ostend, 150

Panama Cigar Hurdle, 91
Pan American Games, 119,120,
  146,149,161,189,192,211,226
Paris, 28,30,31,110,124,134,143,
  150-2,157,166,170,190,195,
  197,202
Paris, Grand Prix de, 25,30,31
Pennine Chase, 99
Perpignan, 153
Perth, 97
Phoenix Park, 28
Piazza di Siena, *133*,166,167,170,
  173,175
Pinerolo, 110,166,170
Plumpton, 82,91
Poland, 154,195,261
Pompadour, 253
Potsdam, 110,119,123
Preakness Stakes, 16,17,52,61
President's Cup, 134,193
Prince of Wales's Cup, 144,186
Prince of Wales's Stakes, 22,25
Prix des Vainqueurs, 173
Punchestown, 73,213,218,220,
  222,232,241,246,250

Queen Alexandra Stakes, 31
Queen Elizabeth II Cup, 148,149,
  176,208,213

Queen Mother Champion Chase,
  105
Queen's Vase, 24

Radnor (USA), 228
Rail Freight World Jockeys
  Championship, 92
Ribblesdale Stakes, *32*
Riem, 222
Rome, 111,113-15,119,122,123,
  127,132,*133*,134,141,143,145,
  150,157,161,164,166,167,170,
  175,176,181,182,189,191,192,
  194,197,201,215,216,219,225
Roodeye, The, 27
Rotterdam, 115,141,143,146,152,
  161,165,177,186,197,199,200,
  201,202,207
Royal Hunt Cup, 24
Royal International Horse Show,
  32,208,237
Rushall, 233

s'Hertogenbosch, 130,202,207
St Gallen, 197,198,200
St James's Palace Stakes, 25
St Leger, 70
St Leger, English, 13,15,22,24,26,
  32,*36*,38,39,43,45,48,55,61,63,
  64; Irish, 57
Salisbury, 9,38,39,62,82
Sandown Park, 13,39,40,74,83,84,
  88,92
Santa Anita, 17,52
Santa Anita Derby, *see* Derby
Santa Anita Handicap, 53,54
Santa Anita Maturity, 51,53
Saumur, 110,150,225,242
Schweppes Gold Trophy, 74,88
Schweppes Hurdle, 105
Scottish Horse Trials
  Championship, 262
Sean Graham Trophy Chase, 98
Sedgefield, 100
Seoul, 111,113,127,*131*,*134*,144,
  145,175,176,178,190,197,199,
  202,*210*,216,217,224,230,237,
  243,245,251,252,255,256,261
Sha Tin, 9
Southwell, 92,105
Spa Hurdle, 84
Spanish Riding School, 118
Spruce Meadows, 192
Stewards Handicap, 37
Stockholm, 54,110,111,119,123,
  131,141,143,144,147,155,*157*,
  161,167,170,188,191,197,209,
  211,213,217,229,231,*240*,242
Stratford, 97,105
Strömsholm, 110
Stuttgart, 202
Sun Alliance Chase, 105

Tampa, 193
Teesside, 97
Tidworth, 247
Tokyo, 111,113-15,124,141,
  143-5,148,152,157,161,176,
  189,191,197,217,220,222,225,
  238
Topham Trophy, 91,97
Toronto, 130,200
Tote Ebor Handicap, 98
Towcester, 105,108
Triple Crown, English, 13,45,61,
  63; fillies, 63; USA, 15,16,52,
  61,63
Tripoli, 204

Triumph Hurdle, 105
Turin, 173
Tweseldown, 219

United States Equestrian Team
  (USET), 154,160,161,192,198,
  216,225,228,229
US Equitation Championship, 160
Uttoxeter, 77,96

Venice, 173,176
Vienna, 126,130,146,173,178,189,
  197

Warendorf, 119,121,123,127,155,
  159,181
Warwick, 54,104,199
Washington, 192,193
Washington International, 13,15,
  17,45,48,55,61
Welsh Champion Chase, 91
Wembley, 121,191,204,207
Wesel, 246
Weston Park, 257,262
Wetherby, 97,100
White City, 111,143,*147*,150,*151*,
  161,167,*168*,*174*,175,176
Whitbread Gold Cup, 74,84,96
Whitbread Trophy, 215,233,259,
  262

Wilfred Sherman Trophy, 72
Wilkinson Sword Trophy, 62
William Hill Golden Spurs, 60
William Hill Yorkshire Hurdle, 98
Windsor, 28,58,71,88,211,213,
  237,262
Windsor Castle Stakes, *32*
Winnipeg, 119, 189
Witton Castle, 262
World Championships, Dressage,
  111,113-15,122,124,126,127;
  Jumping, 132,143-57,164,166,
  173-207,266; Three Day Event,
  213,217-60
World Cup, Dressage, 115,127,
  129,130; Jumping, 132,143-7,
  153-64,175-207; Three Day
  Event, 252
World Equestrian Games, 229,252
Wolverhampton, 38
Woodward Stakes, 54
Worcester, 37,90,91,108
Wye, 82
Wylye, 247,253,258

Yarmouth, 49
York, 17,29,38,45,98

Zuidlaren, 125,199
Zürich, 54,129,144

HORSES

Commercial prefixes have been ommited

Abadir, 186
Abdullah, 192,193,
  207
Abergeldie, 40
Admiral Drake, 32
Adular, 111
Affirmed, 61
Agent, 186
Ahlerich, 124-7
Aiglonne, 153
Airs and Graces, 215
Air Wedding, 83
Aldaniti, 74
Ali Baba, 150,151,
  153,238
All Along, 13,48
Alleged, 45
Allez France, 55
Ally Soper, 80
Alpenjäger, 155,159
Alphabatim, 48
Altesse Royale, 55
Alvaro, 57
Alverton, 97,98
Alydar, 61
Alydaross, *32*
Ambassador, 144
Anderguy, 223
Anglezarke, 142
Anglo, 89
Anti Matter, 105
Any Chance, 242
Apollo, *139*,200,207
April the Fifth, 31
Arcadius, 123
Arden, 108
Arete, 134
Arkle, 71,74,78,*78*,
  85,264

Arlequin D, 144,152,
  153
Aryaman, *76*
Aureole, 39
Bacchus, 181,182
Bachelor Wedding,
  29
Bago, 243
Bally Cor, 229
Bally Hack, 262
Bambi, 151
Bambi V, 213
Barberry, 219-21, *221*
Bar Fly, 108
Baron IV,132
Beacon Time, 103
Beagle Bay, 242,250
Beaver, 87
Beethoven, 177,182
Be Fair, 215,236,
  246-9,252
Bella Colora, 63
Bellevue, 173,174,
  266
Bells of Clonmel, 173,
  174
Ben Arthur, 242
Beneficial, 256
Ben Faerie, 254
Bend Or, 23
Ben Nevis, 81
Besciamella, 97
Big Ben, 147,175,197
Bigua, 151
Bird's Nest, 98
Blue Stone, *216*
Blushing Groom, 45
Bold Minstrel, *134*,161

Bolkonski, 19
Bones, 152
Boomerang, 146
Border Incident, 91
Borough Hill Lad, *69*,
  92
Botany Bay, 250
Bowjack, 173
Boy Desmond, 91
Brains Trust, 71
Brazil, 236
Briacone, 166
Brigadier Gerrard, 10,
  17
Brown Chamberlin,
  69
Brown Jack, 31,32
Bula, 79,91

Calypso, 192
Canadian Club, 190
Captain Cuttle, 29,*30*
Carawich, 229
Carlingford, *34*
Carry On, 88
Cartier, 237,263
Castlewellan, 249
Celtic Shot, 89,105
Cent Francs, 83
Charisma, *238*,241-4,
  251,266
Charles O'Malley, 28
Charleston, 153
Chef, 194
Chicago, 213,232,233
Chumleigh, 38
Chummy's Favourite,
  19
Circus Plume, 48

Citation, 16
Claire Soleil, 83,84
Clear Cut, 97
Clonee Temple, 202
Colledge Master, 215
Columbus, 226,234, 236,237,247
Comanche Run, 48
Consul, 130
Corlandus, *116*
Cornelia, 159
Cornish Gold, 222
Cornishman V, *217*, 218,221,222,266
Cottage Rake, 78
Count Fleet, 15
Countryman, 178
Countryman III, *134*, 213,*214*,215
Crepello, 43
Crisp, 91
Crispin, 213
Crofton Hall, 97
Crow, 55
Crown Prince, 45
Cutting Blade, *32*

Dancing Brave, 11, 57,58
Dawn Run, 81,100, 103
Deansland, 259
Deister, *137*,186,187
Dering Rose, 95
Desert Orchid, 71,81, *81*,100,104,264
Destino, 166,170
Detroit, 57
Devon Loch, 73,84
Diamant, 152
Dibbidale, 11
Dick Turpin, 38
Didi, 207
Diminuendo, 63
Disney Way, 204
Distinctive, 237
Dolly, 96
Donald Rex, 177,182
Doublet, 218,226, 233,236
Doublette, 199,120, 121
Dozent, 152
Dr Peaches, 229
Dundrum, 145
Dramatist, 98
Dubonnet, 253,254
Duke of Richmond, 25
Dunfermline, 13
Durtal, *45*
Dutch Courage, 115
Dutch Gold, 115,*116*
Dutch Wife, 52
Dux, 124

ESB, 73,84
Early Mist, 73
Easter Light, 166,167
Eborneezer, 85
Ekbalco, 99
El Gran Senor, 57
Empery, 45
English Prince, 55
Enigk, 157,159
Espy, 108
Exhibitionist, 32

Fahnenkönig, 145
Fair and Square, 215, 246
Fairy Footsteps, 48
Fare Time, 84
Farmer, 144
Father Delaney, 97
Favour, 236
Fearless Seal, 100
Felix II, 241
Ferdinand, 54
Ferdl, 182
Fermoy, 213
Feuerdorn, 157,159
Fidelitas, 157,159
Fidux, 167
Final Argument, 77
Fiorello, 173,174
First Boy, 161
Flame Gun, 84,91
Flanagan, 147,149
Fleet Apple, 161
Flittermere, 100
Floating Pound, 91
Flying Water, 55,66
Foinavon, 74
Forest King, 77
Fort Leney, 79
Fortria, 86
Fortun, 159
Foxhunter, *139*, 139, 140
Free Thinker, 91
Freiherr, 182
Fresh Wind, *116*
Friendly Alliance, 95

Gallant Man, 52
Gaillard, 24,25
Gallery Goddess, 84
Galloway Braes, 84
Game Spirit, 77
Gammon, 202
Gauguin de Lully, *129-31*,*134*
Gay Crusader, 29
Gay Lord, 37
Gay Moore, 105
Gay Time, 42,43
Gay Trip, 76,79
Gem Twist, 197
General Bugle, 261
George, 234,248,239
Get Smart, 263
Gladstone, 143
Glenamoy, 215
Glenburnie, 256,259, 261-3
Glen Fire, 82
Glenkiln, 100
Glenside, 80
Golden Fleece, 57
Golden Miller, 71
Gone Away', 173
Good Mixture, 226
Goodwill, 218,234, 236
Gowran Girl, 173,174
Granat, 126,127,129, 130
Gran Geste, 189,190
Great Circle, 51
Great Ovation, 22, 232-4,236
Grebe, *140*
Gretna Green, 236
Gribun, 83
Griffin, 256,261-3

Grittar, 81
Grundy, 57

Habitony, 53
Halla, 152,155,157, *157*,158,167,173
Halloween, 83,84
Hatton's Grace, 78
Hawaiian Sound, 53
Heliopolis, 202
Henbit, 13
Hidden Value, 77
Hideaway, *234*,237
High and Mighty, 213,215
Highland Chief, 24
Hollandia, 161
Honey End, 74
Hot Grove, 45
Huipil, 189
Humorist, 29

If Ever, 200'
Ile de Chypre, 11
Iriquois, 23
Irish Cap, 225,226, 228

Jacapo, 176
Jacob Jones, 222
Jappeloup, *137*,165, 175,180,195,197, 198,202
Jason, 253
Jay Trump, 80,89
J J Babu, *175*,229
Jocasta, 241

Kadett, 115,
Kahyasi, 13,*14*,19
Kalaglow, *11*
Karabas, 45
Katie J, 96
Kilbarry, 211,*212*, 213
Kilcashel, *173*,223
Kilgeddin, 134,139, 140
Killaire, 241,249
Killiney, 91
Kilmore, 85-8,*87*
Knock Hard, 73
Kris, 63
Kruganko, 97
Ksar d'Esprit, 161
Kwept, 183

Landau, 39
Lanveoc Poulmic, 83
Lannegan, 178
Lanzarote, 91
Lashkari, 56
Lastic, 199
Last Tycoon, 56
Laudanum, 195
Laurenson, 229
Laurieston, 222,234
Lausbub, 123
Lavendel, 143
Law Court, 142
Law Society, 57
Lean Ar Aghaidh, 74
Leap Man, 73
L'Escargot, 79
L'Historiette, 153
Lincoln, *204*,237
Linwell, 104
Lion Courage, 71

Litargirio, 170
Little Charlie, 20
Lochinvar, 222
Lomond, 57
Lord of War, 54
Lorenzo, 186
Lothian Brig, 97
Lumino, 86
Lutteur B, 152,153, 238

Madras, 126
Madrigal, 248
Magnifico, 170
Maid Marion, 234
Maid of Trent, 20
Main Spring, 161
Mahmoud, 38
Majestic Prince, 15
Majetta Crescent, 97
Malacca, *85*
Mandarin, 85,86,264
Manhattan, 177
Manna, 30
Marcroix, 210,238
Marius, 202
Marmion, 152
Marquee Universal, 62
Marquis III, 144, 150,153
Marzog, 127
Master Craftsman, *240*,243,244, 255-7,263
Match, 55
Maybe, 199
Mehmed, 124,127, 129
Melton, 25
Merano, 170,173, 174,*174*
Merely a Monarch, 148
Merganser II, 241
Merry Boy, 130
Meteor, *142*,143,150, 151,167
Michaelmas Day, 242
Michelozzo, 64
Midnight Court, 99
Miesque, 17
Might Tango, 228, 229,249
Mill House, 74,85
Mill Pearl, *139*,192-4, *193*
Milton, *139*,178,182, 198,202,203,*203*, 207,208
Milton Tyson, 241
Minster Son, 13
Minting, 26
Miramar Reef, *46-7*
Miss Moet, *137*,190
Mix 'n Match, 107, 262
Moët et Chandon, 152
Monade, 55
Monksfield, 98
Monsanta, *170*,203, 207,208
Monteverdi, 45
Mont Tremblant, 82, 83
Monty, 139,140
Mossman, 242
Moxy, 90

Mr Ross, 178
Mr Softee, 176,177
Mr Todd, 245
Mr What, 78
Muley Edris, 22
Multigrey, 90
Murphy Himself, 229,254-6,262, 263

Nagir, 190
Narcotique, 197,198
Nashua, 52
Nashwan, 13
Navarette, 167
Nepomuk, 197
Never Say Die, 39, 43,48
Night Cap II, *253*, 254,255
Night Life, 241
Night Nurse, 79,97-9
Night Owl, 161
Nijinsky, 45
Nizefella, 195,201
Nonoalco, 55
Novilheiro, 202

OK, 199
Oberest II, 132
Oh So Sharp, *62*,63
Old Vic, 64
Opal, 130
Orient, 152,159
Ormonde, 26
Ossian, 25
Our Nobby, 218
Our Solo, 215
Overton Amanda, 204
Owen Gregory, 204
Oxford Blue, 259,260
Oxo, 104

Pagoro, 166
Papyrus, 29
Paradox, 25
Park Ranger, *74*
Pasch, 38
Pas Seul, 85,86
Pass Op, 190
Pebbles, 57
Pedro The Cruel, 243
Pieces of Eight, 43
Pele, 146
Pendil, 77,91
Peppermint Park, 243, 244,256,263
Perkunos, 121
Pernod XX, *120*,120, 121
Persian Holiday, 236
Persian War, 79
Peter, 24
Phideas, 32
Philco, 178
Piaff, 111
Piglet, 259
Pinza, 39
Plain Sailing, 226
Playamar, 236
Pleasure Seeker, 97
Polygamy, 57
Pomeroy, 259
Pommern, 29
Pomone B, 152,*170*
Poor Flame, 71
Posillipo, 174
Preziosa, 64

Priceless, 242,254, 255
Proud Stone, 97
Psalm, 148

Quare Times, 79,84
Quieva du Marais, 198
Quorum, 145,152

Rainbow Quest, 57
Rebell, 155
Red Fox, 167
Red Paul, 90
Red Rum, 78,103
Red Splash, 71
Reference Point, 63, 65
Regal Ambition, 108
Regal Realm, *207*, 250,*250*
Relko, 55
Rembrandt, *113*
Rex The Robber, 144,182
Reynoldstown, 80,84
Rheingold, 17,45
Rhyme 'n Reason, 79
Ribero, 45
Riviera Wonder, 161
Roberto, 17,19,45
Robert the Devil, 23
Rock du Taillan, 198
Rock On, 231-4
Roimond, 73
Roman, 143
Romanus, 157,159
Rosyth, 88
Royal Mail, 98
Royal Tan, 73,83,98
Russian Hero, 73
Ryan's Son, 195, 201-3

St Blaise, 24,25
St James, 200
St Mirin, 26
St Paddy, 43
St Simon, 25
St Teilo, 219
Sabin du Loir, *100*
Saffron Tartan, 85
Salad Days, 215,216
Salmai, 130
Salvanos, 20
Samuel Johnson, 213
Sassafras, 55
Scintillate, 57
Scipio, 123
Sea Pigeon, 95,97,98, 100,*100*
See You Then, 79
Shadeed, 48
Shaef, 82
Shafton V, 51
Shagall, 130
Shahrastani, 13
Shannagh, 261
Shergar, 13,*15*,63
Shining Example, *141*
Shirley Heights, 11,53
Silver Buck, 99
Silvio, 22
Sikorski, *66*
Simbad, 103
Simona, 143
Singapore, *36*
Sinjon, 161

Sir Ivor, 45
Sir Ken, 73
Sir Wattie, *240*,243, 256,259,261-3
Slip Anchor, 63
Snowbound, 161
Sonnenglanz, 157,159
Southern Comfort, 241, 244
Spectacular Bid, 53
Speculator, 223,229
Sportsman, 178
Stallbridge Colonist, 74
Star Appeal, 11
Starlight XV, 211
Stella, 213
Stopped, 92
Stranger, 174
Stroller, 147
Sucre de Pomme, 144
Sunbeam, 167
Sundew, 84
Sunsalve, 175,176
Swaps, 52
Swop Shop, 100
Sword Dancer, 52

Taj Akbar, 38
Talisman, 186
Tally Ho!, *147*
Tap on Wood, 63
Taxidermist, 84
Teenoso, 48
Temperate Sil, 54
Ten Up, 79
Terminus, 159
The Colonel, 71
The Dikler, 77
The Freak, 143
The Irishman, 244, 266

The Minstrel, 45
The Poacher, 222
The Poser, 261
The Quiet Man, 170, 174
The Reject, 92
The Rock, 167,*168*
The Tetrarch, 28
Theyra, 121
Thousandfold, 63
Tied Cottage, 98
Tiger Fleet, 97
Tio Pepe, 253,254
Titus Oates, 96
Tomboy, 149
Tony Lee, 52
Top Hunter, 238
Top Twenty, 84
Torphy, 157,159
Torreon, 100
Tost, 226
Touch of Class, 192-4, 207
Tournabride, 152
Trempolino, 58
Troy, 13
Troytown, 80
Tudor Minstrel, 39
Tulipano, 166
Tulyar, 43
Turnstone, 221

Ultimo, *113*
Uncle Bing, 91
Uranio, 170
Uruguay, 152,166, 167,*168*

Valoris, 43
Valour, 23
Varinia, 43
Velleda, 195

Victor Dakin, 226
Village Gossip, 228, 249,250
Virgin Soldier, 92
Virtuoso, 153
Volunteer, 242,243
Voulette, *151*,153

Walzerkönig, 144, *145*,187,198
Warren Point, 207
Warrior, 218,228,249
Warwick Rex, 182-4, *183*
Wayfarer II, 222
Wayward Lad, 99
What a Myth, 88
Whirlaway, 16
Wideawake, 247-9
Wildfire, 175
Wild Venture, 211
Wiley Trout, 115
Wilton Fair, 243,245
Wimpel, 182
Winsor Boy, 48
Winzer, 143
Winzerin, 127
Woodland Venture, 74
Woodside Dreamer, 258
Wotansbruder, 132
Woyceck, 111,129
Wulf, 146
Wyndburgh, 84

Xanthos, 148

Yair, 261
Young Pretender, 213

Zev, 29
Zucchero, 42

PERSONALITIES

The first names used in the text are retained for the index

Abdullah, Prince Khalid bin, 58
Ahearn, Lt-Col Fred, 132
Allhusen, Maj Derek, 218,222
Anne, HRH Princess, *see* Princess Royal
Ansell, Col Sir Michael, CBE, DSO, 121,134,158
Anthony, Ivor, 31; Jack, 79
Antley, Chris, 16
Arcaro, Eddie, *16*,16,51-4
Archer, Fred, 10,20-6,*21*,27,31, 38,39,42,43,48,50,86
Arrambide, Hugo, 188
Asmussen, Cash, 17,*32*

Bacon, Kevin, 149
Baeza, Braulio, 17,45
Barker, David, 176
Barnekow, Marten von, 132
Barry, Ron, 74,97
Bartle, Christopher, 115
Bartle-Wilson, Jane, 115
Baumann, Matthias, 217
Beard, Donald, 199
Beary, Michael, 38
Beaufort, Duke of, 22; 10th Duke of, 210; 11th Duke of, 215
Beerbaum, Ludger, 194
Behan, Philip, 28

Berry, Frank, 98
Bertran de Balanda, Gilles, 145
Best, Greg, 197
Bicester, Lord, 73
Biddlecombe, Terry, 74,76,77,79, 104
Blacker, Philip, 98
Blixen-Finecke, Hans von, 217
Bohorques, Jose Alvarez de, 188
Boland, Bill, 52
Bolternstern, Gustav, 110
Boyce, Trudy, 242
Brabazon, Aubrey, 77
Bradley, Caroline, 148,199
Bradwell, Judy, 249
Breasley, Scobie, 19,42
Breuil, Bertrand du, 155
Brinckmann, Hans-Heinrich, 132, 133,155,182
Broderick, Paddy, 78,97,98
Brookshaw, Tim, 84
Broome, David, OBE MFH, *134*, 141,146,149,167,175-80,*179*, 182,199,265
Brown, Buddy, 146,192
Buhler, Anton, 215
Bullen, Jane (*see* Holderness-Roddam; Jenny (*see* Loriston-

Clarke); Michael, 115
Bunn, Douglas, 177
Burdsall, Katherine, 149
Bürkner, Colonel Felix, 111,119
Burr-Lenehan, Leslie, 149
Büsing, Dr, 157; Wilhelm, 217
Butler, Helen, 241

Caprilli, Federico, 110,132
Carberry, Tommy, 78,98
Carr, Brig Arthur OBE, 139
Carson, Willie OBE, 11,*12*,13,19, 45,48,50,57,58,63,98
Cauthen, Steve, 13,15,*32*,48,50, 58,60-6,*62*,*65*,72,98,163,264
Cazalet, Peter, 73,89
Cecil, Henry, 19,48,63,106
Chamberlin, Harry, 146
Chammartin, Henri, 113,115
Champion, Bob, 74
Chapot, Frank, 146,*147*,177,188, 190,192; Mary, 149,190,192
Charles II, King, 9
Clapham, Diana ('Tiny'), 259
Clarke, Lorna, 259,261
Coakes, Marion, 147,177
Cochrane, Ray, 13,*14*
Cockburn, Mercy (*see* Rimell)
Coffin, Tad, 226,228,229
Cordero, Angel, 17,50
Corry, Lt-Col Dan, 132
Cortés, Gen Humberto Mariles, 133,134,191
Cottier, Frederic, 145
Crago, Brian, 215
Cristi, Oscar, 151
Cumani, Luca, 13,19,*59*

Dallas, Major Ronnie, 152
Darling, Fred, 38-40,106
Davidson, Bruce, *173*,216,217, 225-30,*227*,242,247,249
Davies, Bob, 74
Dawson, Matthew, 20,23-5
Day, Jim, 146,190
Delaney, Brian, 90
Derby, Lord, 31
Dettori, Gianfranco, *18*,19; Lanfranco, 19
Dick, Dave, 73,83-6
Dickinson, Michael, 99
Donoghue, Steve, 10,15,19,27-35, *28*,*30*,35,37,40,42,48,264
Dover, Robert, 114
Dowdeswell, Jack, 72
Doyle, Paddy, 84
Dreaper, Tom, 78
Drummond-Hay, Anneli, 148
Dudgeon, Lt-Col Joe Hume-, 219, 225
Dunwoody, Richard, 78,*99*,107
Durand, Pierre, *137*,145,165,175, 195-8,*196*,*197*,264

Easterby, Peter, 97,99
Eddery, Pat, 13,19,*34*,45,48,50, 57-9,*59*,63,64
Edgar, Elizabeth, 149,199; Ted, 149,199,245
Edinburgh, HRH Prince Philip, Duke of, 39,88,141,218
Ehrenbrink, Ralf, 217
Eilberg, Ferdi, 256,261
Elder, Jim, 146,177
Elizabeth I, HM Queen, 9
Elizabeth II, HM Queen, 13,39, 40,49,73,83,88,211,*214*,218, 226,234,235,248

Elizabeth the Queen Mother, HM Queen, 73,77,83,84
Elliott, Charlie, 10
Emerson, Denny, 226
Eppelsheimer, Georg, 155
Erhorn, Claus, 217
d'Esmé, Dominique, *116*,118

Fahey, John, 152
Falmouth, Lord, 21,23-5
Fanshawe, Capt Dick, 210
Fargis, Joe, *139*,146,164,191-4, *193*,207,265
Fenwick, Charlie, 79
Filatov, Serge, 114
Fillis, James, 110
Fischer, Gustav, 113
Fordham, George, 10,21
Fox, Freddy, 38
Francis, Dick, 73,74,84,105
Francome, J., MBE, 68,69,74,77, 79,89,90-5,*93*,98,99,104-6,108, 199,224,265
Franke, Kathe, 123
Fresson, Max, 150
Frühmann, Thomas, 185

Galvin, Patricia, 114
George V, King, 29,31,37,38,40
Gifford, Josh, 73-4,76,83,86,92
Glanely, Lord, 38
Gold, Joan, 115
Gordon-Watson, Mary, MBE, *217*,218,221,222
Goulding, Dave, 100
Goyoaga, Francisco, 145,152
Green, David, 250; Lucinda, MBE, *207*,209,215,218,228,236,241, 242,246-52,*250*,256,259,261,265
Greenhough, Gail, 165,197
Grillo, Gabriela, 113,*113*
Grisone, Federico, 110
Guerinière, Francois de la, 110
Günther, Walter, 'Bubi', 113

Hall, Joanna, 'Jook', 115
Hartel, Liz, 111
Hartigan, Martin, 37,38,40,106
Harty, Eddie, 90
Harwood, Guy, 57,58
Hasse, Kurt, 132
Hastings, Lord, 22,25
Hatherley, Sue, 249
Hawkins, Colin, 97
Hayes, Seamus, 145
Head, Alec, 17; Freddie, 17; Capt Richard, 91
Heins, Johann, 146
Hern, Dick, 10,13
Hill, Bertie, 211,213,*214*,231-4
Hills, Barry, 58,61-4
Hindley, Reg, 211,213
Hodgson, Janet, 236
Holderness-Roddam, Jane, 218, 222,228,249
Homfeld, Conrad, 146,*148*,192,207
Hough, Margaret, 213
Howard de Walden, Lord, 63,108
Huck, Karsten, 175,197
Hunt, David, 115,118,247,249; Rachel, 259,261

d'Inzeo, Carlo Costante, 166; Piero, 144,146,152,157,166-9, *168*,173-6,189,201,265; Raimondo,144,146,152,155, 157,167,170-4,*170*,*174*,175,176, 184,188,189,191,201,265,266

Jacquin, Lisa, 149
James I, King, 9
Jenkins, John, 92
Jensen-Törnblad, Anne-Grethe, *118*,127
Johnsey, Debbie, 90,148
Johnstone, Lorna, 115
Jones, Captain Ben, 220,222
Jousseaume, André, 111

Karsten, Horst, 217
Kaspareit, Thies, 217
Kastenmann, Petrus, 217
Kelleway, Paul, 78,91
Khan, HH The Aga, 31,38; HH Prince Aly, 19
Kizimov, Ivan, 114
Klimke, Michael, 127; Reiner, *102*,113,115,122-7,*125*,129,181
Kursinski, Anne, 175,192
Kusner, Kathy, 190,191

Landau, Guy, 74
Langen, Carl Friederich von, 111
Lavis, Neale, 215
Lefèbvre, Janou, 148
Lefrant, Guy, 145,155
Le Goff, Jack, *216*,216,225,226, 229
Leng, Ginny, 209,218,229,*240*, 242-4,251,253-7,*253*,259,261-3, 265
Lemieux, Robert, 261
Lesage, Xavier, 111
Ligges, Fritz, 217
Linsenhoff, Ann-Kathrin, 111, 113,114; Liselott, 111
Lithgow, Lt-Col Bill, 222,231,232
Llewellyn, Lt-Col Sir Harry, Bt CBE, 90,134,*139*,139,140, 219
Longden, Johnny, 15,52
Loriston-Clarke, Jenny, MBE, 115,*116*
Lörke, Otto, 113,119,123
Lütke-Westhues, Alfons, 123,155, 181; August, 123,181,217

McCarron, Chris, 16
McCourt, Graham, 107
McVean, Jeff, 149,245
Macken, Eddie, 142,146
Magnier, John, 45
Maher, Danny, 15,29,63
Mairs, Mary (see Chapot, Mary)
Maktoum, Sheikh Hamdan al, 13, 61
Mancinelli, Graziano, 141,144, 148,177
Margaret, HRH Princess, 73
Marion, Pierre, 111
Marshall, Bryan, 71-2,73,82,83
Mason, F., 71
Mathet, François, 55
Matz, Michael, 146,192
Maupeou, Comte Pierre d'Ableiges de, 150
Meade, Richard, OBE, *173*,218, 219-24,*221*,229,234,266
Mellor, Stan, MBE, 73,*74*,87,92, 104
Mercer, Joe, 10,63; Manny, 58
Millar, Ian, 146,147,175,197
Miller, Lt-Col Sir John, GCVO, DSO, MC, 213
Molony, Martin, 77,82; Tim, 82, 104
Momm, Harald, 132

Monahan, Katie, 149,192
Moore, Ann, 148; George, 19,43
Moratorio, Carlos, 220
Morgan, Laurie, 215,216
Morris, George, 146,160,175,245
Morshead, Sam, 92,105
Moser, Hans, 113
Mullins, Paddy, 100; Tony, 100
Murless, Sir Noel, 19,39,40,43,55, 106
Murphy, Dennis, 192

Nagel, Freiherr Clemens von, 119, 155
Neckermann, Joseph, 111
Nemethy, Bertalan de, 146,191, 192,216,225
Newcastle, Duke of, 110
Nicholson, David, 104-6; Frenchie, 57
Nicoll, Lt-Col Henry DSO, MBE, 139
Niemack, Gen, 181
Nishi, Baron Takeichi, 146

Oaksey, Lord (John), 105
O'Brien, Vincent, 17,43,45,57, 61-3,73,78,79,106
O'Dwyer, Jed, 132
O'Neill, Jonjo, 77,78,81,92, 96-103,*99*,*100*,104,105,264,265
d'Orgeix, Jean, 144,145,150
d'Oriola, Pierre Jonquères, 144, 150-3,*151*,155,167,*170*,188, 190,191,197,238
Otto-Crépin, Margit, *116*,118

Page, Michael, 225
Paget, the Hon Dorothy, 83
Pahud de Mortanges, Charles, 150, 209,238
Parker, Bridget, 222
Pattinson, Aly, 229
Penna, Angel, 55
Perse, Atty, 28,42,72
Pessoa, Nelson, *137*,146, 188-90, *189*,264,265
Petushkova, Elena, 114
Philip, HRH Prince (see Edinburgh, Duke of)
Phillips, Capt Mark, CVO, 107, *204*,213,218,222,226,231-7, *234*,249,263
Piggott, Keith, 42
Piggott, Lester, 10,11,17,19,*32*, 39,40,42-50,44,*46*-7,57,58,60, 61,63,71,98,106,107,158,203, 264-6
Pincay, Laffite, 16,17,50,61
Pipe, Martin, 104-6,108
Pitman, Richard, 76,89-91,237
Plumb, Michael, 216,*216*,226,228, 229
Pluvinel, Antoine de, 110
Podhajsky, Alois, 118
Pohlmann, Ottokar, 220
Porter, John, 25,27
Portland, Duke of, 22,25
Pottinger, Tinks, 242,243
Powell, Brendan, 78,*79*,107; Rodney, 244,259
Price, Ryan, 74,82,83,85,88,89
Princess Royal, HRH The, 218, *218*,223,226,233,234,236
Prior-Palmer, see Green, Lucinda
Purbrick, Lizzie, 243
Pyrah, Malcolm, 142,199

Rau, Dr Gustav, 123,155,181
Rees, F. B., 71
Rethemeier, Helmut, 217
Richards, Sir Gordon, 10,15,19, 25,29,31,35,36-41,*36*,*41*,42,43, 48,82,89,106,265
Richards, Gordon, 96
Ricketts, Derek, 199
Rimell, Fred, 71-4,79,91; Mercy, 71,72,92,105
Ringrose, Col William, 145
Robbiani, Heidi, 148
Robert, Michel, 145,198,202; Michael, 19
Robeson, Peter OBE, 140,*140*, 141,152,176
Robinson, Willie, 85
Rodzianko, Count Paul, 132
Rook, Maj Laurence, MC, 211, 213,220
Rosebery, Earl of, 22,40,82
Roycroft, Bill, 215,216
Rozier, Marcel, 145
Russell, Lady Hugh (Rosemary), 256

St Cyr, Henri, 111
Sachey, Don, 226
Saint-Martin, Yves, 17,50,55-6, *56*,66
Sangster, Robert, 45,57,58,61-3, 66
Sant Elia, Contessa di, 83
Sassoon, Sir Victor, 32,39
Saunders, Dick, 79
Schockemöhle, Alwin, 123,141, 143,144,177,*181*,181-5,*183*, 186,191,265; Paul, *137*,143,144, 183,186-7,*187*
Schridde, Hermann, 143,152,181
Schultheis, Willi, *102*,111,119-21, *120*
Schultz, Karl, 217,248
Scott, Col Alec, DSO, MC, 231
Scudamore, Michael, 84,104; Peter, *53*,54,69,*72*,77,79,89, 92-4,97,*100*,104-8,*106*,199,265, 266
Sederholm, Lars, 208
Shapiro, Neal, 148
Sherwood, Oliver, 81; Simon, 79, 107
Shoemaker, Willie, 15,16,50,51-4, *53*,60,*66*,106,265
Silva, Joaquim Duarte, 152
Simon, Hugo, 143,146,201
Skelton, Nick, *139*,142,178,197, 199-200,*199*,207,256,264
Sloan, Tod, 13
Sloothaak, Franke, 143,144,*145*, 178,187,198
Smirke, Charlie, 38
Smith, Doug, 10; Harvey, 141, *141*,142,146,177; Melanie, 149, 192,201; Tommy, 79
Smith-Eccles, Steve, 78,107
Smythe, Pat Koechlin, OBE, 147, *149*,176
Sönksen, Sonke, 183
Springer, Rosemarie, 113,119,121
Stack, Tommy, 77,91
Stark, Ian, MBE, 107,218,*240*, 243,244,256,258-63,*260*,264, 265
Starkey, Greville, 11,*11*,53
Steenken, Hartwig, 141,143,146, 182
Steinkraus, William, *134*,146,152,

160-5,*163*,177,190,192,264,265
Stephenson, Willie, 73,104
Stevens, George, 70
Stewart, Lt-Col Duggie, DSO, MC, 140
Stilwell, Dick, 90,248
Stives, Karen, 242
Stott, W., 71
Stoute, Michael, 48
Strachan, Clarissa, 256
Straker, Karen, 263
Stückelberger, Christine, 114,126, 128-31,*128*,*134*
Swinburn, Walter, 13,*15*,48

Taaffe, Pat, 76,77-8,*78*,84-6,104
Talbot-Ponsonby, Lt-Col Jack, 132
Templer, Capt James, 220
Theodorescu, Monica, 113
Thiedemann, Fritz, *142*,143,150, 152,155,167,175,176,181,184, 189,265
Thomas, Hugh, 236
Thompson, Arthur, 82
Thompson-Jones, Tim, 97
Thorner, Graham, 91
Todd, Mark, MBE, 150,209,218, 238-45,*238*,*239*,256,263-6
Townsend, Ann, 148
Tucker, Angela, 241,261
Turnell, Andy, 91,98,107
Tuttle, Hiram, 114

Uphoff, Nicole, 113,*113*
Uttley, Jimmy, 78

Vaillancourt, Michel, 146
Velasquez, Jorge, 17

Wade, Tommy, 145
Wahl, Georg, 129,130,131
Wales, HRH The Prince of, 26,219
Walwyn, Fulke, 73,79,83-5,106; Peter, 55,57
Ward, Liam, 45
Weier, Paul, 146
Weldon, Lt-Col Frank, MVO, MBE, MC, 211,*212*,213,216, 231,259,261
Westminster, Duke of, 22,25
Whitaker, John, *139*,142,178,195, 198,201-3,*203*,*208*; Michael, 142,*170*,178,203,204-8,*208*; Veronique, 208
White, Jimmy, 29,37; Wilf, OBE, 140,151,195,201
Whiteley, Capt Martin, 222
Whittingham, Charlie, 54,106
Wildenstein, Daniel, 13,48,55,63
Wiley, Hugh, 146,152
Willcox, Sheila, 215,246
Williams, Brenda, 115; Dudley, 84
Williamson, Bill, 19,45
Wilson, Dorothy ('Dot'), 256,262; Gerry, 71
Wiltfang, Gert, 143,183
Winkler, Hans Günter, 143,146, 152,*154*,154-9,*157*,164,167, 173-7,181,183,184,189,191,265
Winter, Fred, CBE, 73,74,82-9, 85,*87*,90-2-94,97,104-6,265
Wofford, Jim, 229
Wood, Charlie, 25,26
Wootton, Frank, 17
Wragg, Harry, 10,82

Xenophon, 110